Reading for Fun:

*A study of how parents and libraries
encouraged children aged 9-12
to read for enjoyment*

by DINA THORPE

with an epilogue
by ROSEMARY TELLING:

*The after school activities of
9-11 year olds*

Cranfield Press

Price £15.00

 British Library Cataloguing in Publication Data

Thorpe, Dina
    Reading for fun : a study of how parents and
    libraries encouraged children aged 9-12 to read for
    enjoyment.
    1. Children. Reading habits. Acquisition
    I. Title
    028.5'5

ISBN 0-947767-91-6

Cranfield Press
Cranfield Information Technology Ltd
Cranfield
Bedford
MK43 0AL
U.K.

Printed by Cotswold Press, Oxford.

Contents

List of Tables	(Main Text)	(v)
List of Tables	(Epilogue)	(vii)
Foreword	Cecilia Obrist, Former Chairperson of the UK Reading Association	(viii)
Acknowledgements		(ix)
Introduction	Max Broome, County Librarian, Hertfordshire County Council, former President of the Library Association	(x)
Prologue	What is a Family Reading Group?	1
Chapter 1	Researching Family Reading Groups	9
Chapter 2	Examination of Methods	21
Chapter 3	Who comes to a Family Reading Group? *"There is a bunch of four of us, and we all recommended it to a friend called Tom and he has come ever since."*	33
Chapter 4	Reading as a Recreational Activity *"I read when I have some spare time."*	51
Chapter 5	Choosing and Reading *"If someone says — Gosh this is fantastic, sit down and read it — you do!"*	63
Chapter 6	What is 'A good read'? *"Once I read 8-10 chapters in one night."*	81
Chapter 7	Reality and Readership — From I like reading about dogs because I've got one" to *"I felt his feelings"*	91
Chapter 8	Conclusions	101
Chapter 9	Recommendations	111
Chapter 10	Epilogue: the after school activities of 9-11 year olds by Rosemary Telling	117
Appendix 1	Interview schedules	149
Appendix 2	My after school diary	155
Appendix 3	List of Family Reading Group bookstock in order of popularity	161
Appendix 4	Example of data sheet	166
Appendix 5	After school activities mentioned in the diaries	168
Appendix 6	Weekend activities mentioned in the diaries	172
Appendix 7	What the pupils said they liked best of all	175
Appendix 8	Book titles mentioned in the diaries	178
Appendix 8(a)	Fiction	178
Appendix 8(b)	Non fiction	185
Appendix 9	*Woman's Hour* interview with Dina Thorpe	186
Appendix 10	A list of useful organisations and journals	190
Bibliography		193
Index		197

List of Tables   (main text)

2.1	Methods used to examine the effect which running a Family Reading Group can have on libraries	22
2.2	Methods used to examine the effect which attendance at a Family Reading Group can can have on parents	23
2.3	Methods used to examine the effect which attendance at a Family Reading Group can have on children	23
2.4	Time spent by children's librarian on organising a Family Reading Group Meeting	24
2.5	Monthly number of staff hours spent on library activities for children	25
2.6	Yearly number of staff hours spent on library activities for children	25
2.7	After school diary returns	29
2.8	Number of juniors who completed diaries in 1984 (3rd years) and 1985 (4th years)	30
2.9	Number of children who completed diaries in 4th year juniors (1984) and 1st year secondary school (1985)	30
2.10	Number of families interviewed after their first Family Reading Group Meeting and again 6 months later	31
3.1	School representation in attendance at Fleetville Family Reading Group	36
3.2	Library use of a sample of 22 Reading Group children 1984	37
3.3	Library use of a sample of 24 Reading Group parents 1984	38
3.4	Barriers to library use among Fleetville families	41
3.5	Attendance of adults and children over 10 meetings	43
3.6	Attendance at meetings by children accompanied by an adult	44
3.7	Reasons given by children for coming to the Family Reading Group	47
3.8	Attendance at consecutive Family Reading Group Meetings	49
4.1	Difference in incidence of activity of Reading Group Members and non-members	56
4.2	Comparison between after school activities of Family Reading Group Members and non-members in February 1984	57
4.3	Comparison of number of activities of Family Reading Group members and non-members	59
4.4	Comparison between after-school activities of Family Reading Group members and non-members in February 1985	60
4.5	Changes in incidence of activity in the lifestyles of children after changing to secondary school	60
4.6	Comparison of the number of books mentioned over 2 weeks by Family Reading Group members in 1984 and 1985	61

List of Tables / continued..

4.7   Comparison of the extent of book awareness by Family Reading Group members and   62
      non-members in 1984 and 1985

5.1   Reasons for choice of books given by Family Reading Group Members at 'Impact'   65
      nterviews

5.2   Methods of choice preferred by Family Reading Group members   65

5.3   Effect of recommendations of the popularity ratings of Family Reading Group   68
      bookstock — all books available for 10 meetings

5.4   Pattern of books read (R), retained and part read (PR) and retained and not read (NR)   76
      over a five month period

6.1   Reasons given by children for liking a book   86

List of Tables   (Epilogue)

E2.1	To show the number of diaries completed.	120
E3.1	After school activities mentioned in the diaries: breakdown of selected activities by school. I. On getting home from school but before having a meal.	123
E3.2	After school activities mentioned in the diaries: breakdown of selected activities by school. II. After having a meal but before getting ready for bed.	123
E4.1	The frequency with which pupils listed television viewing as an activity.	125
E4.2	Children's television — the programmes mentioned in the diaries.	127
E4.3	Organised activities mentioned in the diaries.	130
E4.4	A comparison of the number of times reading was listed as an activity with the number of organised activities attended.	131
E5.1	To indicate the amount of voluntary book reading undertaken by each of the sexes as evident from the number of titles listed over the two weeks that the diaries were completed.	134
E5.2	To indicate the amount of voluntary book reading undertaken by each of the sexes as evident from the number of days that book titles were listed over the two weeks that the diaries were completed.	134
E5.3	Size of family x number of days book titles were listed.	135
E5.4	Number of non-fiction titles mentioned x sex.	136
E5.5	Comics — number of titles mentioned.	137
E5.6	Comic titles mentioned in the diaries.	138
E5.7	Annuals mentioned in the diaries.	140
E5.8	To show when and how often the pupils read.	142
E5.9	To show variations in patterns of reading between the three schools.	143

Foreword

Family Reading began in the early 1970s. A branch of the Federation of Children's Book Groups found this an excellent way to involve parents and children in leisure reading at a meeting choosing books recommended by a librarian. The books were taken home to read, either separately or together depending on the age of the child. Then a month later at the next meeting the children and the parents gave their views on the books they had read. This led to a discussion and those books praised were eagerly chosen by others.

At this time the Bedfordshire Council of the United Kingdom Reading Association had carried out a survey which found that teachers were concerned about the lack of books in the home, and about lack of liaison between home and school. Since Family Reading Groups appeared to meet both these needs it was decided to try similar Group meetings in schools. These first meetings went well and the project spread to adjacent counties where schools formed groups with children of all ages. Some, in lower schools, were in school time while in upper and middle schools they take place in the evenings. Some are lead by librarians or teachers or sometimes by committees of parents. Each group finds their own most relevant way to run the meetings.

Through involvement in Family Reading Groups it appeared that parents, teachers, children and librarians were coming to know each other in an informal way. Librarians were gaining a wider knowledge of children's opinions of books. Teachers were obtaining a better knowledge of their pupils and their parents and the habit of reading books was being established as a lifetime pursuit.

It had been hoped that research would subsequently validate and enlarge on these hypotheses. One such research forms the subject of this report. It was carried out at the Cranfield Institute of Technology where the School of Policy Studies provides programmes for qualified and experienced professionals to carry out practitioner research projects on matters relevant to their work and professional interests.

This work by Dina Thorpe gives a picture of the out of school activities of children in the nine to eleven age range and asks where reading fits in with these. It is hoped that this work will show the importance of bringing such activities as Family Reading Groups to a wider audience. Dina Thorpe is to be congratulated on her endeavours and for producing this excellent book.

Cecilia Obrist
Member of Research Committee
U.K.R.A.

July 1988

Acknowledgements

I should like to thank especially Cecilia Obrist for her constant support and encouragement and John Blagden for his advice and guidance. Many colleagues in The Hertfordshire Library Service have been involved in this project and instrumental in its completion, in particular: Rosie Dudgeon, Linda Banner and Lesley Cooper, who ran the Fleetville group, Heather Adams and Juliet Maclean who provided background information, and Ann Parker who has always upheld the cause. Kate, Adam and Catherine all contributed much needed practical assistance with bibliographic and mathematical checking, and Marion offered unbiased opinions at the proof stage! Margaret Davies created order out of chaos by typing this manuscript.

A true picture of the lively excitement of the Family Reading Group could not be adequately put into words. Andy Rafferty's photographs are just a few from the many reels of film shot at group meetings and represent only a fraction of his practical and psychological contribution to my completion of this investigation.

I would also like to thank Helen Pain-Lewis of Loughborough University of Technology for her help in arranging the additional analysis of the diary data as well as, of course, Rosemary Telling who actually undertook the work.

My thanks to the BBC's *Woman's Hour* for permission to reproduce the transcript of my interview with that programme. This included a discussion with Julia Eccleshare of the National Book Trust whom I would also like to thank. The Youth Libraries Group of the Library Association gave kind permission to use some of their information in the Appendices.

Finally, I would like to thank Bodley Head, publishers of "Days Are Where We Live" (compiled by Jill Bennett and illustrated by Maureen Roffey) for granting permission to reproduce illustrations for the After School Diary. The Diary also uses illustrations from "Bluebell Hill Games" — I would like to acknowledge David McKee, the illustrator, for these.

Introduction

Hertfordshire's librarians are encouraged to pursue their own initiatives and, as far as possible, given positive support to enable them to do so. This is a policy which grows progressively more difficult to sustain as resources decline. I therefore welcome this book, for it provides eloquent testimony to the effectiveness of this policy by critically analysing one of its manifestations — a family reading group based on a small library in the town of St. Albans. The rigorous assessment of innovative work is all too rare, and Dina Thorpe is to be congratulated on undertaking this and on pursuing it with characteristic enthusiasm and in such a comprehensive manner.

I welcome this book, too, because it reinforces my belief in the value of cooperation between school and public library, and in the importance of librarians as experts in the promotion of books and reading — of which there is no greater exponent than the skilled children's librarian. Today's emphasis is on the librarian as a manager of resources and as information specialist and I do not underrate the importance of these roles. Regrettably, however, these developments have caused some librarians, and not a few library schools, to overlook the crucial need of children for imaginative stimulus through books and the part which the librarian can play in meeting this need.

The services which such librarians provide are seen as highly relevant by parents. They also stimulate use and ensure that the library remains a vital force in the community. They therefore make an effective contribution in the battle for political support and for resources. This fact is not always recognised, nor may it be fully appreciated by all who read this study. The book contains intriguing references to the threat of closure which hung over the Fleetville Library during this period. There are also references to the profoundly discouraging effect of a high rate of fines on the use of libraries by children. Happily both these policies have since been reversed.

The Fleetville Family Reading Group played a part in securing this change of policy, not by political campaigning, but by quietly reinforcing the importance of the library to community life. Hertfordshire Library Service has encouraged parental involvement with their children's reading in home, school and public library for many years. This study shows how shared family reading can tempt "children forward to a stage beyond survival reading — enjoyment."

E M Broome
County Librarian Herts County Council

July 1988

Prologue

What is a Family Reading Group?

The Fleetville Family Reading Group was held on the first Thursday in the month in Fleetville Library at 7 p.m.

"It's a library and you go into it and there are quite a few tables laid out with books, quite a few different, all new."

Commentary by the children and parents of Fleetville
All photographs by Andy Rafferty

Books were spread out on tables, face upwards, for the children to browse.

"It is somewhere where you can talk
to people about books and hear people
talk about books, and
people show you interesting books."

"I showed that one to Mary and then she read it and then I found another one in the series and she
read that as well."

For the first twenty minutes the children could look at the books —

"Perhaps the cover of some of them took his eye that he might not have picked out if he was only looking at the spine on the back of the shelf."

"He picks his books a bit more, not by the picture on the cover, he goes into it a bit deeper".

— and have a drink of orange and a biscuit.

"There's some nosh, some grub and a drink."

"I liked the biscuits,"

"It's more social than anything else."

Parents were specifically invited to come to meetings with their children.

*"The parents seem to sort through
the books quite a lot — the fact that the
parents go, that they go with the children,
encourages them."*

*"It is better if my Mum comes,
because usually while I am looking at one
pile, my Mum looks at another
pile and finds some books."*

Then everyone sat down to talk about their favourite titles.

"I liked hearing the three of you say briefly what some of the books were about, I think that was a good idea, because you can't always tell what a book is going to be like."

"You explained books if you liked them to people — made people laugh if they liked them. If you wanted to make them laugh you read them the funniest bits."

Unrestricted borrowing made choosing books easier, and children could take home as many as they liked!

"You can take as many books as you like, you can read as many books as you like, and after you've chosen your books in a little while, people sit down and talk about some more books, about how they like them and everything, and then after that you are allowed to check in your books, and maybe collect a few more books, and then you can go home!"

Chapter 1

Researching Family Reading Groups

The focus of this investigation was an analysis of how family reading groups can encourage children to read for enjoyment in their spare time. A full explanation of how family reading groups can be established and function will be given, before doing so, however it is necessary to define reading and enjoyment since they are central to the argument, and also to consider what the children are being encouraged to read, and why.

1. Reading

The title of almost every book and article in the bibliography to this survey contains the word 'reading', but it does not always have the same meaning. Most frequently the word 'reading' is taken to mean 'how to read', and, in the introduction to his own examination of *The Reading Process* (Hatt, 1976) Frank Hatt notes that this is especially so in the UK where

> "The teaching of reading, in fact, has generally been taken to mean the teaching of word recognition and common sentence construction."

He continues

> "One seldom finds an attempt to describe what the readers do in their heads, comparable with the lengthy accounts of what they do with their eyes."

In his UNESCO report *The Future of the Book. Part II: The Changing Role of Reading* (1982), Michel Gault defines literacy, or survival reading, as

> "the ability to understand a written message (which as such has no meaning for the eye) and to transform it into an oral message which is comprehensible to the ear."

But he agrees with Frank Hatt that "Literacy alone does not make a reader," for "establishing a relationship with a book requires a quite different activity." This "different activity" is "what the readers do in their heads" and the way in which children relate to books is discussed in the second half of this survey. This survey is not a technical account of what children do with their eyes when they focus on the written word, although it accepts this is an ability which is necessary before they can do anything 'in their heads'. It is concerned with examining a method of tempting children forward to a stage beyond survival reading — enjoyment.

2. Enjoyment

Enjoyment is an unsatisfactory term for that which is achieved as a result of a satisfactory experience — in this case, reading. In his studies on media communication Katz (1973) calls this user satisfaction "gratification" and relates it to user needs. James Britton's article *Response to Literature* in *The Cool Web* (1977) explains

> "We must expect, and encourage, reading to go on for various purposes at various levels, and not concern ourselves solely with performance at maximum effort. 'Reading for enjoyment'... will certainly be an apt description of the lower levels of effort, but is probably misleading when applied to the most demanding kind of reading. Satisfaction... however must be there in the end."

In this way, it is possible to say that children 'enjoy' being frightened by stories — to use the term 'enjoy' is a shorthand way of saying that they related to or were gratified by the frightening experience in the story.

Reading for its own sake, rather than for a practical purpose, is frequently defined in the literature of children's literacy as 'reading for enjoyment'. Frank Hart (1976) calls this "terminal reading" and lists the following motives for it, each of which would bring its own satisfaction or gratification:

1. Respite.

2. Compensation for personal inadequacies and dull circumstance.

3. Confirmation of opinions and values.

4. Enjoyment of enhanced status and prestige.

5. The feeling of belonging to a group.

Hatt, like Katz, sees the reader as choosing the form of media which will satisfy their own need and thus bring its own gratification. In addition the child gains satisfaction from completing the book and practising the new skill of decoding, which reflects Hatt's fourth motive concerning status and prestige.

3.   The reading of fiction

Fiction books almost always fall into Hatt's category of 'terminal reading' as opposed to 'instrumental reading' which is defined as reading in order to be able to complete a task. Children do gain satisfaction from reading a non-fiction or information book; they learn how to recognise butterflies or aircraft, how people lived in England in mediaeval times, or in Africa today, how to build a kite or make a cake, but they do not learn about their inner selves. They do not learn what makes them laugh or cry, love some people, hate others, or even change their minds!

Anthony Storr, whose New Statesman article, reprinted in the collection *Only Connect. Readings on Children's Literature* (1969) speaks of "the emotional effect" which reading stories has for children. This effect

> "rather than conveying information, does not put things into the mind, but rather objectifies its contents... the thrill is one of recognition."

It is easy for literate children with a question to answer to find an information book that will help, for they are providing their own motivation. Children who 'want something to read' — and when they say 'something', mean 'a story' — have only a half-formed motivation, a recognition of a need, (emptiness, boredom, call it what you will) which will soon be filled with an alternative to a storybook if the right one is not produced there and then. If it is not they are in danger of being deprived of that extension of experience and imagination which reading fiction brings. This study, therefore, is concerned with directing children towards a recognition that the reading of fiction will provide the gratification of this need.

4. Why should children read?

The major psychological and developmental reasons behind encouraging children to read noted above, can be summed up by a passage from the introduction to Margaret Meek's *The Cool Web* (1977).

> "the worry that surrounds illiterates focuses on the fact that they become social cripples, as that aspect of their lack is easiest to define, but they are also shut out from a way of looking at the world which other people habitually use as if it were an extension of their perception. Unable to read, a child or adult is cut off from a way of entering into the experiences of other people, the better to understand his own."

However, more often repeated, are the educational benefits of reading, as expressed ten years ago in The Bullock Report *A language for life* (HMSO 1975).

> "Literature brings the child into an encounter with language in its most complex and varied forms and is a valuable source of imaginative insight. It should be recognized as a powerful source in English teaching at all levels."

This basic premise has not changed over the years. However, two issues which were also given prominence in The Bullock Report have changed since then:

1. The involvement of parents with their children's reading in the early years was recommended by The Bullock Report and has been formally developed in schools in the 1980's through such schemes as PACT, described by Alex Griffiths and Dorothy Hamilton (1985) in *Parent, Teacher, Child.*

2. The provision of resources, seen as "increasingly difficult" in 1975 has continued to decline, to the extent that Brian Cox, President of the National Council for Education Standards, writing in the Sunday Times in December 1985, comments

> "During the last few years, the gap between the educated and the uneducated, employed and unemployed, rich and poor, has widened alarmingly. The increase of ill-educated unemployables has vast social implications... By reducing spending on school books, the government is ensuring that more money must be spent on law and order."

Both these developments had implications for this research which examined ways of involving parents with children's reading at a later stage in their reading development than before and at the book supply necessary to support their activities

Equal with this concern over book supply is the concern of those working in the book industry — publishers, booksellers and librarians — that there should be a market for their product. The establishment of the reading habit during childhood is necessary to ensure an adult reading public. This has been shown by Michel Gault (1982) and by the survey *Reading in America 1978* (Library of Congress 1979 ed. Cole and Gold). In the report on this survey, American publishers discussed factors relating to "an early appreciation of the values of books and reading". Martin Goff of the National Book League reiterates these. Speaking at the 1983 Booksellers Association Conference, he asks "all these are words, important words, but what have they to do with us, traders of one sort or another in books? Well, at their most obvious, books are our living. Our interest is vested. But it so happens... that our needs as book traders coincide both with the individual's need as a communicator and with the imaginative and emotional needs of that individual."

As a result of this conference the Children's Book Trust was set up in 1987 to bring the promotion of children's books to the fore with campaigns backed by tabloid newspapers, breakfast television and other major commercial sponsors.

In order to survive economically, librarians and booksellers need to provide children with books they want to read, as Bob Leeson argues in *Reading and Righting* (1985):"

"The very survival of the literature, at any level, depends upon whether it can develop a broad popular appeal and win the backing of the wider audience."

All these surveys and reports on reading concluded that further research was necessary into methods of motivating children to read; this survey is an in depth investigation into one such method.

5.   Family Reading Groups

Organised methods of family reading are not new and go under different guises and titles. They differ from the host of other activities run in schools and libraries aimed at involving children with books in the following ways:

1.   Family Reading Groups create an opportunity for the whole family — parents, grandparents, children and friends to share books.

2.   The meetings are book-based, concerned with promoting the reading of fiction books.

When Eve Astbury (1972) wrote about Family Reading Groups in the East Riding, parents were still kept at a distance by some schools, who preferred them to be relatively uninvolved with the process of children learning to read. The finding of the Plowden Report (1969) that

"Where the interest of parents linked up with the presence of books, the children forged ahead at school"

took time to filter through to some classrooms. Large scale schemes such as PACT (Parents, Children and Teachers) in Hackney and 'paired reading' schemes elsewhere did not occur until the late 1970's and are only just becoming widespread in 1987 alongside schemes for learning to read using 'real' books described in Liz Waterland; *Read with me* (1985). In the meantime a United Kingdom Reading Association Research Sub-Committee pilot study on children's reading highlighted two main areas of concern, quoted by Cecilia Obrist (1984) in her pamphlet How to run Family Reading Groups *as*

"1.   The lack of books in the home.

2.   The lack of liaison between home and school."

As a result reading and reviewing groups — Family Reading Groups — were started in a Junior Mixed Infants school in South Bedfordshire. Other Family Reading Groups have been run by the Federation of Children's Book Groups. The difference between these and Family Reading Groups run in public libraries — such as the Fleetville group under discussion here — is that membership of public library groups is not restricted to one branch of the community, e.g. to children from one particular school, or whose parents belong to a particular organisation. As Chapter 3 shows, many of those attending the Fleetville group were not even members of the Fleetville Library.

6. Family Reading Groups in Hertfordshire

The library service in Hertfordshire has been concerned with running a variety of Family Reading Groups over the last ten years. Like all self-help groups, they take on the characteristics of their members and of their organisers. They have been organised by the divisional Schools Library Services, sometimes in conjunction with branch library staff, and sometimes jointly with school librarians or teachers in schools. Juliet McLean has written about a Hertfordshire sixth form reading group at Mount Grace School, Potters Bar, in her MA dissertation *A study of voluntary reading across the secondary age range and of the role of groups formed in two secondary schools to extend and support pupils' voluntary reading* (1985) concluding that

> "The indications are... that reading groups do offer an enriching dimension to individual reading experiences through the means of shared response."

This "shared response" — the group experience — distinguishes Family Reading Groups from yet another 'book talk' given by the librarian or teacher as an 'expert'. At the Reading Group all members are 'readers' and the recommendations of peers often provoke a greater response than those of the 'experts'.

Wherever the Hertfordshire Reading Groups have developed there have been four major features:

1. Informality.
2. The involvement of home, school and library service.
3. A plentiful book supply with unrestricted borrowing.
4. The public or school library as catalyst.

Over the past five years there have been two Family Reading Groups run in branch libraries in West Hertfordshire. The first was at King's Langley and there were several reasons for making this the first branch-based group:

1. It is a well-defined village community, with one infant, one junior and one secondary school. The community has a good socio economic mix, with some commuting to London, and some local employment in the paper mills or Ovaltine factory.

2 Previous activities — visits from children's authors and illustrators, creative writing and Family Storytelling evenings — have involved all three schools and the branch library.

3. The library is situated in a central focal position in the village, next to the community centre.

A Family Reading Group was also established at North Watford the following year in an attempt to compare reactions to a community group from families in an area which differed in the following ways:

1. This is an industrial area on the edge of a large town. Most families work in local industry — printing and engineering — and there is growing redundancy.

2. The group is promoted in four very different junior schools which have varying links with the local branch library. Holiday activities in the library are well supported.

3. The public library is not situated in a focal position within the community; indeed, it is rather difficult to reach, on a busy road off a feeder highwday to the M1 motorway.

Indications from these two groups seemed to show that the sociological background had little effect on the success of the group, as both were well attended over several years. Important factors which emerged were that the unrestricted borrowing policy encouraged the children to read more widely and that children relied heavily on recommendations from others in the group when choosing a book. The effect which group discussion had on the choice of books made by parents, as well as by teachers and librarians, also called for closer scrutiny, as did the role played by the public library.

Most public libraries have a post for a designated children's specialist on their staff. However, timetabling and staffing formulae often result in their skills being given a limited outlet. It can be argued against this that even when the children's librarian is sitting in the junior section, ready to give advice, the clients (children), may not be there at the same time. Even when the client and the adviser are in the library at the same time, an opportunity often has to be made for them to interact. If specialist skills cannot be shown to be cost effective there is a danger that they could be viewed as unnecessary in the change in emphasis on staffing service points (Helen Pain-Lewins LAR 2/87).

Is the library service in the business of providing books for readers or promoting books to readers? Can it always be assumed that, once inside the library building, confronted by a roomful of books, the reader will be able to make a choice? If this choice becomes too difficult or confusing the reader may leave the building without a book at all and the chances of their return will be slight. This is bad luck for the reader, but the prognosis for the library is even worse.

Libraries, like all client-based services, are dependent on their users for survival — a fact often overlooked by those working in a public service. A policy which implies 'here is the book — take it or leave it' may often result in the book being left. In the budget conscious services of the 1980's, too many books being left will lead to less money for books in the future and the downward spiral of provision will take over.

A passive library service may appear to be cheaper and easier to run, but an active service in which books are consciously promoted to the public may reap its own rewards. This survey of promoting books to one section of the public in one public library touches on the policy and managerial implications of an active as opposed to a passive service and the more effective use of librarians specialising in childrens work.

7. Aims of the study of Fleetville Family Reading Group

It was decided to examine the formation and progress over one year of a Family Reading Group in the Fleetville neighbourhood of St Albans as a basis for research into three main areas: parents, children, libraries.

The case has already been made that children should read fiction and that parents should be involved with this reading process. However motivated children may become to read, and however aware parents may be of their need, they still need access to a ready and comprehensive book supply with guidance on its exploitation. This, then, is where the public library service comes to the fore — a public agency providing books and other materials to encourage reading and please the imagination, completely free of charge for the whole family! Almost any other form of leisure activity carries some kind of levy, even though it too may be provided by the local authority — swimming pools and leisure centres have an entrance charge; arts centres and play schemes a session fee. Reading and using the library is free.

The research sets out to consider the following questions:

For libraries

a) Is the Family Reading Group a viable activity for children in the public library?

b) To what extent can the public library actively encourage children to enjoy reading through running a Family Reading Group as compared with other extension activities such as book clubs, holiday events and storytimes?

c) How far can this be reconciled with administrative and budgetary restrictions?

d) What implications does running a Family Reading Group have for library staff and stock?

For parents

a) How can parents be encouraged to remain involved with their children's reading once the child has mastered the 'decoding' process?

b) How can they be made aware and advised on the material available?

c) What effect did their own childhood reading have on their present attitude to children's reading and use of libraries?

For children

a) Is the Family Reading Group effective in encouraging children to read for fun in their spare time?

It will be shown to be effective if sufficient numbers of children come to meetings, borrow books, read them at home in their leisure time and 'enjoy' them.

b) How do children express their gratification as readers?

Factors which will affect the success of the group include

1. The practical organisation of the Reading Group evening and its promotion.

2. The bookstock available (points 1 and 2 are very much dependent on library policy and budget).

3. The reader's adviser methods used by the organisers.

4. Peer group and other environmental influences.

To measure the effect of the Family Reading Group on the child it will be necessary to examine:

1. Children's ability to choose what they read.

2. Their development as 'readers', in terms of the wider definition of reading given earlier.

3. The extent of their 'gratification' through the way in which they relate to the book.

8. Summary

The first half of this book discusses the practical aspects of running a Family Reading Group. The second half concentrates on the effect that attending the Reading Group and borrowing and reading stories have on the child.

Chapter 2 sets out the various methods used in the research. A range of methodology was necessary to validate the findings and to provide a statistical background for the more qualitative conclusions. Two aspects of the research presented problems:

1. The formal study of an informal practice.
Attempts were made at earlier groups to record the comments of children and parents as they selected their books, but this proved unsuccessful. A straight charting of the use of time at the meetings: "7pm — 7.10pm children came in and returned books, 7.10pm — 7.20pm children and parents selected books" etc. lacked the sense of excitement which is characteristic of the group and a component of its success. It was decided to combine photographs taken at the meetings with comments from the children themselves to describe what happened at a Family Reading Group meeting (see Prologue) and to combine them with more formal statistical and observational records to assess the viability of the group.

2. Questioning primary age children.
This has been found to be a problem by most researchers of children's reading habits, and probably explains why most studies are confined to children of secondary age. Frank Whitehead used questionnaires backed by selected interviews in his national survey "Children and Their Books" Schools Council Research Studies (1977). The youngest children surveyed were 10 or older and he comments

> "The able and intelligent children of this age seemed perfectly capable of giving sensible and accurate questionnaire answers, but one felt less confident when one came to children of lower ability and attainment in this age range."

This inevitably means that the results of his survey relate mainly to the reading habits of the more "able and intelligent children".

A more recent discussion of children's reading by Donald Fry *Children Talk about Books: Seeing Themselves as Readers* (1985), attempts to overcome the difficulty inherent in questioning younger children by using reports of 'conversations' with six children. He states that his work

> "deliberately restricts itself to six young readers in the belief that such case-studies are revealing and helpful because of their particularity".

However, only two of the six children studied are at primary school.

Whitehead (1977) comments that children's memories are unreliable when completing questionnaires about books. The Fleetville project attempted to overcome this drawback:

1.   By keeping records of borrowing from the Family Reading Group. In this way it was possible to know exactly which books the children had taken home.

2.   By visiting children within two weeks of their taking these books home, thus making it possible to know exactly which titles they had read.

The methods used in this project, which will be discussed and assessed in the next chapter, included: observations of meetings; records of stock and of borrowing; informal interviews with parents and children who attended group meetings and diary records of 9-11 year olds in Fleetville.

Chapter 3 uses records of Family Reading Group meetings, together with interviews with parents and children immediately after they had attended their first Family Reading Group in order to establish who participates in such activities. The effect of promotion is discussed as are the effects of the home and school environments in encouraging children to attend meetings. The attitude of the families to library use and to reading which emerges from the interviews is substantiated in part by records of the children's use of Fleetville library and by the incidence of reading and library visits in the After School Diaries. The reasons given by the children for coming to the meeting reflect a strong peer group influence.

The theory that it is the more active child who is likely to become an avid reader is confirmed by the After School Diaries which are examined in Chapter 4. These were completed by children at four schools in the Fleetville area over a period of two weeks in February 1984 and 1985. The importance of group activities to children in the 9-11 year age group has implications for the promotion of reading to them.

Chapter 5 examines the books which the children chose to read and the reasons for their choice. Personal recommendation is shown to be one of the prime reasons for choosing a title. The child is also influenced by the presentation of the book and the level of its reading.

Chapter 6 analyses the findings of the monthly interviews with selected group members. These 'impact interviews' aimed to discover what it was that the children liked or disliked about the books which they had chosen at the Family Reading Group. As they became more accomplished as readers, what children found boring and what they found interesting in a book, changed. This could be one of the reasons why they read the same book more than once. As they developed as 'readers' of fiction — "terminal readers" in Frank Hatt's words

— they used earlier experience gained through their reading to help them; for example they learnt always to read the opening chapters as these give clues to the action. Experience brought more sophisticated gratification. Dialogue and allusion, which may once have been found intrusive, amused at a later stage in 'readership'.

Chapter 7 continues to examine this development of children as 'readers', and their changing perception of reality in the books which they read. Interviews with children at varying stages in their development showed that more practised readers had reached the stage of recognising elements of reality in fantasy stories, and were better able to identify with them.

The final chapters draw conclusions and make recommendations for

1.   Effective library provision and promotion of fiction to children.

2.   Parental involvement with their children's reading.

3.   Children's enjoyment of fiction.

9.   Background Reading

The background reading for this research came from three major sources:

1.   Published surveys of children's reading during the last ten years which have examined

   — Children's Reading Habits 10-15 (*Children and their books*, the final report of the Schools Council research project on Children's Reading Habits 10-15, Whitehead et al, 1977).
   — The Influence of Book Supply in Middle Schools (Ingham, Jennie, *Books and Reading Development* 1981).
   — The Benefits of Parental Involvement With Children Learning to Read (Griffiths, Alex and Hamilton, Dorothy, *Parent, Teacher, Child, Working Together in Children's Learning* 1984).
   — The use of public libraries by adults (Totterdell and Bird. *The Effective Library* 1976).
   — The method used by Westminster City Libraries to encourage children to read (Bird, Jean. *Young Teenage Readers.* B. L. 1982).

2.   — Discussions on the developmental, psychological and philosophical aspects of childrens reading found in *The Cool Web,* edited by Margaret Meek and Aidan Warlow (1978) Nicholas Tucker's *The Child and The Book* (1981) and Robert Leeson's *Reading and Righting* (1985).

3.   — Discussion of the gratification provided by the media in general, Katz E and Blumler, J, *Current perspectives on gratification research* [1973]) and by books in particular, (Hatt, Frank, *The Reading Process* [1976]).

4.   —Articles on minor surveys of children's reading and leisure interests in Europe and America.

This background material was identified in part through a Dialog computerised literature search using the key words Families, Reading, Parent, Child, Library. This was updated through LISA. Non-specialist journals such as The Bookseller, The Times Educational Supplement and The Times Literary Supplement were scanned weekly and some relevant material was also found in the Sunday newspapers! Since the topics covered by the literature search — parental involvement, use of libraries, children's reading and leisure interests — are specifically discussed in separate chapters of the report, previous works will be commented on in the relevant chapters. There will be no separate chapter on the literature survey and all references will be listed in the bibliography at the end of the report.

Chapter 2

An examination of methods used in the research together with comments on their practice

A variety of methods was used to study the Fleetville Family Reading Group and the families who attended. These methods were:

1. *Observational records of*
   a) the setting up of the Fleetville Group
   b) 10 Family Reading Group Meetings.

2. *Statistical records of*
   a) attendance at 10 group meetings
   b) use of Fleetville Library by members
   c) the books borrowed at meetings
   d) the books which the children read from amongst those which they borrowed at meetings.

3. *Records of the cost of*
   a) bookstock
   b) staff time.

4. *After school diaries*
   of the leisure time pursuits of 278 9-12 year olds in Fleetville in February 1984 and 159 in February 1985.

Table 2.1 To Show Methods used to Examine the Effect which Running a Family Reading Group can have on Libraries

	Areas on which Activity Impinged			
Method used to observe activity	*Library Administration* *Staff*	*Stock*	*Library Use* *Image*	*Issue/Membership*
Observation of				
setting up group	X			X
group meetings			X	X
Statistical records of				
group attendance				X
members' use of Fleetville Library				X
book borrowing (from meetings)		X		X
book reading		X	X	
Costing of				
FRG bookstock		X		
FRG staff	X			
After School Diaries				X
Informal interviews				
parents/children			X	X
'Impact' interviews		X		X

5. *Informal interviews*

with 24 parents and 22 children who attended the first meeting in order to assess attitudes towards library use and book reading. These interviews were repeated six months later.

6. *Regular discussions*

with fourteen child group members after the first four Family Reading Group meetings to find out which of the books borrowed were read, and the 'impact' which they had on the child, assessed in terms of understanding and 'enjoyment' as defined in the introduction.

Tables 2.1, 2.2 and 2.3 show how these methods related to the aims of the project, as set out in the introduction.

Table 2.2   To Show Methods used to Examine the Effect which Attendance at a Family Reading Group can have on Parents

Method used to observe activity	Areas on which Activity Impinged		
	Parents' Involvement with child's reading	Parents' Awareness of Materials	Parents' Library Use
Observation of			
group meetings		X	
Statistical records of			
group attendance	X		X
book borrowing	X	X	
Informal interviews			
parents/children	X	X	X

Table 2.3   To Show Methods used to Examine the Effect which Attendance at a Family Reading Group can have on Children

Method	Areas on which Activity Impinged			
		EFFECT ON CHILDREN'S		
	Use of Library	Ability to Choose books	Enjoyment of books	Use of Leisure Time
Observation of				
group meetings		X	X	
Statistical records of				
group attendance	X			X
members' use of				
Fleetville Library	X			X
book borrowing				
(from meetings)		X		
book reading		X	X	
After School Diaries	X		X	X
Informal interviews				
parents/children	X		X	X
'Impact' interviews		X	X	

1. Observational records

(a) Observation of the Fleetville Group's establishment

(i) To meet the needs of the children

Blaise Cronin and Irene Martin write of the social responsibility of public libraries in their article *Social Skills Training in Librarianship* (J. of Librarianship, April 1983), and point out "the fact that library services exist, not in their own right, but as need fulfilment agencies." Barry Totterdell and Jean Bird in *The Effective Library* (1976) writing of the types of need, unactivated, unexpressed and expressed, which the Effective Library should meet, quote the needs of children and young people as prime among the "unactivated" — "the most difficult form to be evaluated, but it cannot be therefore simply ignored."

An internal assessment of Children's Services and stock of the St Albans' libraries (1 main branch, 4 sub-branches, 2 trailers) in 1983 had recommended "a slightly more outward looking philosophy in terms of community contacts" and commented that, at Fleetville in particular, "library activities in the community have been marked by their infrequence". Since Fleetville Library was well placed in the community to serve at least two out of the four schools in its catchment area, there was a very good argument for the need for some kind of service to young people in the community.

(ii) To meet the staffing needs

St Albans libraries have an area team staffing policy. At the time when a Family Reading Group in the unit was being discussed (October 1983) Rosie Dudgeon had just been appointed as Librarian in charge of children's services for the area. This was a new post of responsibility as, prior to this, sub–branches had been responsible for their own children's services. The policy resulting from the internal assessment was that "conscious co-ordination between Rosie and the librarians of sub-branches is needed".

As well as being a new venture in itself for St Albans, it was anticipated that the running of the Family Reading Group might create new links between library staff at the same time as increasing the scope of activities offered to the general public. Rosie's time for children's activities at the sub-branches was limited (20.1 hours per week total) and she had to be convinced that the Family Reading Group would be the best use of her time within the brief of the post, and not an optional extra. Although this particular group was held out of normal working hours, branch time allocated for running a Family Reading Group is working time and has to be claimed back at some other stage during the working week.

Table 2.4 To Show Time Spent by Children's Librarian on Organising a Family Reading Group Meeting

Activity	Hours per Meeting (10 meetings a year)
Preparation of library	½
Group meeting	1½
Maintaining records	1
*Promotion	2
TOTAL	**5**

* Since the group was promoted at 3 schools in the area which were each visited once a term, and there were three Family Reading Group meetings a term, the figure given is an average.

The promotional visits to the schools also served to promote the library service as a whole. When made in conjunction with the Divisional Schools Librarian, these visits also served as a liaison point between the schools and public library services. The promotion of branch library activities to children in schools is important as it is the ideal opportunity for the librarian to come face to face with users and non-users alike — all children go to school, but all children do not go to the library.

It is difficult to quantify staff time spent on library activities for children since, as is shown to be the case when visiting a school, one visit serves many purposes. The librarian may be promoting books, or reading, or the library service in general, or one specific event, or all of these, and is probably also dealing with queries from teachers on the suitability of reading material and the organisation of the school library all at the same time. The most common library activities for children fall into three main groups:

1. Regular story times each week for a particular age group.

2. Library 'clubs' or 'book clubs' which usually involve some form of craft or written activity in conjunction with the books promoted and which are held at regular intervals.

3. Holiday activities or special events — 'one off' sessions involving author visits, book character costumes, theatre groups, etc.

All events often include volunteer helpers, non-professional staff, parents and others. Mark Leach, children's librarian at a large central library, gave the following approximate timings for activities which can be seen here compared with those for the Family Reading Group.

Table 2.5   To Show Monthly Number of Staff Hours Spent on Library Activities for Children

	Preparation	*Presentation*	*Total*
Library Club	1¼	¾	2
Holiday Activity	2	2	4
Story time	½	½	1
Family Reading Group	1½	1½	3

Over a year the number of hours spent on activities would be as follows:

Table 2.6   To Show Yearly Number of Staff Hours spent on Library Activities for Children

	Preparation	*Presentation*	*Total*
Library Club (fortnightly term time)	22½	17½	40
Holiday activites (X 9)	18	18	36
Story time (weekly – term time)	20	20	40
Family Reading Group (10 per year)	15	15	30

This shows that running a Family Reading Group is a relatively economical use of staff time, and as such, well suited to an Area Children's Librarian such as Rosie, who has a limited amount of time available to spend in the sub-branch library.

(iii) To meet the need of Fleetville Library for increased use

Fleetville Library

Fleetville Library was opened in 1959. At the time of this project it was open 25 hours a week — Tuesdays, Thursdays, Fridays and Saturday mornings. On 25th November, six weeks after the inception of this project, it was announced by Hertfordshire County Council that Fleetville Library would close on 1st April, 1984.

It had been understood that one sub-branch in St Albans would have to close when work on a much needed new Central Library began, but the County Committee suggested bringing forward the closure of the library in a bid to save those funds estimated as needing to be cut in order to meet Government spending targets.

On the Saturday after the announcement was made, the leader of the local Conservative Group collected 270 signatures on a petition to keep the library open and spoke eloquently at the County Committee meeting later that week in favour of retaining the library as a community facility. The local papers agreed with him as did the Liberal councillor, who commented to the press that "Fleetville was not the most affluent area in St Albans and had very few community assets, which made the library even more important". An unnamed supporter in a letter to the papers headed "Bookworm blues" wrote, "Fleetville library was custom-built to modern standards to serve a clearly identifiable community which, I hope, will protest most strongly".

At their meeting early in December the county committee took note of this phenomena of cross-party agreement and announced that "while they were prepared to accept that libraries might have to close next year as a money saving measure, they did not wish to decide immediately which ones". (Herts Advertiser 9/12/83 — Library Fate in the Balance.) This was a hopeful sign and the "Review" of 8/12/83 closed its article with the comment

> "The county librarian said that if the decision was not made until the end of the financial year, half the planned savings would be lost".

Accordingly, before the decision date of January 18th, 1984, it was made known that the County's Finance and Resources Committee

> "agreed at their meeting on Monday, January 9th, to make available an additional sum of money in order to avoid the need to close any libraries".

This small drama, centred around the fate of Fleetville library within weeks of the research project being planned, had several results. On the negative side it prevented early plans being confirmed, as had the decision been made to close Fleetville in April, 1984, the Family Reading Group would have had to have been sited elsewhere, probably at London Colney. School visits to promote the group were postponed and even after the reprieve had been given, the first meeting had to be postponed from mid-January to early March, 1984. This in turn, had the effect of reducing the number of meetings used for intense impact analysis.

Positively, the reaction in favour of the retention of Fleetville library gave a very strong impression of the community spirit of the area and the importance given to the need for a local library, particularly for use by the elderly; mothers with young children and children calling in on their way home from school. The library took advantage of this and formed a "Friends of Fleetville" group, one aim of which is to fight any future threats of closure, but which also holds exhibitions and meetings on topics of general interest. The Family Reading Group therefore opened with an unexpected dual purpose of consolidating the library's position in the community as well as promoting its books to the families living in the surrounding area.

b) Observation of group meetings

Systematic observation of group meetings was affected by the informal nature of the group. It seemed important to convey the relaxed, club atmosphere of the groups of parents, children and librarians, and this could not be done by systematic observation. A photographic record was kept of the second, third and seventh meetings. A twelve minute video has now been produced showing Family Reading Groups in a public library and in a secondary school. It is available, (price £4.60 plus post and packing, from Herts Educational TV, Goldings, Hertford, plus post and packing). The photographs, together with comments on the Family Reading Group from the families who took part, appear in the prologue.

2. Statistical Records

a) Statistics of attendance

A record was kept of the children who borrowed books over the ten meetings from March 1984 to January 1985, which provided feedback on the cyclical nature of the attendance. A record was also kept of the total number of children and adults who attended each meeting. Records were able to show whether the transfer from primary to secondary school for ten of the members had any effect on their attendance at meetings, and also whether children whose parents came to meetings had a different pattern of attendance.

b) Statistical survey of members' use of Fleetville Library

In order to assess whether the group was encouraging children and their families to use the Fleetville library it was necessary to discover whether they or their families had actually borrowed any books before the meetings began in March 1984, and whether they continued to borrow from the library independently of the Family Reading Group. If the library issue system had been computerised this would have been easy. As it was, the Browne issue system provided time consuming to check.

The Fleetville issue was checked two days after the first Family Reading Group meeting against a list of members. It was checked again a year later. The findings are discussed in the following chapter, but cannot be taken as a comprehensive indicator of library use since the interviews revealed that families also used St Albans Central, Marshalswick and Cunningham libraries — none of which at the time of the project, used a computer system. Time restrictions made it impossible to check all four outlets, and Fleetville was chosen since it was the use of Fleetville library which was being promoted.

c)   Statistics of book borrowing

Each book had an issue card headed by author and title on which the name of the borrower was recorded each month. If a borrower retained the book for more than one session this was also noted. After each meeting record cards were completed and the titles of books borrowed were also recorded according to borrower. This not only showed the most popular books, but also which books had been handed on from friend to friend since names were often listed in the same order on the record slips of various books — for example, Lucy, Louise and Mary (a girl not included in the interview sample) all read *The Little Vampire, The Little Vampire Moves In* and *Outside Over There*. Ceri can be seen to be borrowing titles such as *Absolute Zero* or *Gowie Corby Plays Chicken* after Andrew and Tom. In this way the records substantiate the observations made at meetings that books are passed from friend to friend, and the children's own assertion that recommendations by friends can account for their choice of book. Borrowing records also showed the frequency with which children retained a book from one meeting to the next. Issue figures for the group, when worked out as an hourly average, can be compared with those generally at Fleetville Library.

d)   Statistics of books read

Interviews with fourteen of the group members as soon as possible after the first four meetings showed which books the children had read from those which they had taken home. This has relevance to the study of how children read (see Chapter 5) and also had practical implications for the number of books to be allowed on loan from a library, and their length of issue.

It was necessary to visit the children regularly, before they had forgotten whether they had completely read a book or not. Relying solely on a questionnaire, as Frank Whitehead (1977) found is not sufficient when dealing with primary age children.

3.   Costing

a)   Costing of Family Reading Group bookstock

Initially a collection of hard back and paperback books was bought costing approximately £600. Compared with the total amount spent on junior stock for the St Albans group this represents 4.5% of the annual junior budget. However, as with promotion of the service, no boundaries can be placed, in this case, on the cost of stock. The collection, though bought for the Family Reading Group, was recirculated into the stock of the branches as it outlived its time of usefulness in the group. It allowed for a flexibility in selection on the part of the librarian, who was able to use the group as a sounding board for new or experimental titles.

b)   Costing of staff

This has already been covered in Section 1 (a) (ii).

4. After School Diaries

In order to assess how reading rated as a leisure time activity, and whether or not the Family Reading Group had any effect on this, children at the schools in which the group was to be promoted were asked to fill in After School Diaries listing activities and, preferably the timing of these activities, between arriving home from school and going to bed at night.

It was hoped the diaries would show how reading, along with other activities, fitted into the timetable of an active child, out of school and before bedtime, and how it compared as a viable alternative to Brownies, swimming, music, gymnastics, etc. Interestingly enough, this was one point which emerged from the correspondence following the *Reading in America 1978 Survey* where John S Zimmer Jr (Senior Editor, Readers Digest) suggested "attempting to interest organisations in starting to think of reading as an activity, like cooking or playing basket ball or camping or sewing or dating".

The diaries were used to assess how far Family Reading Group members were representative of 9-12 year olds in their lifestyle and, subsequently, how Family Reading Groups could be promoted to appeal to this age group. The children's attendance at and comments on meetings show how far this has been successful (See Chapter 3).

Details from the diaries of group members were used along with interviews and records to assess the extent of the children's reading and whether it increased after contact with the Family Reading Group.

The diary format appears in Appendix 2. There was difficulty in making provision for the children to express the concept of time spent involved in an activity. 'A long time', 'not very long' has little meaning to a child and is relative to whether they find that particular activity to their liking! It was decided to provide analogue clocks for the children to fill in, but this also proved fallible. However the dividing of time into "before my meal", "after my meal", "bedtime" and "after bed" helped to place the activities in sequence. The children were asked what they liked 'best of all' to see whether reading featured as a preferred activity.

300 diaries were distributed to third and fourth year pupils at four junior schools in the Fleetville area in February 1984 before the first Family Reading Group meeting (schools 1-4). The Family Reading Group was subsequently promoted in these four schools. In February 1985, 300 diaries were again distributed to fourth year pupils in the same four schools and to about half the first year secondary pupils in the nearest school to be 'fed' by these junior schools (school 5).

Table 2.7   To Show After School Diary Returns

	School 5	School 1	School 2	School 3	School 4	Total
1984	—	39	92	66	81	278
1985	53	14	41	30	21	159
						437

The returns in 1985 were substantially lower than those in 1984 for two reasons:

1.   The diaries lost their novelty value to children and teachers.

2. It would have been too time consuming to trace and distribute diaries to all the original children who completed diaries in 1984 but who had changed schools in 1985.

As a result, 92 children returned diaries in both 1984 and 1985.

Table 2.8   To Show Number of Juniors who Completed Diaries in 1984 (3rd years) and 1985 (4th years)

	School 1	School 2	School 3	School 4
Number of FRG Members	1	9	4	—
Number of Non-FRG Members	7	26	12	6
TOTAL	**8**	**35**	**16**	**6**

Table 2.9   To Show Number of Children who Completed Diaries in 4th year Juniors (1984) and 1st year Secondary School (1985)

	School 1	School 2	School 3	School 4
FRG	2	2	2	—
Non-FRG	4	3	14	—
TOTAL	**6**	**5**	**16**	**—**

By comparing the 1984 and 1985 diaries of members and non-members it was possible to examine whether belonging to a Family Reading Group or the change from primary to secondary school had any effect on the children's use of leisure time, and in particular on their reading habits.

5.   Interviews with parents and children

Twenty four children from twenty two families were interviewed after attending their first Reading Group Meeting, together with one or both parents, to assess their approaches towards books and reading and their attitude towards public libraries and public library use. For twenty of those interviewed, the inaugural meeting was their first but 4 of those interviewed missed the inaugural meeting and were therefore interviewed after the second Reading Group Meeting. Parents were asked about their own reading habits and their use of libraries as children in an attempt to see whether patterns established in their own childhood were continued as adults or had affected their attitude to their own child's reading.

Both parents and children were asked about their initial reaction to the Family Reading Group. (For Questionnaire see Appendix 1). Twenty one follow up interviews were conducted six months later with twenty families, (one child was now at boarding school and the other 2 families difficult to pin down) to assess any change in attitude towards books or reading on the part of the child since attending the Family Reading Group, or any change in awareness of children's books on the part of the parent. (For Questionnaire see Appendix 1).

These interviews also gave feedback information on the timing of meetings and factors which prevented parents or children from attending.

It was decided to interview a sample of 'late starters' who attended the second or third Family Reading Group meeting as their first to see why this was so, hence the spread of first interviews between March and May 1984.

Table 2.10   To Show Number of Families Interviewed after their first Family Reading Group Meeting and again 6 Months Later

	March-May 1984	October 1984	Total
Number of Families	22	20	42
Number of Children	24	20	44

The parents interviewed were especially keen to talk about library provision and opening hours, (particularly because of the recently postponed closure of Fleetville branch). Having attended the Family Reading Group meeting, most felt positively towards the interview, since they had already met the interviewer at the meetings. The informality of the meeting carried over into the interviews.

6.   'Impact' Interviews

These interviews took their name from the need to assess the 'impact' made on the children by the books which they had borrowed.

One of the justifications for an active promotion of books given in the introduction was that it involved the specialist librarian and the client in the choosing of materials. These regular interviews with the children who had received this service provided an opportunity to assess whether or not they were benefiting from it. Were the books which they were selecting at Family Reading Group meetings extending their literary horizons more effectively than books selected at random from shelves at school, at home, or in that same library? What exactly was it about a book which appealed to one child and not to another? Was it connected with the book itself, or with the child's accumulated experience? Even more relevant to this survey was the question of whether the child's experience of the book was coloured by the way in which it was promoted. By creating a group whose aim was to encourage the reading of books for enjoyment, was the library successful in its methods of motivation?

In an attempt to assess how far the Family Reading Group was encouraging children to read for enjoyment, it was necessary to know what reaction they had to the books which they had chosen and taken home from the group meetings. Did they, in fact, enjoy them? Did the children, by their comments, show that they had benefitted from the advantages, listed in the introduction, of becoming a 'reader'? What kind of impact did their reading have on them?

As well as assessing the books which they had borrowed from the first meeting in the course of the first interview, fourteen children were visited as soon as possible after the second, third and fourth meetings to discuss the books which they had taken home. The full questionnaire is given in Appendix 1. Items which caused the most comment were:

1. Why these children had chosen the books.

2. Which titles they had read and which rejected.

3. The way in which the books had been read — in fits and starts or in lengthy chunks, on their own or with friends and family.

As has been already mentioned, it was necessary to talk to children face to face as soon as possible after reading their books in order to gauge their true reaction. The children had the books in front of them, which helped them to remember which they had read, and they often read favourite passages aloud to make a point. The passages which they chose, either to read or relate, then led to discussion of why that particular book was funny or frightening. In this way it became possible to discuss titles in depth. Where children had taken home a pile of books, these informal interviews became quite lengthy, sometimes lasting for up to an hour.

The advantages of these impact interviews over a written reading record or survey were that they allowed the children to give a broader answer to questions about books and avoided the trap mentioned by Whitehead (1977) that only the more intelligent could give written answers to a questionnaire. Jennie Ingham bypassed this problem in the main by the use of the Ingham/Clift Reading Record Form, where children ticked boxes to indicate the extent of their liking of a title *Books and Reading Development,* 1981. However, she also found it necessary to augment her findings from the reading records with case studies of children's reading during the Bradford Book Flood.

In the Fleetville survey the interviewer's increased rapport with the child was aided by the fact that she knew already from the reading records which books the children had borrowed, had probably read them herself and was thus better able to follow the discussion.

Often the children developed their opinions on the book as they spoke and used the interviews to extend their reactions to it; in this way it was possible to see the growing impact which was made by a particular title.

As all the children had the same collection of books to choose from, and the interviews were made over a period of six months, it was possible to compare the reactions of different children to the same title. It also became apparent why some children retained the same book over a long period of time. Altogether a total of 56 interviews were held with 14 children.

It is clear therefore that a variety of methods were necessary to the scope of the research. Written records and observation supported evidence and the ideas obtained more informally through the unstructured interviews with children and their families.

Chapter 3

Who comes to a Family Reading Group?

"There is a bunch of four of us, and we all recommended it to a friend called Tom and he has come ever since."

In her report on *Promotional Activities and Materials for Children in an Urban Branch Library* (Fearn, 1982) Margaret Fearn recommends that:

"Librarians need to develop strategies for promoting the service to teachers that move beyond the library visit".

Before looking at who came to the Fleetville Family Reading Group it is relevant to describe the promotional methods used and at whom they were aimed.

1. Promotion of the Group

(a) To the schools

It was decided to promote the Family Reading Group at all four junior schools in the Fleetville area.

Rosie and I visited each school in February 1984 to talk to the head about the theory behind Family Reading Groups and to leave behind an article on Family Reading Groups by Dina Thorpe *Reading,* 1982 and a pilot diary study to be discussed by staff. Rosie subsequently visited the schools again to leave leaflets for all third and fourth year children in all four schools to take home to their parents. It was stressed that ideally children coming to a group meeting should come with an adult/parent/next door neighbour or whoever looked after them in the evenings. This caused some disappointment among children who knew their parents — for various reasons — would never come. This promotion took two three-hour sessions.

As two of the four schools had new heads during this time, the visits to the schools served a double purpose. They were certainly effective as far as the children who came to the group were concerned, as most of those interviewed, when questioned as to their main reason for coming to the first Family Reading Group meeting explained: "Rosie came to school and told us about it" (see Table 3.80).

School 1

This was the smallest school involved with the Family Reading Group and also the one furthest away from the public library. Built in the early 1900's amidst terraced housing of a similar date, School 1 has a mixed intake with a high percentage of children from multi-racial backgrounds, especially Asian and Italian. The Head is highly committed to books and to reading, an active member of the Schools Library Association, whose Home Counties book group holds meetings in the school. The approach towards books and library use is open and integral with the curriculum; the library, which is centrally positioned in the school, is run by the remedial teacher who also became a regular supporter of the Family Reading Group. Another teacher in the school was a former secretary of the St Albans Children's Book Group. This then is a school where book awareness flourishes, and appeared on the surface to be an ideal field for Family Reading Group members, yet only three children from the school came to meetings and two of them left after a relatively short time.

School 2

School 2 is the largest in the area with 234 children, it is also the nearest to the public library, although on the opposite side of the road. A new Head had been appointed who took up his office in January 1984 and made a point of making contact with the public library at his earliest opportunity. He welcomed the idea of the Family Reading Group and saw it as an opportunity to get to know some of his parents outside the school gates — a priority for him as the school had no PTA or School Association and little history of parental involvement. Rosie and I were invited to visit the classes and to look around the school — including the library!

The school's central library at that time was very antiquated, more suited to the level of the Girls Secondary School, (which the building had housed in the distant past), with a stock which resembed "sets of projects" rather than a balanced collection of books. Fiction collections were in the classroom and varied from teacher to teacher, whose different attitudes to children's reading, the use of books and home loan must have confused many a pupil! As a whole, the attitude of the school at that time to reading could be said to be "formal".

The Head saw the school library as one of his first areas of innovation and as a means of involving parents in the working of the school. This was not easy, as not all members of staff viewed this constructively. However a year later the new library was well underway, thanks to the hard work of a group of mothers, two of whom were Family Reading Group regulars.

The Head admitted that he was a "priorities" man and tended to go from enthusiasm to enthusiam, attending to the library one year, music the next, etc. He came to three out of the ten meetings in the first year. School staff support is reflected in the attendance of the children to the group (see Table 3.1), who enjoy (for the most part!) meeting their teachers out of school. Support for the Reading Group from an interested member of staff — who can remind the children of dates and times of meetings — saves the time of the librarian, who can make a telephone call to the Head from time to time instead of a series of visits to the school.

School 3

School 3 has 213 children in seven classes, but as it is a JMI school only approximately 120 of these are in the junior part of the school. The building is in the middle of an area of 1950's built houses — three long roads with council houses at one end and larger, privately owned homes at the other. It is next door to the main secondary school in the Fleetville area, a mixed comprehensive.

The Head was interested in the project, but usually "very busy" when library staff called and although he agreed to put up notices and to let Rosie talk to classes there was no active backing to the project. This non-committal attitude towards the Family Reading Group reflected the school's approach towards library provision. There is a Junior Non-Fiction library in the small entrance hall to the school and fiction stocks are held separately in each classroom. Separate stocks can mean that teachers may not know what the other classes hold and can lead to frustration among the readers, like Nicola who began reading "Ramona the Pest" at the end of the school year and "had to put it back so that we could change classrooms".

Before the project started, arrangements had been made for the Schools Library Service to reorganise the Non-Fiction Library with the help of the Head and this did eventually result in the involvement of parents.

Table 3.1   To Show School Representation in Attendance at Fleetville Family Reading Group

School	Number of Children at FRG	Number of Staff at FRG
School 1	4	1
School 2	30	2
School 3	15	–
School 4	–	–
Children at other schools	5	–
Children at unknown schools	5	–
TOTAL	**59**	**3**

School 4

This is a Catholic school on the edge of the Fleetville area. It was decided to include the school in the Family Reading Group promotion on the grounds that it was no further away from Fleetville Library than School 1 and could make natural links with Fleetville as the nearest public library.

It can be seen that the school which had the strongest staff support also had the strongest representation at the group. School 2 is also the nearest school to the library and had contact with it before being visited by the librarian.

The complete lack of take up at School 4 was not unexpected as the school was the furthest away from the library and, in addition, had a very wide catchment area, with Catholic families bussed into school. Combining this with the fact that the school was in a state of flux at the time of Family Reading promotion, with a new Head taking over four days before the first meeting, the outcome is not surprising. As a result, further promotion of the group at this school was seen as an unprofitable use of Rosie's time, although a visit was made a year later with the follow up diaries.

The low response from School 1 was disappointing, although not unexpected by the Head in view of the high percentage of Asian children at the school who would be unlikely to go out in the evenings. My hypothesis would also be that children at this school were already receiving stimulus in their reading interests, and because of this found little use for the Family Reading Group. This hypothesis will be supported when we look at the library use by Family Reading Group members and non-members. Of the four children who came to the group from this school only one stayed the course: two of those who dropped out were among those interviewed as "before and after" case studies. It emerged that as well as using the school library, these two were already confident and regular users of the public library.

(b)   Other methods of promotion

It will be seen from Table 3.1 that ten of the children came from schools at which the group was not being promoted. This shows the advantage of holding a Family Reading Group in a public library rather than in a school, where attendance is obviously limited to the children who attend that school. A leaflet was on display at Fleetville Library, together with handbills to take home. In addition, Rosie spoke to the Federation of Children's Book Groups St Albans branch Annual General Meeting on the theme of the Family Reading Group. A consequence of this was that one mother, who was a freelance broadcaster, contacted her to discuss the possibility of an interview for Woman's Hour on the subject. This, in fact, took place before the first meeting and was broadcast in September 1984 and included comments and recordings made during the first meeting. (See Appendix 9)

2.   Where did they live?

Whatever school they went to and whatever public library they used, almost all the Family Reading Group famililies lived within a mile of Fleetville Library with seventeen of the twenty two families interviewed after the first and second meetings living on the same side of the main Hatfield Road as the library. This bears out the findings of Totterdell and Bird in *The Effective Library* (1976) that

> "What have been shown as major barriers to library use are man-made geographised features, in particular lines of communication such as major roads, railways, etc., which people are often reluctant to cross, even were subways are provided"

and they were talking about adults, not children!

The rolling attendance patterns and the small catchment area of the Reading Group show that it became accepted as a local "drop-in" point for reading families. A cup of coffee, a drink of orange and a chat about books resulted in a pile being taken home to be looked at over the next four weeks and talked about with friends. The close proximity and the low key nature of the group meant that it fitted into the routine of young families who did not see it as a formal event. Not only the level of the books but the tenor of the meeting was calculated to encourage a "little and often" approach to reading that was not intimidating.

Table 3.2   To Show Library use of a Sample of 22 Reading Group Children 1984 (100%=22)

Library Mentioned	Fleetville	Marshalswick	Cunningham	St. Albans	Other	More than 1	Books on loan from Fleetville at time of interview
Number of children mentioning use of this library	15	4	1	10	1	13	3
(%)	(68%)	(18%)	(4%)	(45%)	(4%)	(59%)	(14%)

Table 3.3   To Show Library use of a Sample of 24 Reading Group Parents 1984 (100%=24)

Library Mentioned	Fleetville	Marshalswick	Cunningham	St. Albans	Other	More than 1	Books currently on loan from any library
Number of parents mentioning use of this library	14	1	7	8	1	7	10
(%)	(58%)	(4%)	(29%)	(33%)	(4%)	(29%)	(42%)

3.   Did they use a Public Library?

Tables 3.2 and 3.3 show the responses from the parents and children who were interviewed after the first Family Reading Group meeting to the questions "Had you ever been to Fleetville Library before you came to the Family Reading Group?" and "Do you borrow books from St Albans Central, or any other libraries?"

The actual percentage of the fifty nine members with books on loan from Fleetville Library at the end of February when the issue was checked was 14%. However the percentage of the twenty two children interviewed who said they used Fleetville Library was 68%. Because of lack of computerisation of the issue systems, it was practical only to check Fleetville issue against a list of Family Reading Group members' names and not to carry out a similar check on the issues of other libraries in St Albans. The difference in percentage of those who described themselves as library users and those who actually had books on loan from Fleetville at the time of the check is interesting, and no doubt representative of the many children who hold up their hands in class when asked if they use a library. This is substantiated by Peter Mann's findings in Sheffield noted in *Book Buyers and Borrowers* (1971) where 12% of people using the library did not borrow any books.

The hypothesis that the Family Reading Group attracted children who may not have had their reading needs met elsewhere, exemplified in part by the lack of use of the group by children from School 1, is strengthened by the analysis of sample diary returns. 22% of non-members who completed sample diaries in February 1984 listed visiting the library as an after-school activity, as compared with only 5% of children who subsequently became group members. Thus the Family Reading Group can be seen to have encouraged children who had not visited the library during the last 2 weeks of February 1984 to do so when they came to the first group meeting.

In February 1984 ten out of the total of the 59 Family Reading Group members (as distinct from the sample interviewed) had books on loan from Fleetville Library (17%). When the issue was checked a year later thirteen out of the total membership of fifty nine had books on loan (22%). Whilst this represents only a relatively small increase in library use, it must be remembered that these were spot checks on one day only, and, in either year, some children may just have returned books to the library and thus slipped through the net.

"If it is shut on Monday and then you shop on Tuesday and then it's shut on Wednesday and so it's Thursday before you get them back."

Table 3.4   To Show Barriers to Library use among Fleetville Families (100%=24)

Fines	Inconvenient hours	Difficulty in Obtaining new books
27%	27%	9%

5.   Children's perception of the Public Library

The children were asked to describe a public library to a space invader who had landed from another planet. Their consensus on libraries was that they were useful places if you could read, that you had to remember to return the books which you borrowed and that librarians tried to be helpful. Most agreed with Louise's basic description that

"It's a place with lots and lots of books and you can borrow them for a few weeks and then you have to give them back".

One or two thought that a space invader could find the library useful "for reference — finding out about this planet, there are a quite a lot of interesting books there" and Michael added, tellingly, "If he can read them". Being able to read, to these 9/10 year olds, was still a prerequisite of visiting the library, even though some of them would have been taken there long before they could read for under-5's story times. If libraries are to encourage literacy there is still more that they can do to woo non-readers beyond placing an adult literacy sign in the window. The encouragement of literacy should begin at the beginning with children.

Martin certainly began at the beginning by describing a book and then a library to his man from Mars.

"Books are instruments for storing knowledge or facts, they usually are rectangular or square, and you turn the pages and they have letters written on them and the letters form words and the words form the story or the facts and there are hundreds of them in the library and the library is the place where you can borrow them with a card."

Martin's approach to books will be followed up in a later section on readership apprenticeship for he was a relatively mature reader who saw beyond the procedures of stamping library books in and out, to the true sense of them, (and of a library), as a storehouse of knowledge.

Most of the children interviewed would have agreed with the low Sunday Times careers stress rating for librarianship (February 24th, 1985). Librarians are described as "people who help in the library and put the dates on the books". The misconception that they spend a good part of the day reading begins early, "I wouldn't mind being one, you could look at the books a lot". To all, librarians are helpful; to most, knowledgeable —

> "Librarians are rather nice and know where all the books are" — and only Louise came close to some recognition of the readers' advisory role of the librarian when she said: "Librarians help you when you are trying to look for books in case you don't know what you are looking for".

6. Parent participation in group meetings

The House of Commons report *Achievement in Primary Schools* (1986) notes the trend "reflected in official reports and policy decisions and in legislation" towards involvement of parents in many aspects of primary education, from language development through to school government. The importance of parental involvement with their children's reading has been touched on in the introduction. From the Bullock Report (1975) through the Bradford Book Flood Report (Ingham 1981), all agree with Alex Griffiths' and Dorothy Hamilton's statement (1985)

> "We can now say with certainty, from the evidence of both research and practice, that where parents help consistently with reading their children gain both in reading age and in the quality and enjoyment of their reading".

Some attempt has been made to gauge the amount of guidance parents need to be able to do this — sessions in schools can help with the techniques of how to hear a child read and Alex Griffiths discusses several of these. Jean Karl in the International Reading Association report, *Parents and Reading (Perspectives in Reading* No 14) 1971, notes

> "When a child's ability and growing interest make him ready for richer experience, the wise parent will exercise a little guidance so that the reading time will not be wasted"

and continues to suggest various sources. However, anyone who has ever stood in the children's area of a public library or bookshop will recognise that one of the main sources of information on books for children drawn on by parents is their memory of their own childhood reading. How many times are children recommended to read "Pollyanna" or Arthur Ransome? Quoted in a Times article *Oh my Bunter of long ago* (Feb. 19th 1988) Brian Aldeson, children's book reviewer, says "Nine out of ten new books are ephemeral and parents need better advice". Any form of booklist handed out to parents may be fallible if they follow it too closely without sharing titles recommended with their children and discussing their likes and dislikes with them.

When the Reading Group was promoted in the schools, it was stressed that children should come to meetings with an adult. The leaflets, too, were aimed at parents as well as at children. Although it was realised that this stricture would prevent some children from coming to meetings, it was not rigidly adhered to, and children arriving with 'someone else's mum' were not thrown out!

On average over the ten meetings, 31% of the attendance was adults. Since eleven of the families came with two children and one (on occasion) with four, it can be seen that the Family Reading Group was successful in attracting parents as well as children to the meetings. One mother commented:

"I do think if you said the parents didn't have to come it would all fall to pieces"

and another agreed:

"the fact that the parents go, that they go with the children, encourages them".

This is shown by the record of attendance at group meetings where it can be seen that the children who attended most meetings were accompanied by an adult.

Of course, the aim of involving parents was twofold — to encourage the children and to educate the parents.

Many parents agreed that the Family Reading Group had broadened their awareness of the children's books now available, and 62% either borrowed books from the group for themselves or read books which their children had borrowed, such as *The Witches, The TV Kid* or *The Speckled Panic*. One mother felt that the children's books which she had borrowed and read from the group had increased her critical awareness of books in general:

"I never realised that the writing of children's books was of such a high standard. I assumed that children's authors wrote down to children, but a lot, in fact, very many of them, are writing to a higher standard than books which are churned out now for adults — I felt that I had been spoilt a bit by some of the books so I think it has increased my awareness of the standard books".

Table 3.5   Showing Attendance of Adults and Children over 10 Meetings

Meeting	Number of Adults	Number of Children	Total
1	12	20	32
2	19	41	60
3	9	31	40
4	16	36	52
5	16	31	47
6	2	9	11
7	15	27	42
8	8	16	24
9	12	22	34
10	4	13	17
TOTAL	**113**	**246**	**359**

Table 3.6   To Show Attendance at Meetings by Children Accompanied by an Adult

Number of meetings attended	1	2	3	4	5	6	7	8	9	10
Number of children who attended meetings with an adult	10	6	13	7	9	4	6	3	1	–

7.   Parents' own experiences of reading

Jennie Ingham (1981) and Vera Southgate, (in *Extending Beginning Reading* [1981]), both asked children about their parents' present day reading, and related a home with books in it to a child's success in reading. However, there are few surveys of what parents remember of their own childhood reading. It seems relevant here to look at parents' memories of childhood reading experiences and relate them to the reading habits which they are forming in their own children.

Twenty six parents in twenty two families were asked to think back over their own childhood reading habits. Only two said that they had not used a public library at all because there wasn't one where they lived. Nineteen used a public library, and two of these used the St Albans Central Library as a child and still do today. The comment from one of them:

"It was not a lot different to now really, very similar, very large"

probably explains in part why the newer, smaller, less intimidating, sub–branch libraries are more popular with children. One had used a mobile library, one a branch of Boots lending library with a friend, and three had not used the public library much until they were of secondary school age.

Factors which limited library use by children twenty years ago show, by contrast, the progress which has been made by most authorities in library services to children. They included:

1.   Complete separation of children's from adult's books.

2.   Minimum age limit on adult borrowing.

3.   Uniform 'library editions' of books.

4.   Limited stock of children's material.

"Because we lived just over the boundary I wasn't allowed to use the City Library and we only had about fifty books for children and I had read those by the time I was about 9".

"I don't think they had many children's books in those days and then when I was 13 — you were supposed to be 14 — I joined the grown up library."

"I think I had every single book out that my library possessed."

The attractive appearance of library books today compared with the "uniform" library bindings of the post war years was mentioned:

> "It was all standard size books without just jackets — boring".

The library of the 1950's, like that in Kingsley Amis' *That Uncertain Feeling* (1955, reprinted 1985) was a joyless place.

> "There were notices — "Silence" — everywhere, nobody spoke — I don't think I would have dared to take a young child in until they were actually old enough to read a book for themselves — the child wouldn't have gone into the library."

All this, thankfully, is a far cry from Books for Babies schemes, under 5's storytimes and noisy children's activities in present day libraries.

Interestingly, only seven out of twenty six parents interviewed remembered using any kind of school library. One father who retained the reading habit does remember an enlightened teacher bringing fiction into history lessons.

> "In the junior school, round about the age of seven or eight, we were introduced to reading instead of history lessons, there were a lot of books at the time that were popular. They were adventure stories of children our own age that were in various ages throughout history — I think a woman wrote most of them — about Romans against Britons."

Some recall reading or visiting libraries with their own parents, the habit now being passed down through three generations. It is interesting that parents' expectations of the norm for their children is coloured by their own childhood experiences; the mother of the one non-reader in the sample commented:

> "I went to the library when I was young, but like him, I don't think I read an awful lot at that time".

Just exactly what were these children of the 1940's and 1950's reading? The shortage of books in the post war period was mentioned:

> "Books were in very short supply because it was war time and all I remember about books was collecting them up to be turned into waste paper. I remember at school we used to get merit marks or something for the number of books that you could actually carry to school to be pulped up — I think an awful lot of books must have disappeared".

The author who led the popular revival of books in the post war period was, of course, Enid Blyton and she is mentioned by nine out of 26 parents, albeit in a rather guilty fashion! Historical works were also popular (to have been replaced nowadays by those written in "time-slip" guise) with 4 out of 26 parents mentioning Rosemary Sutcliffe by name.

It is surprising how 'pulp' fiction survives over the years along with the 'classics', whilst a whole middle range of reading material disappears into oblivion. Series recalled by parents and still popular today include the *Nancy Drew* stories, Ruby Ferguson's horse stories and *Biggles,* although the *Bobsey Twins* and *Jungle Doctor* seem to have disappeared from the reprint list. Less popular today are the school stories on the Talbot Baines Read model and the wordier action stories such as *Hornblower* and *Treasure Island.* Bearing in mind some of these titles in the light of Bob Dixon's warnings against the proliferation of racism and sexism in children's books of that period *(Catching The Young,* 1977) emphasises the need for parents to be given an antidote to offer their own children.

Lack of time and the emergence of other commitments clearly account for a dropping off in reading among adults. 17 out of 26 said that they were library users as children, but only 10 out of 26 had books on loan at the time of the first interviews.

> "It takes me some months to get through a book because I don't get time to sit and read as I would like to"

would be a representative comment, although some mothers, like some children, would read anywhere, any time:

> "I try to go to bed early and read then and in the evenings when I go babysitting and the odd times during the day before I rush off to school".

> "I read if I travel into London on the train; I read in places like the hairdressers."

Finally, a decadent confession:

> "I'm afraid I read in the day time. I put the washing machine on and I sit here with my book — I feel as if I'm working because the machine is doing all the work".

The reading experiences of parents interviewed are echoed in Joan Aiken's article in the Times Educational Supplement (15.1.88).

What effect, if any, did parents' own reading and library use have on that of their children?

Certainly the only child who attended nine out of the ten Family Reading Group meetings, and two of the three who attended eight out of ten meetings, had parents who were regular library users with books on loan at the time of the interviews, so library habits clearly die hard. Against this can be seen a whole family of four children, two of whom attended seven out of ten meetings, whose mother, a registered child-minder, now has no time to visit the library:

> "I don't go so much now — no books out at the moment — if I get a book, a fiction book, I like to sit down that minute and read it and heaven help anyone who gets in the way — so I tend not to read fiction books very often".

An overwhelming passion for a certain kind of book — animal stories or Science Fiction — can be passed on from parent to child. This can be seen as one thread in the skein of "readership apprenticeship". Children such as Martin or Andrew, well on the way to completing this apprenticeship, had parents who discussed their own childhood reading with them, but were also prepared to read widely in the idom of the child today. One of the conclusions of this survey, that parents who only impress their own reading on their children can be as stultifying as those who never read at all, but those who can — at the time time — share their child's enthusian will succeed in stabilising it in a firm and lasting form.

Table 3.7   To Show Reasons given by Children for Coming to the Family Reading Group (100%=24)

Rosie told us at School	Peer Group Influence	Mother heard about it
58%	75%	12%

8.   Why did they come to the Family Reading Group?

1.   Promotion in schools by librarian

Some children gave more than one reason for coming to the Family Reading Group. However, it is clear from the above table that Rosie's visits to the schools to talk personally to the children in the classroom were effective. It was certainly what most of the children remembered, and they also remembered her name:

> "Rosie came into school and she talked about it in our class and she gave out the little pamphlet things and we all took one home".

Rosie made a point of telling the children she visited in school that she would be at the library for the meetings. After the first contact the children had a link person between them and that impersonal building full of books. They had a name to conjure with, and to ask after when Rosie was away sick at the third meeting. A children's librarian has to gain the child's trust in order to be able to recommend books to them with credibility. The moment of contact is usually brief and if they cannot come up with the goods there and then they are in danger of being written off:

> "I have asked librarians for help once or twice when I couldn't find the book I was looking for. They look and see if the book is out or not and that is usually the end, the book is either there or it isn't."

This statement, incidentally, confirms the need for one member of library staff to have sufficient stock knowledge to offer an alternative title!

The Family Reading Group gives the librarian a chance to develop a relationship with their readers over a period of time and to persuade them that, even though librarians may sometimes be fallible, it is usually worth asking for help in looking for a book. In getting to know the children, librarians can also better gauge the type of material to offer them — both in reading level and in content. As the section on "boring" books will point out later, often a book which is claimed as "boring" may be one which does not live up to the reader's expectations — the chances of avoiding this are clearly greater if reader and librarian share the same expectations. It may very often be the reluctance of adults to lower their expectations of the child's ability to cope with the book which results in this mismatch. Adults may prefer to visualise the romantic picture of "a child reading" through a glow of classical expectations, imagining the title of the book to be *Little Women* or even *Pollyanna* rather than *My Best Friend,* or *Marmalade Atkins!*

2.   Peer Group Influence

Talking about the Family Reading Group at school with friends, both before and after meetings and coming to group meetings with friends ranked high as incentives to membership. One of the motives for this research was to see how peer group activity — so strong among this 9-12 age group — could be harnessed so that children would encourage one another to read. Porterfield and Schlicting had come to the conclusion in their research on *Peer Status and Reading Achievement* in 1962 (Journal of Ed. Rs. 54:6, April 1961) that

> "A significant relationship exists between peer prestige status and reading achievement status".

The Report *Reading in America* (1979) had also pointed out that peer group, parental, home and community influences were factors which contributed to an early appreciation of books.

Evidence to support these statements came from the first series of interviews with children at Fleetville. Some talked about the meeting at school, especially at School 2, where the Head himself generated a certain amount of interest among the children — enough for them to mention it to me —

> "I talked with my friends and with my teacher about it — it was my teacher who was there. And my headmaster was there too. Rosie came round to our classroom and talked about it and Mr Jukes and Mrs Stewart said could you go. There were quite a lot of hands but some of them couldn't come."

Nicola's enthusiasm carried a long way and she was mentioned by more than one person as recommending the group to them.

> "Nicola and Lisa talked about it because they had been there before, they talked about it and said how good it was, they liked it very much."

> "My friends Jane and Nicola at school, they told me a lot about it and they thought that I would like it... Next day at school we looked at the books that other people had got."

Andrew, a noisy born leader was another catalyst:

> "There is a bunch of four of us and we recommended it to a friend called Tom, and he's come ever since — that was about a month after it started".

Going to events with friends is important at this age and can account for swings in attendance. Friends may fail to attend for practical reasons because another activity suddenly seems more attractive. Guides on a Thursday night suddenly prevented three of the girls from coming half way through the year.

Tom gave a rather literary description of how he came to the group with his friend.

> "By our back gate there is a passage, there is a person called Gregory. I went with his mum."

John and Sam were more pragmatic —

"No one could take me so my friend said he would."

"John wanted to go but no one could take him so we went round and picked him up."

Table 3.8   To Show Attendance at Consecutive Family Reading Group Meetings (100%=59)

Number of consecutive meetings attended	2	3	4	5	6	7	8	9
% of children attending	20	27	17	8	3	–	–	–

N.B. 22 children came only spasmodically to occasional meetings, although all came to more than one.

9.   How often do they come?

It has been shown earlier that parental involvement can encourage children to go to Family Reading Groups. Another factor which emerged from the records of Family Reading Group attendance was that members did not often go to more than three meetings in succession. Table 3.8 shows attendance at consecutive Family Reading Group meetings (100% = 59).

Attendance was rolling: children would go to two meetings, miss one, go to another one, etc. This reflects the lack of pressure on children, which is a feature of the group. They are neither made to feel that they must come to meetings, or that they must read the books. If the group is to be fun, it cannot be enforced.

As the interviews with the families showed, it was not always lack of interest which prevented children coming to meetings — sometimes it was illness which prevented them from coming out, sometimes another event, and sometimes the parent was busy and could not take the children. These findings have implications for those holding library activities for children.

Chapter 4

Reading as a recreational activity

"I read when I have some spare time"

1. Previous research

Surveys on children's use of leisure time have usually focused on secondary schools, with the intention of comparing the influences of junior, secondary modern and grammar schools (Himmelweit 1958) and grammar, secondary modern and technical schools (Veness 1962). Marie Wragg surveyed the leisure interests of children in comprehensive schools and the effect which class differences made on these interests (Wragg, *The Leisure Activities of Boys and Girls,* Educational Research 10, Feb. 1968). Others (Himmelweit, Oppenheim and Vince, 1961) have studied the part played by television viewing in the lives of children. None of these surveys set out with the specific intention of studying children's reading habits alone, but only mentioned them in comparison with other leisure activities.

As was discussed in Chapter 2, the co-operation of schools is necessary to surveys of this kind which seek a blanket coverage of a particular age group. In addition, a certain amount of literacy is necessary to complete questionnaires or diaries, and that probably explains why most of the research into leisure interests has centred around children of secondary age.

Barbara H Long and Edmund H Henderson, however, concerned themselves with 9-11 year olds in their article *Children's use of time: some personal and social correlates* (Elementary School Journal 1973). 75 boys and 75 girls kept diaries for two weeks and their spare time activities were coded into seven categories in decreasing order of importance: sleep, TV, free play, organised activity, homework, reading, chores.

Like Whitehead (1977) Long and Henderson realised the fallibility of written records:

> "One question that arises is the reliability and the validity of the children's records. Another problem is that samples are necessarily limited to children who are reasonably literate and sufficiently interested to keep records".

However, they did not verify their findings by personal interviews with a sample of the children concerned, and their results must have a correspondingly limited validity.

The three major recent surveys into children's reading by Whitehead (1977), Ingham (1981), and Southgate (1981) all made some attempt to define the length of time children spent reading. Because the different surveys used different methods of quantifying time, it is virtually impossible to compare their findings, either with one another, or with the present survey. Long and Henderson (1973) asked 9-11 year olds to complete diaries with a fifteen minute grid for activities out of school; children were given ten minutes at school, morning and afternoon to complete the grid. The authors' comments on the fallibility of this system have already been mentioned. Whitehead (1977) bases his assessment on the number of books read by the children in the sample during the month under study, but does not distinguish between whether these books are read at home or in free time at school; moreover, children are told not to count stories which are told mainly in pictures, which, in view of the findings of this present survey, must have excluded quite a few entries! Whitehead's "follow up interviews" only took place once with each child, and do not give a very detailed picture of other out of school interests or activities. Children are categorised by the report as 'light readers' — reading 1-2 books a month, 'moderate readers' — reading 3-4 books a month, and 'heavy readers' — reading over 5 books a month.

Southgate (1981) bases her comments on children's reading habits on the two questions "Do you read a lot at home?" and "Do you read more at home or at school?" As a result, she does not attempt to codify the amount of time which children spend reading or the number of books read.

Ingham (1981) relates the findings from the Reading Record forms with those from interviews with parents, teachers and children in order to define a sample of children as 'avid' or 'infrequent' readers. The numbers of Reading Record forms completed per child during the experiment are used as a quantifier. However, as with the Whitehead report, it remains uncertain whether the books were read at home or at school — used to fill in the odd half hour at lunchtime, or read in preference to television watching or going to a club in the evening.

2. After School Diaries

This survey set out with the intention of calculating the length of time children spent reading, and relating it to the other after school activities of third and fourth year junior school pupils aged 9-11. However, either the "clock" system for recording time or the vigilance of the teachers in encouraging the children to complete the diaries was ineffective, as not all the diaries give an accurate amount of the time spent reading each day. They do, however, give a very rich and varied picture of the way in which these children spent their time after school.

The amount of reading done by the child during the two week period, however, can be assessed by the number of titles mentioned in the After School Diary, or by the number of times that reading is mentioned as an activity. Where the schools allowed the children to take the diaries home, details are often fuller, as children did not have to rely on their memory to complete the entries the following morning. A sample of the After School Diary, together with the notes which accompanied it for the schools taking part, appears in Appendix 2.

The distribution of the diaries and the returns made in 1984 and 1985 have been described in Chapter 2. Where children had returned diaries in 1984 and 1985 it was possible to compare the after school activities from year to year. It was also possible to compare the 1984/1985 diaries of the Family Reading Group members with those of non-members, to see whether attendance at the group had had any effect on their use of leisure time. Twenty Family Reading Group members returned diaries in 1984 and 1985. Two diaries were incomplete. Perhaps it was expecting too much to ask for co-operation from the same schools and children in successive years. The return of both diaries by only 31% of group members was disappointing and limiting to the research. Altogether 92 children (members and non-members) completed diaries in both 1984 and 1985. These diaries represented 34% of the total number of diaries completed. A higher percentage of paired diaries would have provided a broader and more satisfying base for comparison of leisure pursuits from year to year. This low percentage, however, did not only represent a falling off in completion of diaries in the second year, but also accounted for children completing diaries in the second year but not the first! Illness and changing schools accounted for the majority of non-returns, abetted by the fact that it was not possible to track down all the children who had moved from primary to secondary school, but only to issue diaries to that secondary school which had taken the majority of primary school children in the area.

Of the 18 completed pairs of diaries returned by Family Reading Group members in 1984 and 1985, six were from children who had changed schools in September 1984. Diaries from these 18 members were matched by 18 pairs of diaries from children who did not attend the Reading Group, but who had also completed diaries in 1984 and 1985, selected by taking those from every 4th child who had returned both diaries.

The resulting information substantiates Barbara Tuchman's statement in Cole and Gold's *Reading in America* (1978):

> "The heaviest readers are the people most active in everything. The doers are the readers".

As Jan Hajdu says in his PhD Dissertation *An American Paradox: people and books in the metropolis,*

> "Reading books... requires an effort... This in itself makes book reading unattractive to a lonely person whose general interest and activity are considerably lower than that of an engaged person".

Before using the information given in the diaries to compare the lifestyles of Family Reading Group members and non-members, it is interesting to look at a general picture of the lifestyle of 9-13 year olds in Fleetville. The diaries were completed in Winter time (February 1984 and February 1985) and this is reflected in the children's pursuits. There is little mention of playing outside — and sporting activities are probably less well represented because of this. Most children only mention going out if it is for a specific activity — youth club, music lesson, swimming — and so two separate analyses have been drawn up, the first listing 'indoor' activities, and the second listing attendance at organisations, ('organised activities').

1.   Indoor activities

The indoor activities, taken in decreasing order of popularity over a total of 36 children in 1984, members and non-members together, were as follows:

> TV; reading; games; family activities; craft; music, helping at home; school homework; playing with friends; computers and pets.

Some categories for this section are self-explanatory, especially the two most frequently listed — watching television and reading.

(a)   Television

Three children out of the sample of 36 came from families without a television set. The remainder regularly listed children's programmes, early evening comedy programmes, soap operas and 'educational' nature programmes such as *The Living Planet* and *On Safari*. One girl gave synopses of several television programmes each day in her diary which stress the appeal of their episodic structure, for example:

> "6.30 Whatching Cross Roads (sic)
> The new secerty has a headace the garage is a bit behind in its work. Sid dose ofer time instead of Carlo because she is going to tea with David and Sharon. Lots of arguments take a long time at the garage."

There is a very strong sense in some diaries of the television continuing as a background to other activities and not preventing them, as here:

"I watched In Loving Memory while I was colouring in my diary"

and again the same girl writes:

"I watched the end of Crossroads while doing my Topic. I practised my spellings. Watched part of Russell Harty's show."

Five out of the sample of 36 mention videos in their diaries. On each occasion they mention watching television programmes which have been copied by parents rather than commercial videos. Some programmes taped are schools programmes which the child may have missed, such as *Look and Read* — others are adult programmes screened after bedtime such as *Dallas* and "*Spitting Image* which is about important people and cartoon puppets".

(b) Reading

It comes as no surprise to find that the favourite place for reading is in bed — except when the television is taken to bed instead of a book. Several children mention reading as soon as they get in from school, and it can be surmised that the book which is read then has been brought home from school. One boy mentions reading regularly to his mother and another notes stories read aloud by parents. Reading stories to younger siblings is mentioned too. A more detailed analysis based on what children say about reading in their diaries can be found in Chapter 5.

(c) Games

Most popular are the small electronic games such as *Pac-man* and *Donkey Kong* which are played by the child on it's own. Board games such as *Monopoly, Cluedo* and *Scrabble* are usually played with other members of the family. It was difficult to decide whether to classify *Dungeons and Dragons* — the fantasy game which may be played alone with a dice and a 'programmed' adventure story book or in groups with a host of model figures and other accoutrements — as 'reading' or 'games'. Eventually it was decided to include it as reading where children subsequently entered 'read' at each stage in the diary and as a game when they went to a friend's home to play. Imaginative role-playing games, involving dolls, friends and siblings, such as 'schools', 'hospitals' and even, in one diary, 'libraries' still prevail, especially among younger girls.

(d) Music

Practising an instrument — piano, clarinet, flute, recorder, trumpet, and, — usually when mum went out — drums, featured in the 'music' section. Also included here was listening to music, on tape or record, which was more popular with children in the older age range.

(e) Family

Going out with other members of the family is still important to children of this age, and one of the lifestyle features on which the Family Reading Group tried to capitalise. Outings range from simple shopping trips to a yearly visit to Crufts. Accompanying siblings to their organisations — open evenings at Scouts, ballet lessons or swimming lessons — occurs frequently and shows how complex timetabling can be for an active family with several children. Visiting and being visited by relatives, especially at weekends, is all conventionally reassuring!

It is interesting to note that children often entered 'talked to Mum' or 'chatted with Dad' in their diaries, and considered it worthy of note.

(f)   Craft

'Craft' was taken to include colouring in pictures, drawing and painting as well as more complex tasks such as knitting and weaving, which were in the minority.

(g)   Helping at home

This usually meant setting the table, washing up and tidying the bedroom, although one girl from a large family spent a considerable amount of time looking after younger siblings.

(h)   Homework

School homework usually meant learning spellings or completing topic work. Reading a book was not mentioned as homework. Like reading, homework was usually done at once on returning from school, or at the end of the day, in bed.

(i)   Friends

Friends proved of importance and were often mentioned in relation to other activities. Cubs, Guides and youth clubs are often attended with a friend. Visiting friends' houses to play games and for tea is also noted.

(j)   Computers

Computers and computer games appeared in a minority — expensive as yet, and a novelty.

(k)   Pets

Pets included dogs, cats, hamsters and guinea pigs, with no exotica. They were fed, stroked, cuddled, played with — and taken to Crufts!

Table 4.1   To Show the Difference in Incidence of Activity of Reading Group Members and Non-Members

Members	Non-Members
TV	TV
Reading	Reading
Games	Games
Family Activity	Helping at home
Music	Family Activity
Craft	Craft
Friends	Homework
Helping at home	Music
Homework	Friends
Computers	Pets
Pets	Computers

It is interesting to note that activities involving both family and friends are rated higher by Family Reading Group members. Helping at home could be hypothesised to have prevented some non-members from taking part in other activities, possibly because they came from larger families. Music also comes higher up the list for group members, who also, as will be seen later, show a preference for organised activity.

2. Organised activities

In the examined sample diaries (of both Family Reading Group members and non-members) twenty-two different 'organised activities' were listed. An 'organised activity' for the purpose of this survey was taken to be one which would:

(a) Involve the child going out of the house at a certain time in order to complete the activity, i.e. which needed planning.

(b) Involved other people.

The activities mentioned were as follows: youth clubs; St John's Ambulance; Cubs; Brownies; Guides; Scouts; Royal Society for the Protection of Birds; cadets; netball; swimming; gymnastics; ballet; ice skating; football; music lessons; band practice; discos; Scottish dancing; dog training; Badminton Club; Judo and going to church. In addition, three children mentioned going to the Family Reading Group in their 1985 diaries. It is realised that some activities, such as ice skating and discos, are organised by schools, but they are included as they were held in the evening and were not compulsory. It is possible to group the activities into:

(a) Those which involve belonging to an organisation, i.e. Cubs, Guides, Scouts.

(b) Those concerned with physical exercise (including the ice skating and the disco trip).

(c) Going to music lessons, as opposed to listening to music or playing an instrument.

(d) Going to church.

Table 4.2 To Show the Comparison between After School Activities of Family Reading Group Members and Non-Members in February 1984 *(Figures are for the number of times the activity is mentioned over a two week period)*

	Clubs	Physical Exercise	Music Lesson	Church
Members	26	26	6	3
Non-Members	11	17	1	1

The Family Reading Group project in Fleetville set out to discover whether reading would become more popular among 9-11 year olds if it were disguised as an organised activity! We wished to see whether we could take advantage of the clubbable nature of children at this age and their tendency to go around in groups and so form a group which was specifically intended to promote reading, but which was fun at the same time.

Table 4.2 shows that the Family Reading Group certainly attracted children who already took part in organised group activities. Since the children who completed the diaries all went to the same school and lived in the same area, it can be assumed that the activities, some of which were associated with the schools, were equally available and several were free or very cheap. It can therefore reasonably be concluded that children who enjoyed taking part in organised activities were attracted by yet another in the form of the reading group and fitted it into their already busy social lives. Nicola, a group member, talking about her week said:

> "I have netball on Mondays after school, Tuesdays I have Brownies, on Wednesdays I have flute, on Thursdays I sometimes have Gym Club, on Fridays I don't have anything."

Another member charting gymnastics on Monday, Tuesday and Wednesday evenings in his diary, added on Thursday:

> "Have you noticed, I haven't been to gym club today?"

All activities listed took place between 3.30pm and 9.00pm on weekdays. To introduce yet another club. (a further demand on parents who often spent a high proportion of their time ferrying not one but often two or three children backwards and forwards to and from these activities) appears foolhardy in retrospect. Furthermore, this club — The Family Reading Group — was concerned with reading, an activity which all children met to a greater or lesser extent at school. The figures in table 4.2 show that it was highly successful in attracting those children who were active, lively and 'clubbable' and encouraged them to see reading as an alternative to Brownies and Cubs, swimming and gymnastics, flute playing and football.

Peer group influence, as discussed in Chapter 3, has a part to play in guiding a child's choice of activity. Several children attended other groups with the same friends with whom they came to the Family Reading Group — this could have the effect of decimating group attendance on gang show night! While peer group pressure could encourage children to come to the group, it could also encourage them to leave it for an alternative activity. When several girls became old enough to change from Brownies to Guides, they all left the group together. Louise was one of this group:

> "I stopped coming because of Guides — you could either go to the First St Andrews or the Second. My sister went to the First St Andrews so I went to the First."

Question: Did any of your friends come to the group because you recommended it to them?

> Louise: "I think Susie came."

Question: Does she go to Guides as well now?

   Louise: "Yes."

Jane was another girl who left because Family Reading Group night clashed with Guide meetings, but, as her mother said:

   "She has enjoyed the books and the evenings, it's a shame there's the Guides and that she was just nicely into it, but it's just at such a bad time, there's no way round it at all."

Jennie Ingham (1981) found that:

   "What links the hobbies and interests of avid readers is, first, a preference for indoor activities."

This does not seem to be true of readers in Fleetville. The same number (26), recorded taking part in some kind of organised physical activity as recorded attending clubs of some kind. Non-members preferred physical exercise (17), to clubs (11), possibly because of the less strictly ordered nature of the former.

The number of Family Reading Group members involved with learning music could reflect the 'faddy' nature of some, who are ready to try anything for a short time. One group member gave beginning to learn the piano as a reason for stopping coming to the Reading Group.

Children often took part in more than one activity.

This table shows that Reading Group members preferred to be active, sometimes super-active. The only member who did not record taking part in any organised activities at all was the group's only non-reader. He had come to the group because his teacher had recommended it and his mother brought him, whereas the majority of others had come because they wanted to. This picture of a Family Reading Group member as active and extrovert is confirmed once more by the diary evidence that they play far fewer indoor games than non-members.

Table 4.3   To Show Comparison of Number of Activities of Family Reading Group Members and Non-Members in 1984

Number of Activities	Members	Non-Members
0	1	4
1	2	4
2	4	7
3	5	–
4	6	3
5	1	–
6	1	–

3. Comparison of 1984 and 1985 diaries

The drop in the number of Reading Group members involved with music has already been mentioned. Equally dramatic in the comparison of Tables 4.2 and 4.4 is the 50% drop in organised physical exercise mentioned by group members, although they still mention it more times than non-members. Non-members' mention of clubs (such as Guides and Scouts), drops by over 50%. The greater part of this drop in organised activity (among members and non-members) can be accounted for by the fact that one third of the sample changed from primary to secondary school in September 1984. The change to secondary school also accounted for a notable falling off of membership of the Family Reading Group, although we had hoped to sustain their interest in the group — and in reading — through the transition from primary to secondary school. Eleven out of the 59 group members changed from primary to secondary school in September 1984. Seven of these did come to the September 1984 meeting, but only four continued as members until the end of the survey period. This drop in organised activity is reflected in the diaries. Every one of the six group members who completed paired diaries and changed schools records a drop in this area and this is also seen in the 1984/1985 diaries of non-members.

Table 4.4   To Show the Comparison Between After-School Activities of Family Reading Group Members and Non-Members in February 1985

	Clubs	Physical Exercise	Music Lesson	Church
Members	21	13	3	–
Non-Members	5	12	1	1

Table 4.5   To Show Changes in Incidence of Activity in the Lifestyles of Children after Changing to Secondary School   *(Activities listed in order of popularity)*

1984 (Junior School)	1985 (Secondary School)
TV	TV
Reading	Reading
Games	Homework
Helping at home	Games
Craft	Helping at home
Music	Family activity
Family activity	Music
Homework	Pets
Friends	Friends
Computers	Computers
Pets	Craft

It can be seen that homework rises from eighth to third place. Craft and music suffer as a result, and even "helping at home" drops a place — a case of "I can't wash up, I've got my homework to do!"

For most first year secondary children diary entries alternate between homework and television; there is little mention of crafts such as weaving or board games, which involved

60

playing with friends or family. On the whole this presents a rather depressing picture and only those children with an overwhelming interest for *Dungeons and Dragons* for example, appear to retain it through the transition. Tom, one of the keener Family Reading Group members, clearly found this frustrating. One evening's diary entry begins with almost two hours television, followed by one and a half hours homework, a meal (half an hour), then a quick 25 minutes reading before back to the homework for 55 minutes with the comment:

> "Still doing homework, boring really." The entry after bed time at 9.30pm says: "Mum says no time for reading — I give up!"

In the diary section "This is what I read today," the reason for the frustration is explained:

> "Trying to finish Spellcoats — reading madly."

Table 4.6   To Show a Comparison of the Number of Books Mentioned over 2 weeks by Family Reading Group Members in 1984 and 1985

	1984		1985	
	Members	*Non-Members*	*Members*	*Non-Members*
Number of books by primary age range	42	32	51	35
Number of books by transfer children	23	26	29	20
TOTAL	**65**	**58**	**80**	**55**

4.   Reading books at home

The difficulty in measuring the amount of reading done by children from their own records has been discussed earlier in this chapter. The After School Diaries did have a section for the children to record "These are some books I read today", and reading was also mentioned by children as a listed activity. Usually children seem to read in bed, hence the space for an entry in the diary for 'This is what I did in bed' — although some watched television in bed, or fought with their brothers and sisters. Occasionally they will read as soon as they arrive home from school, but more often than not, as some commented, it depended on what was on television. Incidentally, if there was one thing which readers and non-readers, group members and non-group members had in common, it was watching television — children's programmes were all listed by name in the diaries. Table 4.6 shows a comparison of the number of books mentioned by the sample of eighteen group members and eighteen non-members over a two week period in 1984 and 1985. The diaries had been completed in 1984 before the Family Reading Group had begun to function, and so, in speaking of 'Group Members' in terms of the 1984 diaries, it must be remembered that these were then, in fact, prospective members. Since one of the objects of the research was to see not only whether attendance at a Family Reading Group helped children to consolidate the reading habit, but also whether this consolidation could be seen even in children who had the added distraction of starting at secondary school, the figures for those who transferred to secondary school are given separately.

It can be seen that, overall, Family Reading Group members showed a greater awareness of books by mentioning substantially more titles in their 1985 diaries than in 1984, and this is as true of children who transferred to secondary school (29 against 23) as of those who remained at primary school (51 against 42). Non-group members transferring to secondary school mentioned fewer titles than in the previous year, (20 against 26), and this in spite of the fact that in 1984 the same children had mentioned more books than prospective reading group members (26 against 23).

The figures given on previous page show the following average number of books mentioned in the diaries:

1984: members 3.6 books over two weeks, non-members 3.2 books.
1985: members 4.4 books over two weeks, non-members 3.1 books.

According to this calculation, all children completing diaries would have come into Whitehead's "heavy reader" category — reading 5+ books a month.

Since individual children who are heavy readers can distort the statistics, it is interesting to make use of the number of books mentioned in the diaries to calculate the percentage of children who mentioned more or less titles than the previous year. The figures show that Reading Group members consistently increased their reading after one year, whilst non-members read less.

An incidental factor, however, was revealed through the way that the children completed the rhyme on the first page of the diary: "Down the garden, over the wall, this is what I like best of all". Five Family Reading Group members in 1984 and 1985 mentioned reading here, although only two mentioned it on both occasions. Of non-members, four mentioned reading as a favourite activity in 1984, one girl going so far as to mention C S Lewis books by name, but only two of these expressed a similar preference the following year and one of these was specifically for fantasy role-playing books.

Library use

It does seem, perhaps, as though some non-members were already meeting their reading needs through visits to the library and so had less need for the stimulus of Family Reading Groups. Four mentioned going to the library in their diaries — one conducted visits to Marshalswick and Fleetville libraries on the same day. One girl even mentioned playing at libraries! Among Family Reading Group members, one mentioned visiting the library in both diaries and two mentioned it in 1985 diaries only.

Comparing this incidence of visits to the library with that of other activities in the diaries would make it appear yet again that Family Reading Groups encourage children with already busy lives to make more time to visit the library and choose books by presenting them with an organised method of doing so.

Table 4.7   To Show a Comparison of the Extent of Book Awareness by Family Reading Group Members and Non-Members in 1984 & 1985

	Members	*Non-Members*
Read more in 1985	72%	39%
Read less in 1985	22%	44%
Read the same in 1985	6%	17%

Chapter 5

Choosing and Reading

*"If someone says — Gosh this is fantastic,
sit down and read it — you do!"*

Choosing, making decisions is a most complex and difficult task, even for adults. It is easier to cling to what is safe and familiar than to take a risk. Very often, choosing can become a process of rejection rather than selection. Calvino describes this process in the opening chapter of his book *If on a Winter Night a Traveller...* 1981). He categorises 'Books you Haven't Read' as:

"the Books You've Been Planning to Read for Ages
the Books You've been Hunting for For Years without Success
the Books You Need to Go with Other Books on your Shelves
the Books Read Long Ago which it's now time to Reread
the Books You've always Pretended to Have Read and Now
It's Time to Sit Down and Really Read Them."

He then hones in on more specific reasons for choosing a book from amongst: "New Books Whose Author Or Subject Appeals To You", "New Books By Authors Or On Subjects Not New"... and "New Books By Authors Or On Subjects Completely Unknown".

Surveys on adult reading quoted by Michel Gault in his UNESCO report, *The Future of the Book (Part 2 — The changing role of reading* [1982]) give the following reasons for choice of book among adults surveyed in France in 1967:

29% borrow from friends and family
22% borrow from library
38% choice determined by word of mouth
30% radio/TV
29% from book reviews
 3% from librarian recommendation.

He also lists the answers to an unspecified UK survey in 1979 asking "How did you come to hear of the latest book you read?" as:

26% library/bookshop
23% word of mouth
10% from newspaper or magazine
 9% TV/radio
 5% gifts
 4% each — random, favourite author, book club, advertising
 1% through further education
 9% miscellaneous.

Mervyn Horder, writing in the *Bookseller* (June 30th, 1984) about the 1982 Consumer Research Study on Reading and Book Purchasing, (presented to the USA Library of Congress), confirms that the number of people who choose a book through familiarity with the author has declined (which would disappoint Calvino!). The Library of Congress Study quotes the following reasons for choice:

80% recommended by friend/relative
70% by book jacket synopsis and description
61% read a few pages
58% book on best seller list.

Few surveys of children's reading have looked specifically at how a child chooses books, only at what they have chosen, or, at an even greater remove, how the librarian or teacher can choose for them. The Ingham/Clift Reading Record Form, used in Jennie Ingham's Bradford Book Flood survey (Ingham, 1981) asked the children, "Where did you get this book from?" and "Why did you choose this book?" She concluded that, for the experimental and the controlled schools in her survey "In every case, a greater percentage of favourite books was chosen because the child already had some knowledge of the book."

As part of the impact interviews after each of the first four Family Reading Group meetings, the children were asked what had influenced their choice of titles. These interviews took the form of informal discussion. Because the answers were given in the course of conversation and not merely written down, it was possible for the child to give more than one reason for the choice of a single title — for example Ceri said that he had had the *Bagthorpe Saga* recommended to him by a friend, he had heard it discussed at school and he had seen it on television! Tom had chosen *The Power of Hoodoo* because he liked the sound of the blurb on the cover and because he had read other books in the same series. The reasons which the children interviewed gave for their choice of titles were as follows:

Table 5.1   To Show Reasons for Choice of Books given by Family Group Members at 'Impact' Interviews

Reason for Choice	Number of Times Reason Given
Recommended by friends	15
Subject appeal	12
Seen on TV	11
Recommended at Family Reading Group	10
Met with before at school	10
Read another in same series	9
Recommended by family	8
Cover looked interesting	8
Read another book by same author	6
Read that book before	6
Synopsis looked interesting	5
Title sounded interesting	3

Table 5.2   To Show Methods of Choice Preferred by Family Reading Group Members (100% = 14)

Personal recommendation by friend/family at FRG	86%
Book seen before (at school, on TV or read before)	79%
Book unseen but author, subject, series recognised	71%
Book unseen, but cover, blurb or title appeals	64%

The figures given in Table 5.1 are for the number of times a book was chosen for that particular reason.

1. Personal recommendation

It is clear that recommendation by word of mouth — whether by friends or family, at school or at the Family Reading Group — plays a major part in the child's choice of book. As Tom put it:

"If a few people say this book is rather good — I usually read it."

Peer group pressure is such that even Ceri, who did not usually read fiction by choice, took *The Machine Gunners* home:

"I had heard about it and was one of the only ones who hadn't read it."

The *Little Vampire* books became very popular and were passed around by a small group of girls:

"I showed that one to Mary and then she read it and then I found another one in the series and she read that as well."

The same group also took over *The Great Smile Robbery* passing it from house to house — Louise said she had borrowed it because:

"Frances had it from Family Reading Group and I saw it at her house, but only had time to look at the pictures."

At this age, Mum's advice does not yet bring on an urge to do exactly the opposite and parental involvement and help with choosing books are welcomed. Michael talked about *Kidnap* by Alan Evans as one of the most exciting books he had read, although:

"I didn't pick it up, Mum did. She showed it to me, I hadn't actually seen it." Roger said, "It is better if my Mum comes, because usually, while I am looking at one pile my Mum looks at another pile and finds some books."

And the Mother of Peter, our non-reader, welcomed the opportunity help him:

"choose with my help, ones which are going to be up to his standard and not too much reading in one chapter so that he can read one a night."

Enabling parents to help children choose in this environment is one of several positive aspects of parental involvement produced by Family Reading Group methods.

Sometimes, hearing about a book from more than one source can encourage a child to read it for itself. This was so with Roger. He chose the *Just So Stories*.

"We had one of them read to us at school, and my granny has got one which she told me."

The Family Reading Group provides an opportunity, both formally and informally, for personal recommendation of books, from child to child, parent to child and from librarian to both. Such recommendations are an equal exchange of opinion. Here no one is really the expert, and adults and children are heard alike. As the popularity table of books (Table 5.3) shows, those recommended by children are often borrowed more frequently than those recommended by adults. Stephen commented:

> "It's easier to choose a book at the Reading Group because other people are recommending them — authors, and all kinds of books that you want are there and if they are not you can request them."

This point was also picked up by some of the parents who talked about the group.

> "Nothing helps you want to read a book more than personal recommendation," said one, "If someone says, gosh, this is fantastic, sit down and read it, you do." Another added, "I have noticed that he has brought home one or two books that have been talked about by people in the group, he wouldn't have thought of reading."

However, sometimes a recommendation can cause chaos as is described here:

> "We were looking for the *Marmalade Atkins* books and we all hopped up on top of the table, but everybody had got them and there aren't that many any more. There used to be loads of them, but that man showed us one of them and that was the only one there at that time."

Such is the demand that the recommended title immediately achieves scarcity value!

Records of the children's book borrowing over 10 meetings were collated and the titles listed in order of popularity. Those titles with a popularity index rating of 15 or over are listed in Table 5.3, which shows the incidence of recommended titles. The full bookstock used is listed in order of popularity in Appendix 3.

The calculations for the popularity listing were dependent on the following factors:

a) Number of children borrowing that title — this is the number of different children who chose that title over a period of 10 meetings.

b) Number of times issued — each title may be issued 10 times — where 2 copies of the title have been made available it has the possibility of being borrowed 10×2 times, etc. Very often the reader will bring the book to the meeting and ask to borrow it again — the equivalent of borrowing a book and renewing it at the public library. If a book remains on loan for two or more meetings, it is still counted as being on issue for two or more issue periods (issues in mobile libraries, school libraries, centres etc. are usually counted in this way).

c) Popularity rating — this is calculated by adding together the number of children borrowing the title and the issue rating.

Observations

Most outstanding is the percentage of recommended titles found at the top of the popularity scale. This substantiates the children's own observations (Table 5.1) that personal recommendation can often account for their choice of title. The recommendations charted are only those made officially during the discussion part of the

Table 5.3 To Show the Effect of Recommendations of the Popularity Ratings of Family Reading Group Bookstock — All books available for 10 meetings

No. of Copies	Title	No. of children Borrowing	No. of times Issued	Popularity Rating	Rec. Child	Rec. Adult
2	Witches Daughter	10	11	21		
2	What difference does it make Danny	10	11	21	C	A
2	Absolute Zero	10	11	21	C	
2	Marmalade Atkins in Space	9	11	20		A
1	Bogwoppit	9	10	19	C	
2	Cartoonist	9	10	19		A
2	Grinny	8	11	19		
3	Pinballs	9	10	19	C	A
3	House that sailed away	8	11	19	C	
2	My best fiend	9	9	18		A
1	Animal ghosts	9	9	18		
1	Witches	8	10	18		A
2	Great piratical rumbustification	9	9	18		A
2	Dragons live forever	9	9	18		A
2	TV Kid	8	10	18		A
2	Necklace of raindrops	8	9	17		A
1	School trip	8	8	16		A
1	Little prince	8	8	16		
2	Pyewachet & son	8	8	16		A
2	Revolt at Ratcliffe rags	8	8	16		A
2	Bongleweed	7	9	16		
2	Ogre downstairs	7	9	16		A
1	Benjamin & Tulip	7	8	15		A
2	Clever Polly & the stupid wolf	7	8	15		

meeting, and do not account for 'unofficial' bookswaps or comments during the choosing part of the meeting, from child or adult.

Of the top ten titles in the popularity Table 5.3, eight were formally recommended at meetings. Of these, 2 were recommended by both a child and an adult, 3 by children alone and 3 by adults alone.

Table 5.3 shows that books have been borrowed from the library by children, but not necessarily read!

Table 5.4 shows that children, in common with many library users, often borrow books which seem attractive at first sight but appear less so on closer inspection. These books are those which remain unread or are only partly read. Thus a survey of reading preference which relies solely on issue figures can be shown to be misleading. Just as the number of library borrowers can give a false picture of library use — since many people walking through the library doors do not necessarily borrow books — so too can issue figures give a false picture of book reading.

The impact interviews provided data on what the children read as opposed to what they borrowed. Discussion with the children at these interviews incidentally revealed the reasons behind the high postion of some titles in the popularity ratings which would otherwise have appeared puzzling.

Witches, ghosts, Grandmas and animals are constantly popular subjects amongst 9-11 year olds, and titles such as *Witches Daughter* or *Animal Ghosts,* which appear high in the popularity tables, may do so on the strength of their title alone, not their content or readability. Among the 13 children who were interviewed on their choice of books were two who had borrowed but not read *Witches Daughter* and one who had borrowed but only partly read, *Spell me a Witch.* Another clue to the position of *Witches Daughter* at the top of the list was provided when Ceri said that he had chosen the book because it was on a school reading list, but he had not read it. This is an example of adults presenting children with 'worthy' books which, far from encouraging children to broaden their reading interests, limit them by raising expectations which are then dashed by the true subject matter or style of the book.

Similaly, *Animal Ghosts* proved to be a title which few could resist, suggesting as it does that the stories combine two subjects which children find fascinating; *My Favourite Animal Stories* appears much lower down the ratings, as does *Ghosts & Shadows* — the next highest rated title using the word 'ghost'. However, the sample of readers interviewed had only dipped into the book, finding the content much less attractive than the title. Collections of ghost and animal stories, especially those reprinted in paperback, are often compiled from 'classic' stories which were never intended for children and are often far too wordy (and worthy!) and thus lead to disappointment. Books which Dad (or Mum) read when they were young can be disappointing too. *Just William* , and others of the William saga were returned unread or only partly read by the three of the sample interviewed who had borrowed them — Dad's rosy memories reflected recently on the television screens prompting borrowing of titles of a series which made disappointingly anachronistic reading.

2.   Books seen before

Children who gave as a reason for choice the fact that they had seen the book before at school were also influenced by friends who had read that book before them at school. Books which teachers had read in class, such as the *Just So* stories and *Black Jack,* (both titles which may be daunting to a child coming across them on it's own), were taken home from the reading group, although not always read from cover to cover! Sometimes reading at school can have a less positive influence. Nicola had been unable to finish reading *Ramona the Pest* as she had changed classrooms and the book had become unavailable!

Titles which had been serialised on TV were eagerly borrowed, especially if the programme was recent and the publication a 'tie-in' edition with a photograph from the series on the cover. However, such titles were often disappointing, taking more time to read than the programmes did to watch.

The televising of a 'classic', whilst making the story known to the children and encouraging them to borrow the book(s), does not always result in the book being read, as will be discussed in Chapter 6.

The motivation of children who borrow a title because they themselves have read it before is completely different. It can be seen most frequently in the under-fives, who borrow the same picture book over and over again. The pleasures of recognition and the security which this brings are the reasons most often given for repeated reading of the same title. However it can also be seen as one aspect of an apprenticeship in readership and this too is discussed in Chapter 6.

3. The attraction of a known author, series or subject

Children rarely speak of a book in terms of author and title — that they came to do this towards the end of the impact interviews may be taken as a sign of their growing book awareness. Gene Kemp, Betsy Byars and Diana Wynne Jones were authors mentioned by name by the children interviewed. Series are far more easily recognisable and children do not usually realise that books in the same series are often written by the same author. Series of books about *Marmalade Atkins, the Bagthorpe Family* and *Ramona* were popular, but children rarely mentioned the names of the authors who had created these series.

Subject matter is a more obvious reason for choice. Tom went in search of fantasy, and chose *The Wizard of Boland, Sea Green Magic* and *Wizards Mountain* from the same meeting because:

"I like a lot of wizards, favourite spells and that."

Ceri, who preferred facts, chose *What Difference does it Make Danny?* because:

"I was curious about how someone could write a book about being epileptic."

Perhaps Sam gave the most pragmatic reason of all for his choice of *The Gocart Robbery* when he said:

"Well, I've got a go-cart, well it's just wheels really, and I wondered whether it had any pictures or a design and I thought well, that looks alright, and then I like books about robberies and stories like that, and I picked this one up and I looked on the back, read on the back, and I thought this was a good book. This was the first book I picked up."

4. Choosing a book by its cover

A child needs practice at judging what a book is going to be like, and one which does not live up to expectations can lead to dissatisfaction with reading in general. Some of the children interviewed made a successful choice from looking at the cover and reading the synopsis on the back of it:

"I sort of liked the picture, it looked quite good by the picture and I looked inside and it looked quite good — it says in the bit here that they lock her up, but I've got another six chapters to go!"

"The blurb gave you such detail it made you want to read it, but didn't tell you what the end was, so you really had to find out."

There is certainly an art in successful synopsis writing.

Children who chose a book by the cover without looking inside were disappointed. Michael looked for high adventure in *Stephen and the Shaggy Dog* because:

"It has a dog on the front and they look as though they are chasing or being chased, but they are not!"

Louise saw conventional excitement in the cover of *The Short Voyage of the Albert Ross* which shows two boys on a raft:

"It looked exciting and I thought he was going to find treasure"

she said, and was disappointed when he didn't.

Jan Mark's title *The Short Voyage of the Albert Ross* holds a literary joke and the accomplished 'reader' will catch all the clues as to the content of the book from cover, title, blurb and even the first few chapters. However, as surveys of child readers from J A Green, in 1913 *(The Teaching of English Literature, What Boys and Girls Read* Journal of Experimental Pedagogy), through Marie Rankin in 1944 *(Children's Interests in Library Books of Fiction)* to Bob Leeson *(Reading and Righting* 1985, agree, most children are neither so subtle nor so discriminating.

5.   Reject titles

The Family Reading Group bookstock on which analysis was made totalled 275 books which represented 255 different titles. They are listed in decreasing order of popularity in Appendix 3. According to the records, each book in stock was taken home at least once. This does not necessarily mean that it was read (see Table 5.4).

It would be relevant here to look at a few rejects — books which were presented at Family Reading Group meetings but borrowed very infrequently. Most would appear to have been rejected because of their low visual appeal. Spread out on a table they present a sombre display of dark colours — green, grey and black predominating — with black line drawings and much cross-hatching. Where covers bear photographs, they are from outdated TV series, such as *The Amazing Mr Blunden,* or *Dr Who* — the 1970's model! The titles of some give no clue as to the contents — *Astercote, Fireweed, The Eyes of the Amaryllis.* Oddly enough, the paperback/hardback controversy does not seem to apply here and dull-looking paperbacks were 'remaindered' along with the hardbacks. Neither did the children express a preference for paperback or hardback books, although they did talk about "thick boots" and "thin books" and a paperback version does usually appear to be thinner.

6.   The Family Reading Group Bookstock

This was a stock of specially selected titles, chosen by librarians drawing on the experience of borrowing among children in other Family Reading Groups in West Hertfordshire, which are described in Chapter 1.

Unlike other surveys in which children's reading interests were recorded, this project was able to present the children with a selection of material, from picture books to Science Fiction, and to monitor its use over a period of twelve months (10 meetings). Previous surveys, such as Frank Whitehead's *Children and Their Books* (1977) and Vera Southgate's *Extending Beginning Reading* (1981) did not establish whether the books mentioned by the children had been read at school, as part of a lesson, or at home; they also noted popular but not unpopular titles. One of the criticisms of Jennie Ingham's Bradford Book Flood project has been that the books with which the schools were flooded were an arbitrary selection presented by publishers.

The range of books for the Fleetville Family Reading Group was broad enough to present the children with an opportunity to choose but at the same time narrow enough to allow monthly monitoring of its use on record cards. Whilst deliberately seeking to avoid the Blytons and Willard Price pop/pap titles, which are constantly and easily obtainable in newsagents, bookshops and most public libraries, there was also an attempt to avoid the classic Arthur Ransome/Polyanna syndrome. In other words, the intention was that the books offered to the children would present a wide range of interests and of reading levels. Librarians, teachers and others who present books to children have every opportunity to take advantage of selection tools such as *Books for Keeps,* (published by the School Bookshop Association in London), and *The School Librarian,* (published by the School Librarian Association in Oxford), both of which have 'review in use' sections, or Hertfordshire's own review: *Material Matters,* published nine times a year. For parents there is *Books for Your Children,* published quarterly by the Federation of Children's Book Groups and the annual *Good Book Guide to Children' Books,* both publications managing to present the best in popular children's reading, without slipping into worthy exhortations. It could be said that the move in the 1980's to involve parents with their children's reading and to raise their level of interest in the material available has resulted in the decline of the esoteric presentation of books for children by adults who were more concerned with the book as a work of art than with the child. This literary approach to children's book selection of the 1960's and early 70's is mocked by Penelope Mortimer in her article *Thoughts Concerning Children's Books* in *Only Connect: Readings on Children's Literature,* edited by Sheila Egoff (1969). Here she points out that reviews and lists of children's books were:

> "written by adults, usually selected by adults, paid for by adults, published and printed and reviewed by adults"

and she continues to ask:

> "are children's books a form of literature which owes its continued existence to a minority of grown ups who might as well be circulating Family Planning leaflets to guinea pigs for all that they understand the requirements of the average child?"

Bob Leeson agrees in *Reading and Righting:*

"What counts is where the centre of gravity of the library and, eventually, the literature is seen to lie — whether the literature is for young people or whether the children's library is a haven for non-viable literature which is judged worthy of preservation — the "time-capsule" approach."

It is becoming clear that there needs to be a balance in collections of books for children between what adults think is 'worth reading' and what children enjoy.

Table 5.3 Appendix 3 of the Family Planning Group Bookstock list books in order of popularity. They show that the most popular material is that which is instantly accessible because of:

1. Presentation — large print, the use of pictures inset into the text or short chapters, as in Robert Swindell's *Dragons Live Forever*.

2. Humour — involving incredible incidents such as those in Ursula Moray Williams *Bogwoppit* or *Marmalade Atkins in Space* by Andrew Davies.

3. Wordplay — of a sophisticated kind in the puns and family jokes of *theBagthorpes* as in Helen Cresswell's *Absolute Zero* or of a more obvious kind in the rhymes in Roger McGough's *Great Smile Robbery*.

Books which naturally appeal to adults because of the moral or complex nature of the story appear much lower down the list — Russell Hoban's *The Mouse and His Child* and *Greyfriar's Bobby* by Eleanor Atkinson, being examples.

It was pointed out earlier in this chapter that personal recommendations played a large part in influencing the child's choice of books. It is interesting to note however that even adult recommendation cannot raise the popularity of books such as Nina Bawden's *The Peppermint Pig,* or Robert O'Brien's *Mrs Frisby and the Rats of Nimh* above the midway point. Both have won awards and are rewarding to the 'practised' reader, but intimidating to the 'beginner' because of the complexity of the characterisation or plot. Collections for children which are overweighted with such books, which it must be said are valid in their own right to practised readers, can prevent less practised readers from establishing the reading habit. This is because there is often not enough of the immediately accessible material in such a collection to give 'beginner readers' the opportunity to establish their skills.

7. Borrowing patterns

The Family Reading Group had no restrictions on the number of books which could be taken home, or the length of time for which they could be kept. Meetings were at four or five week intervals, and although members were asked whether they still had a book at home each month they were not told to return it immediately. The number of books which could be borrowed was one of the factors about which children commented after the first meeting:

"One of my friends got about eight books, the other got about three."

"Two of my friends went and they said it was really good and they got hundreds of books — one of them got about twelve and another took about six."

The theory behind this was that once they had a wide selection of books at home to browse through, the children would be better able to make a choice of a book suited to their mood or the time available for reading. This freedom brought out two salient points, one about a child's choice of books and the other concerned with how they read them.

(a)   Beginner readers

Children who took home a large number of books were more experimental in their selection. Lucy — a 'beginner reader' — gained confidence at the second meeting. She took home three 'safe' titles linked with reading at school: *Prince Caspian; The Voyage of the Dawn Treader* and *The Magician's Nephew*. To this she added two short, quick reads: *Ronnie and the Great Knitted Robbery* and *The Ice Palace, Danny Fox,* which she read with her mother, and a science fiction story *Dragonfall 5 and the Hijackers,* for her brother. She also took home two books which her mother had chosen for herself, *Revolt at Ratcliffe Rags* and *Witch's Daughter.* Of these she only read one completely, (*The Ice Palace* a short, easily-read fantasy which had been introduced at the meeting), partially read the three C S Lewis books.

Louise, another 'beginner reader' took home six books from the second meeting and kept back two from the first. Of these, two were completely read that month; *Outside Over There,* the Sendak picture book, which she found puzzling, and *The Little Vampire* — the cult book among her particular peer group. *Raging Robots and Unruly Uncles,* which she had chosen because of the "funny pictures" on the cover was one of the books which was kept for a second month, but only partly read because "it went on a bit and was rather muddled". A book of short stories *And So It Went On....* went on and on for several months, being dipped into over and over again. *Horse* — a first story book in the Blackbird series — was finished in the third month, left until last because the title proved disappointing — it was not about a real horse after all, but a white horse carved into a hill! Three other titles — *The Eyes of the Amaryllis, The Ghost in the Water* and *The Haunting of Cassie Palmer* were read by her mother and elder sister.

These two 'beginner readers' were typical of those at their particular stage of reading, halfway through the third year at junior school. They were remarkably persistent in their reading and became quite indignant when asked whether they skipped boring passages in a book. Often they continued reading the lengthier books interspersed with stories which were easier to read. Lucy talked about her teacher reading books of a far heavier nature (in both senses of the term) to them at school — *The Runaways* and *The Flight of the Grey Goose —*

"They're sort of thick books and she reads some every day."

To Lucy, her present book, *The Little Vampire* is:

"quite a thick book and I've been reading it — just ten more short chapters to go".

She achieves gratification from finishing a whole book. Pictures make life easier:

"Sometimes when you're a bit tired of reading you can look at the book and just look at the pictures."

(b) Extending into fiction

Ceri's choice of books was different because it showed a gradual weaning from fact to fiction. When first interviewed he said that he read only non-fiction books and was particularly interested in history — two titles mentioned in his 1984 diary were, *Italy under Mussolini* and *Totalitarianism and the Great Depression!* The books which he borrowed from the first meeting (with one exception) either had an historical background — *Black Jack* and *The Strange Affair of Adelaide Harris;* were based on fact — *Animal Ghosts, Ghosts and Hauntings;* or subjects which he wanted to learn about, in this case epilepsy, in *What Difference does it make Danny?* The one exception was *ordinary Jack,* the first tale in the *Bagthorpe Saga,* which another boy had recommended with great gusto at the meeting but which Ceri found disappointing when he read it for himself. At the second meeting his choice broadened slightly to include the science fiction fantasy *The Wizard of Earthsea,* which had been introduced at the meeting — but which he only half-read, starting his reading that month with *The Machine Gunners* which "everyone else" had read and continuing the wartime theme with *Carrie's War.* However, the two books which he enjoyed most that month were two which he identified with most easily because he had a dog himself — *Lassie Come Home* and *Greyfriars' Bobby,* which topped his list as "best book of the month" and was based firmly on fact.

The number of books which Ceri took home from each meeting increased as he became more experimental in his reading. Although he often only dabbled and dipped into types of story to which he was not naturally drawn, he was able to broaden his awareness because of the unlimited number of books he was allowed to take home. Somewhat lacking in inspiration himself, he relied heavily on recommendations from others, and five out of the nine books which he borrowed from the third meeting had been discussed before. The Family Reading Group formula was allowing him to play safe and experiment at the same time. Although, once he got them home, he often rejected stories which were outside his normal sphere of reference, and although he never really managed to come to terms with fantasy, he did come to extend his imagination to empathise with Ben in *The Cartoonist.* Furthermore, although he stopped coming to the group when he transferred to secondary school, he was still reading fiction the following Spring. He notes in his 1985 diary "Reading" as one of his "best" occupations and lists *Alice in Wonderland* and Robert Westall's *Fathom Five* alongside *Marx for Beginners* and *Imperialism and World War I!*

The unlimited number of books which the children were allowed to borrow meant that they could be somewhat flippant in their choice and succumb to whims and fancies — in other words, they could really begin to enjoy books in a light-hearted way. Andrew took home twelve books from the first meeting, covering a wide range of reading abilities and subject matter. Starting from the heavier end there was *The Hobbit* and Richmal Crompton's *William Again,* two titles in the *Bagthorpe Saga,* two in the *Jesters* series, one *Choose Your Own Adventure* type — *Encyclopaedia Brown* — two "thick" comedies, *Mr Browser and the Comet Crisis* and Hildick's *The Great Rabbit Robbery,* two quick reads and one near picture book, *Dragons Live Forever.* This is how he described his choice:-

"I was being a bit silly when I took this one, I was just going round picking up everything I thought looked good, luckily I picked up ones which were good. These are the ones I picked up on purpose, but the rest, I just happened to pick up and that one *(Encylopaedia Brown)* it's three books in one. I didn't pick that one *(Adventures* of the ABC Mob) because of the picture, but because of the author, Forrest Wilson; these (Jesters) I read quite a lot of when I was a bit younger and that one (Hildick, Great Rabbit Robbery) looked quite interesting. That one (Mr Browser and the Comet Crisis) was on our booklist at school, that one (The Day They Stole the FA Cup) I read the bit on the back."

What was most interesting was that, by the time I visited him the following week, Andrew had read six out of his eleven books and they were all those that he had picked up when he was "being a bit silly" not the *William* book, which his Dad had talked about, or *The Hobbit* or even the two *Bagthorpe* titles which he enthused about the following month. Had he only been allowed to borrow two, the chances are that conforming to the school book list would have had precedence and the excitement of rollicking through several "fun" books would have disappeared.

The way in which Reading Group members developed a cumulative reading pattern, holding some books over and part reading them from month to month whilst eagerly devouring others or rejecting them outright, can be seen in the following record of books read, part read and rejected by children interviewed after the first five meetings. (Table 5.4).

Table 5.4 To Show the Pattern of Books Read (R), Retained and Part Read (PR) and Retained and Not Read (NR) over a Five Month Period

Child	1			2			Meeting 3			4			5			Total		
	R	PR	NR	R	PR	NR	R	PR	NR	R	PR	NR	R	PR	NR	R	PR	NR
Tom	–	–	–	4	5	5	9	5	3	9	2	4	7	2	5	29	9	17
Andrew	10	2	0	3	2	2	3	3	0	4	1	2	3	2	0	23	10	4
Ceri	–	–	–	4	2	0	5	1	0	4	4	1	5	2	0	18	9	1
Roger	3	2	2	5	1	1	2	1	0	5	2	1	–	–	–	15	6	4
Michael	4	0	2	5	0	1	2	0	4	3	4	2	–	–	–	14	4	9
Stuart	2	3	2	2	2	0	5	1	0	4	1	2	–	–	–	13	5	6
Louise	2	1	2	2	3	3	2	4	2	1	4	5	3	4	2	10	15	11
Stephen	4	2	1	2	0	1	1	2	1	–	–	–	2	2	0	9	6	3
Martin	4	0	0	0	1	0	2	1	0	–	–	–	2	0	0	8	2	0
Lucy	2	1	2	0	5	7	1	2	0	0	4	0	3	3	2	6	15	11
Jane	1	2	0	1	4	1	2	3	2	1	3	1	–	–	–	5	12	4
Nicola	0	3	1	2	4	0	1	2	2	0	3	0	–	–	–	3	12	3
John	1	1	1	1	0	1	–	–	–	–	–	–	–	–	–	2	1	2
Clare	–	–	–	0	2	3	1	2	3	0	3	1	–	–	–	1	7	7

TOTAL 156 113 82

It was quite common for children to keep a book at home for two or even three months and to mention it each time they were interviewed. They clearly did not see themselves as failures because they had failed to finish a book, nor did they view that book as a non-starter. They just read backwards and forwards amongst different types of books and at different reading levels, as these comments show.

"I read easier ones in the middle," (Andrew)

"I don't like those (Enid Blyton books). When I start to read them I can't finish them, I start on another book, there is one book which I read twice." (Jane)

"Nicola seems to jog between books," said her Mum, and Nicola explained why when she was discussing *The Talking Parcel,* which she kept at home for several months:

"I leave it alone for a bit when I get bored with it and go back to it when I want to have a read and don't know what to read!"...

...a situation which most of us would recognise. Constraints at school and in the public library which make children return one book before they are allowed to borrow another militate against this flexibility in reading. Margaret Meek says in *Learning to Read* (1982):

"Children and adults who have had a long break in their reading need to be able to read themselves into reading by interspersing attempts at reading longer stories with satisfying, encouraging "quick reads" which reassure them that they can do it and that reading is fun. These "quick reads" may be books which they have read before and which need no struggle to recognise characterisations or plot or may be picture books or very easy but very funny stories. Their presence in the desk or on the bookshelf is reassuring — I have read these, I can read these — and a child struggling with a less satisfactory reading experience can return to them and repeat an experience which he had found to be good."

It can be seen that accomplished readers, such as Martin, Andrew, or even Ceri, have a far greater success rate in terms of finding the boo that they take home readable than beginner readers such as Louise or Lucy. Roger started off as a slow and unwilling reader, but as all the books which he borrowed were well within his reading capabilities, and had some 'fun value' as well *(Dracula's Bedtime Storybook, Fungus the Bogeyman, The Great Smile Robbery),* he gained a sense of achievement through completing the books which he had taken home. The high figure for books which were 'part read' reflects the experimentation which readers were allowed by the unlimited loan system; this figure also represents the proportion of titles which were held over from one meeting to the next.

8. What and how they read

Although the use of the time clocks in the After School Diaries was not consistent enough for a comparative record of length of time spent reading, it does give some insight into how some children read and this substantiates what has just been said about children's patterns of reading.

Lucy mentioned reading only once in her 1984 diary, when she was in the third year at junior school. A 'beginner reader' who took part in the impact interviews and who came regularly to Family Reading Group meetings with one or other of her parents, she features reading heavily in her 1985 diary, often timetabling two or more books a day from the seven which she mentions over the two week period. She seems to be reading from one heavy and one more lightweight book each day — during the first week alternating *The King of the Copper Mountain* with *The Little Vampire* and, during the second, with *Winnie the Pooh.* After the Reading Group meeting on the Thursday of the first week she clearly 'dips' into titles which she has just borrowed, looking at *The 13 days of Christmas* for 10 minutes on the Friday evening, *The Great Piratical Rumbustification* for five minutes on the following Wednesday and *Oggy at Home,* for a marathon 55 minutes on Thursday. It is worth noting that *Oggy at Home,* (which, together with *The Little Vampire Moves In,* she records reading for a far longer period of time), is in fact written at a lower reading level than the other titles which she records as reading, usually for only ten or fifteen minutes at a time. She finishes the second Friday with a flourish "I finished *The King of the Copper Mountains*" — and then goes on to pick up *Winnie the Pooh* once more after tea. Like most children who completed diaries, she appears to read most consistently at bedtime and also at 'infill' times, whilst waiting to go out, for example.

At the other extreme, Tom, who gave as his favourite occupation in his 1984 4th year junior school diary "Reading, while drinking a very cool glass of un-fizzy lemonade", reads each day for several 45 minute periods, pausing only to have his tea, watch *Dr. Who* or tell jokes to his Dad. He usually reads after Children's TV programmes have finished, except on Mondays when he notes "4.35–5.15 — read a book. TV is boring on Monday". He usually reads from more than one book in a day, although the impression is that he finishes one before starting another. The random choice element of choosing a book, mentioned by Andrew earlier in this chapter, appears again as Tom writes in his diary: "8.45 started a domino rally with paperbacks, made another domino rally with paperbacks. 9.00 found a paperback I wanted to read" — or did he! At 9.15 he "Gave up on one book, started a thick magazine". The obsession of a really avid reader comes over well in the entry for Friday, "9.00 got ready for bed. 9.20 picked up my book again. 9.30 told to get into bed. 9.30-9.40 sneaked a few more minutes."

Tom's rate of borrowing was erratic: at the first meeting which he attended he borrowed 14 books, read 4 and part read 5; at the second he borrowed 17, read 9, part read 5; and at the third he borrowed 15, read 7. Perhaps one of the reasons for his voracious reading was his continued gratification by the experience — the books which he took home were mostly well within his range of reading ability and understanding, and when they were not, like *William IV* or Anne Schlee's *The Vandal* he had enough confidence to give up on them. His Mother commented on the Family Reading Group's ability to meet his reading needs:

> "I am amazed at the number of interesting paperbacks that he brings back and also there do seem to be books directed at his age group and with his range of interests, which I had thought never existed."

The diaries asked children to fill in what they did "After School", but Andrew found the best time for reading was early in the morning.

> "I read most of the them in the morning. I wake up at about six o'clock at the moment; I listen to the radio and read a book; quite a lot of the time I don't read a book I just listen to the radio. I'm quite lazy at the moment, I don't get up and do anything. Last week I was reading books, but I've stopped a bit now. I have got half way through some of the game books, but I get stuck in the middle of that; I don't know where I am."

Although this is a survey of children's reading out of school, it must be remembered that, for some, school can provide the only uninterrupted time for reading in the whole day. Some schools take up this challenge; sadly, others don't:

> "One of my friends reads almost every day at playtime."

"One of my friends reads almost every day at playtime."

"Can you stay in at playtime and read?"

"No, she takes a book out into the playground and sits down somewhere."

"I read a book about this thick at school called *'Moominland Midwinter'* and I've been reading that about ten weeks, but we don't normally get enough reading time, only about five minutes."

Chapter 6

What is a "Good Read"?

"Once I read 8-10 chapters in one night!"

In *Reading and Righting* (1985) Bob Leeson suggests that

> "The so-called 'reluctant' reader was, in fact, the great unrecognised critic of the 1960's and 1970's."

Paradoxically, this period has also been seen as a second "golden age" of children's literature. Margaret Spencer makes the link between reading and readers in her article in *Reading: Implementing the Bullock Report* (Grundin and Grundin 1978), when she states that:

> "Literature is the driving force of learning to read... We cannot have theories of children's literature separate from theories of literacy"

and Elizabeth Hunter-Grundin carries this even further in the same report:

> "If the 'best' books for children are defined exclusively so that only a few children can read them, what do the others read? Can critics of children's books ignore the developmental aspects of reading?"

Michel Gault takes up these developmental aspects of reading in *The Future of Books: Part 2, The Changing Role of Reading,* UNESCO (1982), defining "literacy" as:

> "the ability to understand a written message... and transform it into an oral message which is comprehensible to the ear. This is... survival reading... Establishing a relationship with a book requires, however, a quite different activity: the corresponding reading strategy only affects at most 30% of the population. In current conditions, the remaining 70% will always be non-readers, unless they can be given access in one way or another to these reading strategies which can turn them into real readers."

The children interviewed at Fleetville were at different stages in mastering these strategies towards becoming a real reader and it is salutary to look at what they had to say about it. The conclusions drawn in this survey come as the result of successive interviews with 14 children, all aged between 9 and 11 at the time. The questionnaire which was used as the basis of this interview is given in Appendix 1, but the sessions themselves, each lasting about 45 minutes, took on an unstructured conversational form, during which the children talked about their books. As Nicholas Tucker writes in *The Child and the Book* (1981) of 7-11 year olds:

> "It is still not at all easy for them to explain what they get out of their reading, should the question ever be put to them. In this sense stories are something to be entered into and enjoyed, but rarely to be thought about in any more detached way — we must generally wait until children are over the age of eleven and better able to stand back from their immediate experience in order to assess it in more abstract terms."

Even over the age of eleven children — and adults — find it difficult to discuss their books objectively; one of the parents interviewed said that he did not introduce titles at the meeting as he 'found it difficult to see the story from the child's viewpoint' — without realising that it was his own views which were asked for! There are many parallels with the difficulty of interviewing children about reading as made apparent by the problems that Hilary Wigmore *(The Captive Reader,* Cranfield Press) encountered when attempting to interview the housebound about their reading.

However, I was able to balance my conversations with the children against the reading records from the Family Reading Group meetings and to substantiate what they told me with references to their diaries, thus constructing a more complete picture of the impact which reading had on them.

Michel Gault recognises:

"The major obstacle remains the difficulty they have in choosing"

and I have talked about this in the preceding chapter, but, once the book is at home and in their hands, where are the clues which help the children to begin to relate to it? The popularity index shows that the title of the book can often give the first clue and that, where it does not do this, children are less likely to jump into the void and borrow the book. Knowledge gained from folk and fairy tales of early childhood, rhymes and myths can help here. One of the titles in our stock was *The Nine Lives of Island Mackenzie* and two children picked this as a pointer not only to what the book was about, but to the fact that its action would continue right through the book:

"That one gave me a clue, nine lives, so he obviously loses them somewhere."

"If you don't believe in nine lives it's a bit stupid to read it."

1. Understanding and reading

One of the reasons given by children over and over again for not continuing to read a book is that the introduction, the first few pages, or the first chapter is 'boring'. Couple with that the honourable disinclination of most of them to "skip" passages and the fact that many are reading at such a slow rate that the ten or fifteen minutes which they give to that book may be all taken up with the scene setting, and quick-reading adults may begin to understand why. Much has been written recently about the need to teach children study skills, the ability to extract from a passage its essence and pass on to the next chapter, but most teachers would accept that children find this very difficult. Michel Gault has a theory to explain why this happens:

"Rapid speech uses 10,000–15,000 words an hour, reading averages 20,000–30,000. At less than 15,000 the reader begins to flag and the mind wanders."

For the "decoder" who cannot go beyond this speed, use of the written word is valueless, except for "survival reading". This is a scientific explanation for the feeling of bewilderment which Clare, a 'beginner reader' is describing when she says:

"Sometimes it goes on and you don't know what it's talking about, you don't understand."

Louse, at a similar stage in her reading apprenticeship gave up reading one book because:

"It was getting very long and I wasn't very fast at reading and I had a lot of others I wanted to read".

Her addition there is telling. Despite an unsatisfactory experience with one book, she was able to reject that book and start again with another one; had she only been allowed one book at a time, and been told to persevere, she might have viewed reading a lot less positively than she does now. Like Louise, Stuart related the time spent to the amount of gratification gained from reading and preferred to cut his losses and stop reading one particular book when:

> "I didn't have time and it got boring and they mentioned some bits they had mentioned before."

More experienced readers understand that:

> "You have to read the boring bits as well, because sometimes you miss out and later on in the book the boring bits help you to understand what's happening."

Martin, who was perhaps one of the most accomplished readers in the group, agreed that the first chapter was often:

> "boring, but I always read that because very often that is the key page. Without that you wouldn't know what was going on (like when I write a story) so I always try to understand it."

Michael, who had read *Emil and the Detectives* twice, was even more explicit about the part played by the opening of the book:

> "You need to have an introduction because you've got to get to know his Mum first, because she comes in later on as well, and he's got to get on the train because he gets robbed on the train on the way to Berlin."

He has learnt, too, the importance of recognising a sequence of events.

2. For and against series

Some children read the same book twice because they gain satisfaction from foreknowledge. They find a similar satisfaction in reading series; they have already met the characters, know what to expect of them and can concentrate on the action (hence the success of *The Famous Five, Nancy Drew* and the more recent "formula" books, the *Fighting Fantasy* and *Choose your own Adventure* series). Other, more experienced readers, look for originality in the plot. Andrew chose Hildick's *Deadline for McGurk* because he had already read his *Great Rabbit Robbery,* but he was disappointed.

> "He had written too many about the same person because they always seem to be similar stories — once it was painted rabbits and this time it was babies and dolls being nicked. The characters are exactly the same — like the *Famous Five* they keep on going on about the same people doing the same things — a nine year old may enjoy it."

And many nine year olds have done so! The need to meet with a book at an appropriate stage of reading development, to match the literature to the state of literacy to use Margaret Spencer's term, is something which caused comment from one parent reading children's stories for the first time:

> "It's a bit difficult for parents because they think differently — I read one of those space things, *Dragonfall 5* and it was absolute rubbish; when I thought about it, to a ten or eleven year old boy it might have been the height of excitement, you look for different things."

A far cry this, from the C S Lewis theory that a children's story which is enjoyed only by children is a bad children's story. Nevertheless if children are going to read themselves into reading they are going to have to pass through several stages of literacy.

3. Catching the right phrase

Children are also going to pass through several stages of ambiguity — when they comtemplate... lack of it! A beginner reader who has only just managed to master the "decoding" stage can sometimes feel thwarted by rhyming stories:

> "because you can't find well known words to fit in and they have to choose different hard words that sometimes I can't understand."

In this search for understanding, the beginner reader needs to know exactly what is happening in the story and who it is happening to. Flashbacks can be confusing:

> "The beginning was good and then it went off and back again."

Passages of dialogue, which more experienced readers delight in, can confuse beginners. Nicola talked about enjoying:

> "muddly book where they start talking about something and then change the subject again and then someone comes up with that subject again and that doesn't mean anything — it's mainly talking."

On the other hand Clare complained of her book:

> "Sometimes it didn't tell you which person was speaking."

It is significant that Nicola was talking about Pat Hutchins' *The House that Sailed Away* in the Puffin *Beginning to Read* series, whilst Clare was referring to Bernard Ashley's *A Break in the Sun* written at a much higher reading level. Following Gault's theory, Nicola would probably have been reading her book much more quickly than Clare was reading hers, and therefore she was better able to grasp the intricacies of the dialogue.

4. The televised version

Television adaptations of stores such as *Break in the Sun,* whilst encouraging children to read the book, often arouse false expectations in the reader when the text proves too difficult.

> "On TV it was good, but it didn't go into so much detail and you just had to listen — the book is long"

complained Clare. On the other hand Stephen, who is further advanced in his readership apprenticeship, would obviously take the details in Helen Cresswell's *Absolute Zero* in his stride, and missed her descriptions in the screen version.

> "The book paints a picture and you get a different impression of people than on the telly — Helen Cresswell goes into detail, like "The paint was peeling off the walls", but not the most obvious things, like saying 'it was pitch black' and later on 'it was dark'.

I imagined it different on TV. You just see it and they don't tell you anything about it — you just see it."

Technology has the advantage over print when it can show two things happening at the same time. Tom preferred the film of *Freaky Friday* to the book because:

"it showed the mother and the child doing the same thing at the same time."

Although this study does not set out to compare television viewing with reading, (as earlier surveys have shown that avid readers do both), it is significant that television has accustomed children to expect more instant gratification from their entertainment — including their reading.

In 'the good old days', there was much more time to spare and perhaps that was why the children who took home the *William* books because their fathers had read them, or because they had seen the televised versions, found them "lengthy and wordy". As an example of what he meant, Michael quoted me the phrase "both luxuries could be indulged in" from one of the William books and explained that, although the words made it funny, they also made the book "difficult to read to yourself". Andrew and Tom both found the *William* stories rather tame by today's standards, much preferring the more "outrageous" and equally televised *Marmalade Atkins,* whose exploits transferred more easily and identifiably from screen to print and had more street credibility. As Andrew scoffed,

"William was old-fashioned, he kept pretending he was a pirate and he didn't have a bike — he plays pirates when he was 12!"

Table 6.1   Reasons Given by Children for Liking a Book   (100%=14)

Relating to characters in some way, especially when they are naughty	84%
Funny incidents	77%
Being frightened	54%
Action	38%
Being made to feel sad	31%

5.   Reasons for enjoyment

If that is what the children interviewed found "boring" (and for "boring" read "muddled and incomprehensible", as well as dull and lacking in action), what did they find interesting and attractive in the books which they took home from the group? During the interviews in which they talked about what they had read, they mentioned certain incidents, characters and parts of the style of the stories which stuck in their minds and made an impact on them. Because their outlook on reading was positive as a whole, they agreed far more on what they liked than on what they disliked.

Referring to Table 6.1, if the percentage who related to the characters in some way were split into those who related variously to naughty children and others, the 84% becomes 54% who relate to characters anyway and 30% who only relate to their naughty side.

The discovery that children find gratification in stories which reflect their own experience is nothing new and Whitehead charts it thoroughly in the chapter *The Books Children Prefer* in *Children and Their Books,* (1977), concluding that the child's identification with the character in the book may not be totally empathic but may be evaluative as well as emotional. What does emerge strongly from this present survey is the high percentage of children who related to a book because they had found it funny. This, surely, is a pointer towards the type of story that the nine or ten year old may be wooed and won by — not because it reflects their problems in a world of one-parent families and school closures, but because it is fun. Of course, the two are not necessarily mutually exclusive and some of the titles mentioned are, to quote the title of Max Fatchen's poetry anthology for this age group, *A Wry Look at Troublesome Times.*

6.   What was funny about it?

The children surveyed in Vera Southgate's *Extending Beginning Reading* (1981) would agree with the Fleetville Group, as "amusing" topped the list of their reasons for liking a particular book: Southgate also recorded the popularity of adventure books, and the "funny" parts of the stories which the Fleetville children mention are more often related to the action than to particular characters. Their preference is for situation comedy. The following are a few of their examples:

"The things that happened were funny, not the characters."

"The funniest bit was when Michael locked Mr Browser in the cupboard and the children in the classroom."

"There's some really funny bits, like tying to hide the vampire under the bed."

"The sisters — Sister Conception and Sister Purification — stuck to the seat with super glue."

One of the attractions of the stories about 'naughty children' like *Marmalade Atkins,* is that their escapades are funny as well as awesomely awful! The children's laughter also springs from their knowledge of the plot, from being 'in' on the joke — they know that there is a spider in the sandwich in *My Best Fiend* and can laugh from a sense of superiority.

From the very earliest years children appreciate jokes, riddles and wordplay and often it is the style of the author which they find "funny". Examples of this are the alliteration used by Roger McGough in the joke names given in *The Great Smile Robbery,* and the short rhymes in Allan Ahlberg's *Please Mrs Butler* or Michael Rosen's *Down Behind the Dustbin.* Allusive jokes, too, are picked up even by 'beginner readers', no doubt with an ear tuned to telelvision dialogue — Lucy enjoyed the fact that her favourite *Little Vampire* book had the vampire reading *The Revenge of Dracula* and that his enemy... "wanted to be the first man in Europe to have a "vampire free cemetery".

Unlike beginner readers, who found it confusing, more experienced readers picked out the speed and subtlety of dialogue as factors which made them laugh:

"I like the way she cuts a sentence off when it's funny and drifts off — and she said."

"The conversation builds up and adds on — 'With a box of matches — and a little dynamite — it shouldn't be too difficult to blow up the Houses of Parliament.'"

Pat Hutchins' books *Follow That Bus* and *The House that Sailed Away* and Helen Cresswell's *Bagthorpe Saga* are particularly enjoyed because of their wit and pace and their use of plot and sub-plot.

"There was something big happening and something small happening at the same time."

in each.

Illustrations add humour to the stories. This is true for older as well as for younger children and they are particularly useful in helping reluctant, or beginner readers, through the book:

"Sometimes when you are a bit tired of reading you can look at the book and just look at the pictures."

funny pictures in the style of Quentin Blake or Tony Ross are so easily identifiable that children take it for granted that the story will be funny too:

"I chose that one *(Cat and Mouse)* with Nicola because the picture on the back was so funny and the other pictures — he's so fat, a big balloon. We read it in the car going home from the group. The story's not that funny, it's just the pictures made you laugh."

In some books, however, the stories and pictures are inextricably linked as in Raymond Briggs' *Fungus the Bogeyman* or Victor Ambrus' *Dracula's Bedtime Storybook* and it is an advantage that for beginner readers these books can be taken at different levels:

"It's quite hard to read with the descriptions — my sister just looked at the pictures."

7. Liking to be frightened

"Make them laugh, make them cry — that's entertainment", and laughter often comes as a relief from tension. The frightening passages which the children talked about can be divided into those which resulted from the action (mentioned mostly by "beginner readers" such as Lucy), and those which depended on the reader relating to the character (mentioned by Tom and Martin, both more experienced readers).

The Little Vampire caused some little shudders:

"It was very frightening where Tony heard someone come in his bedroom window and rip down the posters — he expected a burglar but found the little vampire."

Michael talking about *Stephen and The Shaggy Dog* said:

"The best bit was frightening"

and read aloud a lengthy passage in which Stephen found the dog in the shed and it howled at him, adding:

> "you have to wait a bit before you go on to the next chapter."

Louise was on the brink of a deeper understanding of people and events around her and groping at expressing the links between her life and her books, as will be discussed in the next chapter. She was fascinated and frightened at the same time by Maurice Sendak's *Outside Over There,* making up her own gloss for the illustrations and going back to it over and over again.

> "Her Mum has got a letter, the little girl is called Ida, the baby hasn't got a name probably because the Father went off before it was quite old and the Mother couldn't choose. The ice baby is horrible, the faces are horrible."

She is also beginning to relate character and action and finds the combination frightening in this passage which she relates from *The Short Voyage of the Albert Ross:*

> "I liked it when John was saying 'I'll tell your Mum' and teasing Stephen. I thought at the beginning they were friends, but in the middle of the book it tells you they were not. I was a bit frightened when the raft drifted off, I thought he would drown and those horrible things eat him."

Here it could be hypothesised that it was the bullying of Stephen by John which, like the ice babies, alternately frightened and fascinated her, but that she hooked this fear on to the actual fact of drowning.

'Beginner readers' could often be thought of as 'beginners' psychologically too, who can only accept a limited amount of charcter identification at a time, if it is likely to be disturbing. This reasoning could also account for the length of time it takes them to read a book, because they have to keep reverting to the safety of less demanding stories. Jane, comparing the *TV Kid* with *Follow that Bus,* explained:

> "Once I read 8-10 chapters in one night (of *Follow That Bus*), from 9 oclock to about half past, but this one (*TV Kid*) I could only read two chapters at a time, you felt as if you'd had enough of that story for the night."

8.   Relating to the story

More mature readers are not only able to decode more complex stories, but to cope with their messages and to identify with the characters' feelings as well as their actions, even though they may find them disturbing. Tom felt this way when he read *The Vandal:*

> "Starting the fire was a bit scary, the footballs exploding — I felt his feelings, emotions gaining over him when he lit it."

Nicola also found both actions and emotions frightening in *The Multiplying Glass,* where the glass reflects the three sides to the heroine's personality, which are embodied in Lisa, Liz and Elizabeth.

"It's very scary at some points, Liz locks Elizabeth up and leaves her there. I liked it. I think it's because sometimes you feel as though one part of you is being normal, another part is saying do something bad and another part — be soppy."

Martin recognises this power of the story to release emotions and speaks of its cathartic effect in the ending of *The Wizard of Earthsea:*

"for the last few chapters you think Ged is going to die, or all the magic will be drained from him, or Aran will go mad. It leaves you in suspense until the last page and then you find he just loses his power."

This is the response of an accomplished reader, able to decode without difficulty. Unlike the beginner readers who go backwards and forwards from book to book, taking the more demanding titles in easy stages, he read right through *Earthsea* with no need for diversion in between. He is one of the lucky ones, others may never reach this stage, but can still gain satisfaction through reading more simple stories in their entirety. The ability to 'read right through' inevitably affects the readers' response to books and also, their ability to manipulate the story and the levels of reality and fantasy which they find there. This will be discussed in the next chapter.

Chapter 7

Reality and Readership

From "I like reading about dogs because
I've got one"
To "I felt his feelings"

1. Relating to reality

Reality — relate — with only a slight juggling of letters, one word becomes the other. One of the most recognised reasons for children's enjoyment of reading is that they relate to the experiences of those "in the story". Helen Robinson and Samuel Weintraub in their paper on *Research Related to Children's Interests and to Developmental Values of Reading* (Library Trends 22: 2 October 1973), conclude that children read for identification, to solve problems and to reinforce views that have been accepted already. Peter Mann lists five types of gratification which adults receive from reading — instrumental, prestige, reinforcement, aesthetic and respite, but comments that:

> "Books and reading mean different things to different people."

Section one of the *The Cool Web* (Meek 1977) is concerned with the reader and their relation to *Kinds of Fiction: a Hierarchy of Veracity* to quote the title of Aidan Warlow's essay. In this, Warlow gives a

> "categorisation of children's books according to the similarity or dissimilarity of the stories to the world as it is usually seen to be."

The popularity listing of Family Reading Group titles shows that the majority fall into that section where normal laws of nature are maintained. To use the terminology of The Cool Web, readers who chose these books are more concerned with the Primary than the Secondary world of belief (which concepts are explained later in this chapter).

In the final paragraph of his essay Aidan Warlow argues:

> "If we attempt to identify the 'proper relation to reality' of other types of story and describe their conventions along the lines I have so briefly suggested above, then we will be getting very much closer to an understanding of the notion of readability. Up to now, elaborate and costly research has been applied to texts in order to describe 'readability' in terms of typography, vocabulary and syntax. Very little thought has been devoted to the question of whether one story can be read more easily than another... Future research might be more usefully applied not to how a text is written but to what sort of a world the story-teller is inviting the reader to enter."

Michel Gault augments this by qualifying his theories (quoted in previous chapters) on 'survival reading' and illiteracy as follows:

> "In depth research has shown that a written text, in order to be readable requires its target reader to possess at least 80% of the information it conveys, thus enabling him to assimilate the remaining 20% of information he previously lacked. On the other hand, a very good acquaintance with the subject involved can offset a poor command of reading skills in this and only this respect."

The veracity of both these statements can be shown by the attitude of the Fleetville children towards reality and fantasy in the books which they discussed. As their ability as a 'reader' develops so too does their perception of reality. At first reality is defined by beginner readers as that which is immediately recognisable and identifiable — i.e. children like them in a world like their own. From here they progress to an indentification with "feelings" rather than actions, or what Aidan Warlow calls "value systems and behavioural characteristics of the protagonists", which will lead them to an understanding of a Secondary world of fantasy.

Felil L Shirly expresses the same theory more simply in her article on *The Influence of Reading Concepts, Attitudes and Behaviour (Reading Today and Tomorrow*, Melnik and Merritt 1972) when she says:

> "Those reporting plot as influence made lower scores in group intelligence."

Looking at the Fleetville children's perception of reality, we can chart a development from beginner reader to complete reader.

> "When I used a word, Humpty Dumpty said... it means just what I choose it to mean, neither more nor less."

> "The questions is, said Alice, whether you can make words mean so many different things."

> "The question is, said Humpty Dumpty, which is to be the master, that's all."

Beginner readers take the words at their face value. After all, they have just mastered the art of learning what words mean, and are hardly likely to invalidate that art by allowing that what the words tell them is not true! Hence the swing away from fairy stories at this age, together with the rejection, at around the age of eight, of what Aidan Warlow quotes as:

> "Piaget's stage of intuitive pre-operational thought."

This is the stage at which children will relate to a story by applying a rigid moral framework such as that contained in fairy tales. Often this bears little relation to real life situations and values. At around nine or ten years old and sometimes before, most children have a grasp of what is real and what isn't and will call a spade a spade and a fairy story a fairy story. Evelina Ness's picture story *Sam Bangs and Moonshine*, firmly states the difference between "real" and "taradiddle" and the dangers of mixing up the two. Of course, many books are written at several levels and the child who returns over and over again to a story may read something quite different into it the second time around. That is the art of the writer referred to by Jean Rhys when she says:

> "One should write in an ordinary way and make the writing seem extraordinary. One should write too, about what is ordinary and the extraordinary behind it. Sometimes we only realise the 'extraordinary' later, but for the time being the 'ordinary' will suffice."

2. How the Fleetville children defined 'reality'

Analysing the impact interviews with the Family Reading Group members, it is possible to note three major definitions of reality, which gradually increase in their complexity. A story is real:

1. If it is about children who are roughly the readers' own age, with families, doing what they do — or would like to do. It must have situations which can be paralleled almost

exactly by their own at home and school. Sometimes the plot can even be re-set in their own classroom or bedroom.

2.   If the readers can identify with the characters' feelings and emotions, even if they do not always act, or speak, in the way that the readers do. This identification may be so strong that is will carry over into situations which are not always entirely probable or immediately recognisable.

3.   If a secondary world is created in its entirety in which the plot and characters are internally consistent, develop within them and are sympathetic to the reader's emotions.

To comment on these at length:

1.   "I could have been there"

The first definition of reality by the children, especially those who were 'beginner readers', was in terms of their simple daily existence which revolves around home and school, friends and relationships. The diary records discussed in Chapter 3 show how little time there is in most of these children's lives for introspection, and the boy who recorded "sat on the sofa because I felt sad" was certainly in the minority. Visiting and playing with friends, going on school outings, being told to tidy their room or go to bed by Mum — this is what life is made of and this is what is seen as "real" in the stories which they read and enjoy. At this most basic level:

> "I like reading about dogs because I've got one."

said Ceri. Before coming to the Family Reading Group, he had only read information books and was still trying to keep his reading as close to the truth as possible, appearing to fight off the intrusion of feelings which he sometimes let slip into his discussions:

> "I think you would understand the story more if you've got a dog — my dog would be too lazy to do that."

Events in the organised activities with which many children are involved are transposed by them into what they read. For example, in *Absolute Zero* by Helen Cresswell, competition fever reaches such a pitch among the Bagthorpes that the whole family take the labels off tins of food for entry forms and they are reduced to shaking them to guess the contents. Stephen recognised this confusion, commenting:

> "It's bad enough at camp."

To children living firmly in a consumer society and who can sing you the jingle from any TV advert, brand names bring instant identification.

Readers commonly seek to relate the story to their own lives in a practical "how to do it" way (Peter Mann's "instrumental gratification"). How many *Secret Seven* clubs have teachers noticed in school, even today, and how many stories about gangs and groups of children are emulated — remember *A Clockwork Orange* (Burgess, 1962)? *Encyclopaedia Brown* is a story in which:

> "the boy solves the crime before his father."

It not only made Michael feel superior because he too could solve the crimes in the book, but set him off to:

"start this detective agency — it didn't go very well though."

Emil, in *Emil and The Detectives*, was another child sleuth with whom Michael identified because:

"he didn't know anything that I didn't know."

On the other hand, Michael found Cyril Bonhamy, the hero of *The Spy and the Mission of Terrible Importance*:

"impossible, unrealistic — he was reading and writing books all the time but he didn't know anything."

Michael is not yet ready to accept the fantasy super sleuth because he is still taking his own life so seriously, and only boy detectives are within his bounds of credibility. He was unable to see the humour in the character of the anti-hero — a much more sophisticated concept.

School life was one area to which most of the children related, especially beginner readers like Jane. She could accept the spaceship in the playground in *Mr Browser and the Brain Sharpeners* because of amazing similarities between the classroom activity in Philip Curtis's story and that in her own school.

"Half the children at school are like that. There's a girl in our class called Victoria Jones and she's always breaking pencils, she's like that and she's always breaking pens, either that or the nib goes."

Andrew, a more extensive reader, related to the school and, through that, to the characters, in *Tyke Tyler*:

"It's a pretty proper school because they got punished for being good and punished for being bad and at the end of term they said goodbye and weren't just pushed out."

For the most part, the children interviewed in Fleetville appeared to come from stable family backgrounds. It is interesting that, to most of these children, families such as Gowie Corby's *(Gowie Corby Plays Chicken)* with the father in prison and a brother in Borstal are far removed and incredible. Ceri:

"felt like giving up after the first few chapters because I didn't know what it was about."

He preferred *Tyke Tyler*, where there were "nicer characters" and more with which he could identify. However, it is a reminder that to some children, books like *Gowie Corby Plays Chicken* extend reality as much as the more elaborate fantasies! Bob Dixon has shown the dangers of such preconceptions in his book *Catching Them Young* (1977).

American family stories such as those by Judy Blume and Betsy Byars are always popular. In particular the Fleetville children discussed Betsy Bayers' *The Cartoonist* and *The TV*

Kid, which had high ratings in the Popularity Index. The fact that these are American stories worried Jane far less than the fact that there was not a Father there to control the situation (and possibly raise the standard of living!). She commented:

> "The mother was a bit ragged, always wearing jeans. When they had their meals they had really cheap things, they didn't have things like mince, they had fish and chips and that. In this one *(Cartoonist)* they had more money. Neither had fathers in it — in this one *(TV Kid)* there was no need for a father, but in the other one *(Cartoonist)* there should have been. In this one *(TV Kid)* I think the father died."

Her excuses for the Father's absence show a concern for all to be right with the world, which echoes Louise's reaction to Maurice Sendak's *Outside Over There*, mentioned earlier. The mother in *The TV Kid* she finds truly annoying because:

> "she turns the TV off and makes him work at the most interesting bits in the quiz programme and I wanted to know what happened next as well."

Jane related so literally to the story in *The Cartoonist* that in her mind she situated it directly in her friend's house:

> "because there's a bend in the stairs just like that and then the attic."

Like Ceri, who cautiously appeared to be protecting himself from the psychological upheaval of sharing too closely in fictitious emotions, but admitted to "feeling sorry" for the beleaguered father in *Absolute Zero*, Jane recognised that the situation of the boy who had to turn out of his bedroom in *The Cartoonist* made her "feel sad". However, she protected herself from these feelings, firstly by only reading:

> "two chapters at a time, you felt as if you'd had enough of that story for the night"

and secondly by drawing the parallel between Ben and herself so strictly that it became absurd:

> "I'd feel like locking myself in the loft, but the trouble is I'd fall right through the ceiling because it's rotten, our loft."

There is, in fact, quite a bit of psychological angst in *The Cartoonist*: Ben, feeling neglected and second-rate because he has to turn out of his attic room to make way for his "no good brother" — the returning prodigal son — barricades himself in the loft and plans in his mind ways of keeping his independence. At heart he longs for his Mother to continue to urge him to come downstairs and to make a fuss of him. He is, as the title implies, a would-be cartoonist, and the cartoons which he draws in his attic express his philosophy — especially the last one which has the caption "Nobody can make me come down — but somebody could try", altogether a rather complex message. Several children in the group borrowed the book and recommended it to others at the meetings, but only one of the boys, Stuart, told me the full story of the cartoons, including the final caption. Others, like Jane, concentrated on Ben's hiding from his Mother or, like Ceri and Stuart's younger brother, Roger, found:

> "the end, where he goes in the loft, far too long. I only liked it when he wouldn't come down."

2.   "I know how they feel"

Children who are not ready to relate to the feelings of the characters in the book will talk about it only in terms of "what happens next" in the story. This was apparent at the meetings, where younger children "recommended" their books to others by re-telling the story rather than isolating factors from it. Michael told me the whole story of *Kidnap*, described in its blurb as:

> "A tense thriller set in France — action from the very first page"

and said that it was his "best book ever". However, he found *Conrad's War,* described as "true to life" by the publisher very difficult and could not accept the fantasy that Conrad could build a full size tank in his bedroom:

> "there was nothing inside it to make it go. I don't think it was in his imagination because it describes how he started to make it. I stopped reading then, I thought 'This is silly' and put it away."

He could not relate to Conrad's feelings of frustration at his father's indifference to his exploits sufficiently to accept that they, and not the plot, were "true to life".

More practised readers talk about books in terms of character rather than action and realise with Tom that:

> "it is characteristics that make them do it."

They are able to distinguish between feeling what the characters feel and acting as they act. In this way they gain the vicarious gratification discussed in the previous chapter from identifying with "naughty children". The "naughty child" par excellence of 1984 was Andrew Davies' *Marmalade Atkins* — the appeal of the book to one child being that his Mother would not allow him to watch the television series! Unlike *William, Ramona (the pest)* or *Charlie and Angela* in *My Best Fiend, Marmalade Atkins,* scourge of the Convent of the Blessed Limit, is completely amoral and is presented with the author's promise that she will "never turn good". She is described with gusto, and seemed to capture the imagination more of boys than girls:

> "She's quite rude and mucks around a lot. Her mum and dad get all these people to talk to her. Roger's naughty, I'm quite naughty. I wouldn't like to be as naughty as that. She's a different person," said Stuart.

Tom, a practised reader, said:

> "She really did all these things, not like *Just William* — she has a good time non-stop, anything that comes to her mind she does — I couldn't do that"

— he is clearly able to separate his wish that he could be as naughty as Marmalade from the possibility that he ever will be, the distancing which comes with a recognition that fact and fiction are two different things.

Marmalade Atkins knows she is doing wrong and so does the reader.

Andrew's comment on *More William* was:

"I don't like the way you think he's not doing anything wrong and he is — it kind of made me feel he was a hero or something"

a very sophicticated reaction, once more viewing the character from a distance, admiring and morally condemning the character at the same time.

A reader has to be quite experienced, both at decoding and at the techniques of literacy to be able to comment on a story in this way, and in order to accept the story in one sense as valid and yet to remain outside it sufficiently to be able to say with Tom:

"I would never do that,"

or with Nicola:

"I knew it wouldn't really happen — I feel as though I'm part of this story, actually in the room with Omri (in *"The Indian in the Cupboard"*) because of the way he tells the story. I knew it couldn't actually happen, but it seems true to life."

It is safer by far to identify with a character like Ramona who:

"says what she thinks and what she wants to happen, but it doesn't happen."

In this way, stories can extend the reader's perception of what might happen, their view of a possible reality, but encourage them to suspend their disbelief and remain within the bounds of normality. Stuart says of Betsy Byars and her characters that:

"She describes their feelings alright, but I don't know whether they would act like it."

The appeal of characters like Ramona or Ben is that the reader has probably already met with their situations and can view them not only with recognition but with a sense of superiority as well:

"Sometimes I thought — Oh, I know better than that."

Once more, the extent of recognition depends on the reader's own development. Lucy and Louise both were impressed enough by the same incident in *Ramona The Pest* to talk about it to me. Ramona's arch-rival in the kindergarten, Susan, has copied Ramona's drawing of an owl and Ramona, in despair, screws up her own owl and puts it in the wastepaper basket. Lucy could not understand why she had done this, but Louise could because:

"people sometimes copy me at school."

Louise also enjoyed the bits where Ramona was shouting at her teacher: (" I sometimes shout"). She was not sure whether Lucy would like it or not, because:

"she's more into made-up stories."

But the "made-up story" which Lucy enjoyed most was one which relied on a little fun and a little fear for effect, rather than on identification with feelings, since she had not reached that stage of perception but was still tending to take fairy tales — and little vampire stories — at their face value:

> "The first time I read it I thought I'd better not take it to bed in case a vampire comes through the window and gets me!"

3.   A whole new world

So we come on to the third stage of reality in fiction, the creation of a Secondary World which appears to be "real" because its plot and characters are internally consistent. The children did not express it in this way, but Tom came near to it when he was trying to explain to me about fantasy which was overdone:

> "Fantasy is OK, but not if they get too wild with everything happening at once — for example 'As I was walking along, this space cat fell on top of me and the centre of the earth was turning hot and about to explode and so I rushed away, took an ice cream and threw it down'."

In this example of "bad" fantasy Tom is also, incidentally, omitting any mention of character or feelings — his scenario is pure action! Martin also gave an admirable example of consistency within a fantasy story:

> "If you have King Arthur and spacemen, that's not right, but Flying Dutchman sort of suits the Homeward Bounders. If Neil Armstrong suddenly walked through it, it would spoil it."

This is the reaction of a sophisticated reader who has some knowledge of literacy sources to back his reading.

One of the more easily read stories which came high in the popularity index and was rated by beginner and practised readers alike was Pat Hutchins' *The House That Sailed Away*, for exactly this reason:

> "It was brilliant. It was meant to be unlikely and silly and it was."

> "It was silly or funny all the way through."

> The characters were real but not the story."

W H Auden, whose article *Afterword — George MacDonald* is reprinted from *Forewords and Afterwords* (Faber 1973) in *The Cool Web*, takes longer to say the same thing in a more literary manner:

> "A secondary world may be full of extraordinary things (fairies, giants, dwarfs, dragons, and enchanted castles) and extraordinary events may occur in it... but, like the primary world, it must, if it is to carry conviction, seem to be a world governed by laws, not by pure chance. Its creator, like the inventor of a game, is at liberty to decide what the laws shall be, but, once he has decided, his story must obey them"

— and this was ten years before *Dungeons and Dragons*.

Martin compared crude Science Fiction with fantasy:

> "Science Fiction is large, metallic objects lunging towards you, objects in space; fantasy has more accoutrements (his word). I read *Space Hostages* in one session, I didn't enjoy it. It's like the films — if you have Luke Skywalker, he's the hero and you know he's not going to get killed. Sometimes you think she should really have had it, but he comes through. All the characters are kids of about eight to twelve but people in that story just aren't real, unless I've been misled all my life."

Here the wheel has turned full circle and far from accepting a book as "real" because it contains children of his own age having adventures, he rejects it for that very reason, just as Andrew condemns *Deadline for McGurk* as:

> "incredible, because they spent all night in this house without their Mum knowing."

The last word in this chapter on reality and fantasy goes to Martin:

> "In *Earthsea* there is all lifespan and what he did and how he grew up and a whole map of the world... You don't want to finish it but do at the same time. In *The Furthest Shore*, (sic) in the last few chapters, you think Ged's going to die, or all the magic will be drained from him, or Aran will go mad, it leaves you in suspense until the last page and then you find he just loses his power — a good ending. Some stories are great but in the end they get blown up in a train crash or something like that, or it's a real ending but so disappointing you feel like rushing to the author and asking him to write the next chapter."

Chapter 8

Conclusions

1. The child

Chapter 7 attempted to show the individual child's growth in "readership" as reflected in their definition and acceptance of reality and fantasy in the stories which they read. The ability to relate to the product of another's imagination and use it to extend one's own for one's own gratification dintinguishes this definition of "a reader" from that of "reader as decoder". It follows that an assessment of how far the Family Reading Group has succeeded in helping children to become readers demands qualitative rather than quantitative judgement. Success could not necessarily be claimed on the sole basis that the children were reading more books — although for the most part they were; it was also dependant on their ability to choose books and to relate to what they had chosen.

One of the major conclusions to be drawn from studying the records of books borrowed and books read, and from observing the meetings, is that the children became more relaxed in their choice of books. Often they were more prepared to take the chance of not borrowing what was expected of them — the school reader, the "manly" adventure — but to choose a book which looked as though it might be fun. One of the Mothers interviewed suggested that this was:

> "because all the books that were there were all for his reading ability and age group, so he was not reluctant to try them."

Nicola said the same thing in a different way:

> "I read more books, I think it was because there were more books that I could read than before."

Children who were presented with a wide range of material that was within their reading ability gained confidence not only in their own increasing skills as readers but in their ability to choose. This growing boldness could result in their attempting to read a book outside their normal sphere of reference. Stephen borrowed the heavier *Shadow Guests* along with the *Battle of Bubble and Squeak* (because he had just bought a hamster) and *Blackbeard the Pirate*, a cartoon pirate book, at the fifth meeting. Boosting his confidence in reading by 'practising' on the easier titles, he eventually finished *The Shadow Guests* after three months. Similarly Jane borrowed *Grinny* — a complex fantasy title — at the third meeting, as well as two books written at a much easier level, *It's Too Frightening For Me* and *Follow That Bus*, and a picture book *Cat and Mouse Story*.

The relaxed atmosphere of group meetings affected the children's choice of books. Librarians, taking their cue from the children's favourites, increasingly included in their recommendations titles by well known authors which were easily read and not necessarily written at classic award winning levels; the children listened to each other's comments and encouraged one another to speak. This helped the children feel that it was acceptable to enjoy silly rhymes, such as those in *The Great Smile Robbery* or picture books such as *Dracula's Bedtime Storybook*. In other situations and at other times they might have been made to feel that books like these were "babyish" — told "there are not many words for you to read in that, are there?" — but introduced at a Family Reading Group they increased the "fun" value of reading and the confidence of the reader.

With this self-reliance, it became easier for children to make their own recommendations to the group and several parents commented on the effect of this:

"I have noticed that he has brought home one or two books that have been talked about by people in the group that he wouldn't have thought of reading."

One thing which most children who came to the group mentioned was that it had broadened their range of reading:

"When they talked about space I went and got all these space books out — I wouldn't read those books if you didn't talk about them"

said one, and another added:

"It's good to be able to go with your friends because then they have read some and can start you on other writers."

Parents were appreciative too:

"You introduce them to such a lot more than the ones that they would have discovered of their own accord — they tend to be stuck in certain channels — he tended to go for the ones that he knew, so I think that it has been good that it introduced him to more – a much bigger variety."

This breadth of reading can be shown to be a direct result of the unlimited loan system as discussed in Chapter 5.

The children became accustomed to discussing books and to identifying them, not by the colour of the cover, but by author and title and to relate books written by one author to those written by another — *Richmal Crompton* to Judy Blume, E W Hildick to Enid Blyton. The author ceased to be a mystical being and the children began to be aware of the author's style of writing and relate it to their own. In a more sophisticated manner, they even began to relate the author's own experience to their writing:

"At the back of this one it's about the author and you don't imagine the author to be like this, you imagine her fairly young, but she's got four children. She might get it off her children"

said Clare; who felt that Betsy Byars exaggerated situations for effect in her story *The Cartoonist*.

The preceding chapters have described the way in which members served their apprenticeship in reading — in learning to follow the clues which lead to a fuller understanding of the book. The table of number of books mentioned in the diaries of Group members and non-members in 1985 (Table 4.4) shows without doubt that Group members are looking at, if not reading, more books than non-members.

It would seem that, through attending Family Reading Groups, children are on the way towards not only reading "more books with more satisfaction" but are also "reading books with more satisfaction". To quote James Britton's article in *The Cool Web* (1977), it is fulfilling the need which he recognised:

"to foster. . . wide reading side by side with close reading."

2.   The parents

And what about the parents? Certainly their awareness of present day fiction available for children increased, both through borrowing books from the meeting for themselves and through listening to the children talking about their books in the Group. Several still read aloud to their children and chose longer books from the meeting, such as *The Song of Pentecost* or *Goodnight Mr Tom*, to read together. Most parents "looked at" the books which the children brought home, although often:

> "not all of them, I couldn't keep up with him."

Other groups, particularly in secondary schools, have stressed the therapeutic benefits of reading stories together. Stan Bunnell, in his article *Family Reading Groups in the Secondary School* (1981) quotes a parent who said:

> "I was most gratified to see how my daughter coped with quite adult ideas and concepts of morality and was able to voice opinions that we might otherwise not have shared."

Although discussions at the lower age level might not seem to follow such a clear moral path, it can be enlightening for adults to listen to children talking about their books. They can often recognise the doubts, fears and exhilarations of the characters which the children are describing as belonging to their own child. One book which did raise discussion between parents and children on a topic which might not otherwise have arisen was *What Difference Does It Make Danny?* on its treatment of epilepsy.

The assessment of parental involvement with children's reading through the group was twofold. One question asked was straightfoward — "Do you read children's books?" The results indicated a rise in those who did — (79% as compared with 54% the previous year.) The other issue addressed was to what extent the parents became involved in the meeting itself and in introducing and discussing books. The number of adults constituted an average 31% of the attendance at the meetings (see Table 3.5). As would be expected, the first meeting had the highest adult attendance, and one of the lowest (excluding the August Summer holiday meeting) was accounted for by a PTA meeting at Fleetville School which was attended by several Reading Group parents — a significant fact in itself! So, if parental involvement was calculated by attendance, it was present and consistent.

When families were interviewed six months after the Group had begun, the parents were asked whether they felt that they were involved sufficiently in the meetings. Since, for the most part, the active participation came from the children in the formal section of the meeting, the positive response came as a surprise. Most agreed with the Mother who said:

> "I think it is important that the adults are there at all — the fact they are spending an hour there with the children just for choosing books — that in itself is quite significant."

They seemed to see the parents' role as helping their own children to choose their books and discuss them on an individual basis rather than as introducing a book to the whole group.

> "They seem to sort through the books quite a lot — the fact that the parents go, that they go with the children, encourages them and they help them sort through the books and if they didn't go perhaps the children would lose interest."

Another Mother agreed with this view of the parents providing the staying power of the group:

"I do think if you said the parents didn't have to come it would all fall to pieces".

Unlike their children, who are constantly being asked to voice an opinion at school, many adults are unused to speaking in public. As Lucy's Mum said:

"It it was the policy for everybody to say something — nobody would turn up."

And Martin's Mother added:

"I don't think many of the Mums particularly want to talk, they all say 'Oh gosh, what am I going to say?' the ones I sit next to."

However, parents were sufficiently in sympathy with the ideas behind the formation of the group to suggest a similar group for adults:

"It might be worth asking the adults who come whether they would like, not a regular thing, just to say what's new and what's around."

"I think perhaps we could do our own little book list — I enjoy books whether they are children's or adults'."

3. The library

(a) Use

When the Fleetville issue was checked for Family Reading Group members' names in March 1984, 18% of members has a book on loan: in March 1985 26%. The number of adults who said that they had a book on loan from any library at the time of the family interviews in March and October 1984 decreased slightly from 70% to 63%. The large difference in percentage between adults and children could be accounted for by the fact that with the adults any public library was taken into account, but with the children only Fleetville. 25% of the adults belonged to more than one library, two Fathers using the public library nearest to their place of work.

By coming to the Family Reading Group, 100% of the children and 66% of the adults surveyed could be termed "library users" (the children received this definition automatically). The Reading Group did attract to Fleetville Library some families who had not visited it before and, in the case of others, such as Roger's family, the Group renewed an interest in visiting the library which had lapsed since pre-school play-group storytimes. When checking the branch issue in March 1985, it was interesting to note the names of brothers and sisters of Reading Group members — one person in the family coming to Group meetings meant that others felt they had 'missed out' and so visited the library the next day. There was further evidence for this in the sample interviews with parents and children, where younger children made a point of asking at the interview whether they could be taken to the library too! Family Reading Group members themselves tended to have their needs for fiction books met by attendance at the group, and only used the library as card carrying members for non-fiction books. The advantages of borrowing from the group — specialist advisory service, longer loan period, no fines — made this preferable.

Overall the junior issue at Fleetville Library rose by 13.7% in 1984-1985 as compared to 1.4% over the rest of the unit, and it is not unrealistic to surmise that the Family Reading Group had some part to play in this!

In the course of the interviews, parents highlighted several factors which mitigated against library use per se and library use at the same time as their children.

Saturday afternoon opening was remembered as one of the few occasions when parents and children could visit the library together. As the diary entries have shown, children's "after-school activities" leave little time for visiting the library and the permutations of activities in families with two or more children make it almost impossible. Jane's mother said of Jane:

> "She is so involved in the evenings and Saturday mornings we don't seem to get anywhere really. The afternoons used to be so handy, you see my husband works every other weekend and it used to be something to do with them in the Winter, and they used to like to go up to the library on their bikes and we don't go now so much in the evenings. By the time she gets home it's tea time; and she seems to do more after school activities than when she was little."

When children were of pre-school age, several parents took the opportunity of going to the library for storytimes and also for their own books.

> "I used to go to Fleetville every Thursday afternoon. I used to take them down to storytime and that was a weekly thing, and of course I used to browse through the books while they were having a story and it was nice, because having made the effort for them I was there to look around for myself. I don't go so much now."

Setting aside a specific time for parents and children to use the library vanishes as the children grow older.

The spasmodic opening hours of small branch and sub-branch libraries not only make it difficult for working people to use them, but also make returning the books difficult:

> "The libraries don't seem to be open when I want to use them."

> "He's not back till 7 o'clock so Saturday mornings are about the only chance; getting them back is awkward too, if it is shut on Monday and then you shop on Tuesday and then it's shut on Wednesday and so it's Thursday before you get them back."

"Getting them back" is a constant problem, aggravated by fines on children's as well as adult books. Children mentioned fines or "overdues" in their description of a library and they were also mentioned by their parents as a deterrent to borrowing books:

> "The last time I went I was fined. They were only two days overdue, but by the time you have added up all the children's books as well and you have missed one day, and they are closed the next, and it happens quite often, and every time I find myself only borrowing half the books next time."

There is ample justification here for the removal of fines from books for children, which has now, happily, taken place. In view of this project's findings on the length of time a child may take to read a book, library policy on overdues and renewal systems, as well as length of issue, could be re-assessed.

Another factor which affected library use was the proximity of the library to the user's home:

> "We are lucky because the library is very near and so we can go round, as soon as they need a book for school we go round."

All Family Reading Group members lived within walking distance of the library, although even then distance is relative, and one Mother felt that they lived close enough to the library for her children go on their own in Summertime, but not in the Winter when it was dark.

(b) Cost effectiveness

(i) cost

The costing of the running of the Family Reading Group has been discussed in Chapter 2, Section 3. The hard edges of the accounts are blurred by several factors:

1. As far as stock is concerned, the £650 spent on buying books provided not only a selection of reading material for the Reading Group but also additional titles for stock at St Albans Central and Fleetville Libraries. As a title outgrew its usefulness in the Group, it was transferred to branch stock. Conversely, throughout the year books were added to the Reading Group stock from branch stock to boost a particular area of interest, or as titles which the librarians brought along to introduce.

2. The leaflets which were produced came from the County promotions budget and not from branch funds.

3. Orange, coffee and biscuits were paid for, as for any other library activity, from petty cash.

4. Staff time involved in actually running the group and in keeping records has been quantified in Chapter 2 (Table 2.6). Staff time spent in promoting the Group is made difficult to quantify by the multi-purpose nature of visits to schools by librarians.

(ii) Effectiveness

If quantifying the cost of library activities for children is a hazy prospect, quantifying their effectiveness is even hazier. Vickery describes the effectiveness of a system as "the degree to which it achieves its stated objective" and also "the degree to which the system contributes to user needs".

The objective of library activities for children is to encourage them to become readers and library users, and the Family Reading Group has been shown to be effective in this.

The needs of the children of Fleetville and their families were:

1. An opportunity to visit the library together, at a convenient time.

2. Access to a collection of books which were well within the reading ability of an average 9-11 year old, but which were also fun to read.

3. An advisory service from a librarian or other book-knowledgable adults.

Were they aware of this need? The three points above are in order of awareness of necessity. Many families, as has been seen, mentioned the first and the second. They were not as aware of the concommitant need for the third. Moreover, the third could not have been given or accepted as readily without the first two. Some parents attend PTA talks on their children's reading — what they always hope to find at the end is the key which will begin to motivate their own particular child. They are looking for a personal advisory service which will not only tell them what type of book might be suitable for their child and where they might find it, but which will actually put that book in their hands there and then. If it is accepted that children should be involved in choosing what they read, that occasion should include the child too.

Why should the library service be the agency which meets this need? Primarily because it has trained professional staff whose main task it is to be aware of this need and to investigate ways of satisfying it within the constraints of the orgnisation. A teacher is a trained professional, but teachers have other demands on their time and other priorities. Not even an English teacher in a secondary school is, or should be, as concerned with general contemporary fiction for young people as the children's librarian. The library service is the prime agency for book supply, the children's specialist within a unit should be allowed sufficient time and assistance to make this supply accessible to the users. Since parents are concerned and are now encouraged to be concerned with their child's literary input from babyhood, the 'users' include both parents and children.

Issue comparisons

The focus of this study has been on trying to assess the impact that a particular book has on a particular child. However intermediate indicators of success such as issue statistics can also be helpful in comparing the effectiveness of Family Reading Groups with traditional branch library services.

For example the Family Reading Group averaged 148 issues per one and a half hour session, i.e. an hourly issue of 99 books. The average hourly issue of books through the Fleetville library was 65. Of course there is a certain element of self-fulfilment about this comparison, in that inevitably if you invite a large number of children at a specific time and allow them unlimited borrowing, it is not surprising that the issue per hour rate is higher than branch issues.

It is perhaps more interesting to note that during the first twelve months of the Family Reading Group (April 1984-March 1985) the total figure for junior issues increased by 13.7% compared with average branch increases of 1.4%. Clearly the Family Reading Group contributed to this increase both in terms of the issues themselves as well as by raising the profile of the library in the community. Furthermore, increases in issues can result in improvements in the level of staffing and also protect a library from either threats of closure or reduction in opening hours.

It could be argued that the reason for the high issue rate at Family Reading Group meetings as compared with average hourly branch issues was due to the policy of unlimited borrowing. Issue figures prove that this is not necessarily so — 66% of the 59 group members borrowed an average of 6 books or less at each meeting and the average number of books borrowed per child over ten meetings was 5.8. In Hertfordshire branch libraries children are allowed to borrow a maximum of 6 books for a period of 3 weeks, and of course they may return and change their books as often as opening hours allow within that period of time. In borrowing an average of 5.8 books every four or five weeks at the Family Reading Group, children were actually borrowing less than the maximum they could have taken home under normal issue conditions from the branch library over the same period of time.

Generally it is difficult to assess the effect of the other "one off" library activities for children in terms of book borrowing. They certainly bring children — but not children and their parents — into the library. The borrowing of books after a holiday activity — particularly an author visit — is observable, but only on that occasion. The only regular activity for children and adults which could be compared with a Family Reading Group would be the Under-5's storytime, which was mentioned by several Mothers as the last time that they had regularly visited the library with their children.

In practice, children of that age can be observed rarely to take home more than two or three books from the public library at any one time because of the following barriers to use:

1. Fear of fines

2. The difficulty of choosing suitable material.

3. Inconvenient opening hours for family visits.

Family Reading Groups offer the means of breaking all three barriers. It is the quality of the service which distinguishes the Family Reading Group from the facilities offered during normal library opening hours, and which results in the quantitative output of this particular service being greater.

Final output

How did the Family Reading Group measure up to Totterdell and Bird's criteria for "final output" — "community attitude towards the library — library image — library performance"?

The future of Fleetville Library is still uncertain; and the foundations for the new St Albans Central Library have already been laid. Did the Family Reading Group help at all to consolidate the library's position in the community (this being one of the questions this survey set out to address)? It brought together a regular set of families who came to identify themselves with Fleetville Library and with the library activities and who were not "Friends of Fleetville Library". The families who were interviewed certainly appreciated the familiarity of a community library — in particular as far as use by children was concerned — and were reminded once more of the services which it offered to adults. The large increase in junior issue for the year 1984-85 (+13.7%) set against the drop in adult issues of 4.1% resulted in a total drop in Fleetville issue of only −0.8% compared with the unit average of −2.8%. The links with the two local schools, in particular School 2, were consolidated and a remedial teacher from School 3 attended the Summer 1985 meeting with four children in the hope that the group's enthusiasm for reading would be contagious.

Library performance depends to a large extent on library staff and an imaginative and effective use of their specialist skills. The specialisms of the Children's Librarian are often overlooked by those who judge a post by the salary scale at which it is offered. A thorough and up to date knowledge of materials is necessary to provide a bookstock relevant to the needs of children today — one which reflects their interests and environment and is accessible in terms of reading levels. Once selected, the stock needs to be exploited, and there should be time for the children's specialist to do this. For effective library performance this time should be when there are most children available. Such a time may have to be created to maximise the contact between Librarian and client.

The Fleetville Family Reading Group seems to have succeeded as a model for others in the area. The staff at School 1 are considering the possibility of starting a group there. Another library in mid-Hertfordshire is planning to start a Reading Group along similar lines, and in Autumn 1986 Rosie anticipated handing over the Fleetville Group to one of the schools and starting a new group elsewhere in the unit.

Chapter 9

Recommendations

Although children are the main subject of this book, the recommendations which can be made as a result of studying their reading habits through the Family Reading Group concern adults. It is adults who create a reading environment for the child and who need to provide the books and the opportunity to choose and read them. Liaison is necessary between those who best know the children (the parents) and those who best know the books (the librarians). A practical advantage of this liaison is that in the process the librarians learn more about children, and the parents learn more about books. Some recommendations apply only to those who provide the books (the library, or school), others to those who have most influence with the children, and some to both.

The major recommendations which can be made from examining the Fleetville Family Reading Group are for the library service or supplier of books, whether in the public or school library. They concern:

1. Provision.

2. Access.

3. Staffing.

4. Promotion.

1. Provision

(a) Much has been made in this study of the value of presenting children with a wide range of books in order to stimulate an enjoyment of reading. It has also been stressed that children should be allowed unlimited borrowing power. This could conjure up a nightmare vision for librarians of a budget overthrown by over-spending on children's materials which were then taken out of the library in armfuls and never returned. This could not be further from the truth. Certainly the children were offered a wide range of books — but a range which had been pre-selected to meet their needs in terms of interest and reading levels. The group operated on a little over 250 books which, over a year, generated an issue of almost 1,500. As has been pointed out in the preceding chapter, the whole project became cost-effective because of the quality of the service (the promotion of the books), rather than because of the number of books involved. A limited stock of books does not necessarily result in a limited number of books being borrowed. How often can members of the public be observed to make straight for the 'returned books' trolley in order to make their own choice from a small number of tried but trusted titles!

It has been observed in a small branch library recently, where a quantity of books have been removed from the shelves each week in order to be processed for automation, that library issues have gone up, not down, when the public have fewer books to choose from. Offering a selection of books to children at a Family Reading Group has the same effect of focussing the attention on a smaller number of books.

Of course this has implications for book selection, and means that the stock which is offered to the readers has to be relevant, of a high quality (which does not necessarily mean a high reading level), and in good condition. Following on from this is the necessity for staff to be more concerned and better educated in stock selection techniques. Children's specialists are usually enthusiasts for their material, but are not always allowed enough time to maintain their book awareness, and there is the danger that their stock can then become dated and irrelevant.

A smaller stock of books on the library shelves is not an excuse for cutting budgets but a reason for the Librarians to think more carefully about what they are buying and to discard stock rather than accumulate.

(b)   Those who are in a position to offer books to children are often misled by their own reading experiences as children, or by over zealous application of 'literary' ideals. They should be aware of the middle range (the popular titles available) and not under-estimate its value in providing the child with reading satisfaction. It is also important to remember that tastes change, and that this year's top ten titles will not be the same as last year's. I am only too conscious that the titles mentioned in the bibliography were those in vogue in 1985, when *Just William* and *Marmalade Atkins* were first being serialised on TV and Roald Dahl's *Witches* was newly published. If reading is to be seen by children as a popular alternative activity, it is not helpful if the adults who are concerned with their reading only to view it in an earnest and profound manner. The recent Times compilation of a list of 50 recommended titles (Times 19/2/88) offers 26 which were published over a quarter of a century ago, and only six in the last 10 years!

(c)   It should be remembered that children, like adults, read at different levels. To continually present them with a book which will "stretch them" — which will always be just too difficult either to read or to understand — is not going to make for reader gratification. Conversely, to place before children mediocre milk and water stories with standard illustrations and in a dull format is not going to make reading interesting, fun, or the 'in' thing to do either. Publishers should be encouraged to produce more short, exciting or funny stories, such as those in the *Banana Books* or *Cartwheel* series, published by Heinneman and Hamilton respectively, and libraries should ensure that their stock includes such series. Although not a new message, it is still necessary to repeat this, as many schools, homes and libraries still cling to the 'excellence' theory or alternatively present children with badly written shoddily produced material. A story which is easy to read does not have to be uneventful. Children should be allowed to choose books from a broad range and to vary the level of their reading, not to be perpetually striving to reach the next highest shelf in the reading scheme.

2.   Access

(a)   *Community libraries.* There was a strong feeling among families that the small community library still had a part to play in their lives. Large, central libraries were difficult to visit with a family — the very size of their stock, as discussed in Section 1, made them difficult to use. Smaller libraries should not be hostages to 'progress'.

(b)   *Opening hours* which allowed for family visits would encourage parental involvement. Saturday afternoon opening is important to families, as are evening opening hours. Where libraries are not open on Saturday afternoons, one afternoon a month would be sufficient to reinstate family visiting patterns.

(c)   *Fines* are a definite barrier to borrowing and library use, especially fines for children, where it is the parent and not the child who bears the brunt of the penalty. The removal of fines from child readers would be a positive step towards encouraging them to use the library independently.

(d)   *Issue periods.* The findings of this study show that children gain from keeping a book at home for six, eight or even ten weeks. This should be taken into account when loan periods for children's books are set. Longer loan periods mean books missing from the shelves for longer periods of time. Bearing in mind that children find it easier to choose from a smaller selection of books, this recommendation could also have implications for stock selection policies — buying multiple paperback copies of popular titles, for example.

(e) *The number of books* allowed on loan from the school or public library is relevant to a child's development as a 'reader'. Children who are forced to read books piecemeal, one at a time, can end up reading nothing at all. An allowance of at least 4-6 books is not extravagant, but, if used, will allow for consideration and rejection of some titles at home, whilst others are read and the reader's gratification met.

3. Staffing

(a) Wherever there is a collection of books for children there should be access to a children's specialist Librarian, who is readily identifiable.

(b) Where library staffing entails one professional Librarian to initiate and maintain service to children within a multiple branch unit, their time is best spent in activities which provide a broad interface with the user, but which result in intensive promotion of the product (the book). Where time and resources allow, a broad based programme of activities is fine; where both are at a premium the essence of Children's Librarianship should be expressed through activities which are "book intensive". If the Children's Librarian can only spend x hours a week in one particular part of the unit, it is essential that the contact which they have with their section of the users should be as wide as possible and should make the fullest possible use of their especial skills.

(c) As has been mentioned earlier, in order to maintain a quality stock, the librarian needs to be given sufficient time for, and support in stock selection. This would include regular updating training sessions for staff.

4. Promotion

The essence of a quality service lies in its promotion to the public. The term 'promotion' covers all contact with the client over and above the taking in and issuing of books. Helping a child to find a book which they can read and enjoy is promoting the service — hopefully they will come back for more. Opportunities for readers advisory services occur daily and librarians should be trained to recognise and not to run away from them.

The effect of active promotion of services is difficult to gauge accurately, hence the analysis of this particular promotion in the Family Reading Group at Fleetville. It appears that it could be the quality of the promotion — the interaction between librarian and client — which resulted in the comparatively high borrowing record of the members and the subsequent gratification of their imaginative reading needs. This, in turn, was reflected in Fleetville Library's annual issue figures and could have a positive effect on the library's issue/staffing ratio. Thus the whole community and not just the children could benefit from the Family Reading Group promotion. In other words, advertising pays! Taking into consideration the difficulty which families find in visiting libraries together during normal opening hours, and the fact that small libraries often do not have space for activities during those hours, it is preferable to set aside a time outside hours for regular promotional events such as Family Reading Groups. In this way the library will be making a time and a place for the specialist to meet the user and exploit the stock.

5.   Parental participation

The most regular reading group members were those who came with their parents. Parental participation can stimulate and help the child to maintain their interest in reading. Parents can make opportunities for the child to read (does the light have to be turned off exactly at 9.45 p.m.?) and to visit the library to choose books. The point was made by parents more than once that by visiting the Family Reading Group with their children they were demonstrating involvement with their reading. A similar involvement can be shown by participating in school reading activities. Parents who actually read some of the books which their children bring home can be pleasantly surprised at the standard of writing and of 'story telling'. Sometimes reading the same book as the child can lead to a discussion of a topic which they might otherwise be reluctant to bring into the open. Alternatively, 'sharing books' may mean sharing jokes and allusions and building on the foundations of literacy. Parental involvement with children: reading should be positive and constant and not affected by educational politics which blow hot and cold over strategies for learning to read (see 'Reading between the lines' Guardian 2/2/88). The neutral support for parents from librarians is becoming ever more necessary.

6.   Reading with friends

Reading is not one isolated activity. The Family Reading Group shows that it can become part of the highly organised life of a child, a team expression of 'activity' — as opposed to 'passivity' — which can be shared with friends. In fact Reading Groups can build on the instinctive urge of children of this age to go around in gangs and to join clubs, and can present libraries, books and reading in a positive manner.

In addition to this the reading group can take advantage of the fads of pre-teens; to consolidate looking at books as part of their lifestyle and to begin a lifetime habit.

7.   Recommendations on recommendations!

Choosing books is difficult. Making use of other people's recommendations is easy and sometimes exciting. Making an opportunity for children to recommend books to one another in an informal manner keeps up the momentum of choosing, reading, recommending and coming back for more.

In short, the Family Reading Group can provide the blueprint to prevent any child in any family coming to believe Hilaire Belloc's cautionary dictum that "literature breeds distress".

8.   The future

Peter Bagnall, reporting to the Booksellers' Association Conference on the work of The Children's Book Action Group (Bookseller, May 10th, 1986) sees the future of literacy —

115

and of the book trade — depending on the future of children's books. The type of public relations programme which he envisages would:

> "address parents and children" and "needs to provide an age bridge for teenagers. Such a programme calls for research, on a routine basis, into reading habits, literacy, use of books and training for their use, improvement of books, valuation placed on books, and attitudes to books."

The creation of the Children's Book Foundation has been the Book Trust's (former National Book League) response to this.

Like Carolyn J Carter (1986) in her article *Young People and Books: a review of the research into young people's reading habits* (Journal of Librarianship 18: 1 January 1986), he realises that some of this work has been done already. Development of this particular research could include:

1. Further monitoring of the Fleetville year of 1984 Family Reading Group members in five years time, as they are about to leave secondary schools, to gauge whether their reading habits were, indeed, stabilised at ages 10-11.

2. In view of the findings on the length of time a child may find it relevant to keep a book, the introduction of bookshops selling books in libraries would make possible a comparison of titles and amount of books bought/borrowed. Liaison between libraries and the book trade can only be advantageous for both.

3. A study of the use made by families of community libraries as compared with central libraries, and the consequent allocation of resources.

4. A study of the further development of school/public library links to extend children's reading and borrowing habits.

The 1980's has seen a growth in the number of awards offered by companies for 'the best' in British Publishing. If the reading public is to continue to appreciate the reading product, equal funding should be made available to research projects concerned with the motivation and reading facility of both children and adults to make sure they are getting it right!

Chapter 10

Epilogue:
The after school activities of 9-11 year olds by Rosemary Telling

THE AFTER SCHOOL ACTIVITIES 9 - 11 YEAR OLDS:

READING — WHERE DOES IT FIT IN?

E.1 Introduction

In the academic year 1985-86 Dina Thorpe submitted an MPhil thesis to the Department of Social Policy, Cranfield Institute of Technology, entitled *Family reading groups: a critical analysis of the part played by parents, public libraries and their peers in encouraging children aged 9-12 to read for enjoyment.* In the course of her research and

> in order to assess how reading rated as a leisure time activity, and whether or not the Family Reading Group had any effect on this, children at the schools in which the group was to be promoted were asked to fill in After School Diaries with activities and, possibly, timing of these activities, between arriving home from school and going to bed at night.

These diaries were distributed to third and fourth year pupils at four junior schools in the Fleetville area (Herts.) in February 1984 and then again in February 1985. As the previous years fourth year juniors would by now have changed schools, diaries were also distributed in 1985 to first year secondary pupils in the nearest school to be fed by these junior schools. In all 537 diaries were collected of which only a small proportion were actually used – those completed by pupils who became members of the Fleetville Family Reading Group, and for comparison, a similar sized sample of non-members. The format of the diary that was used is included in Appendix 2.

The completed diaries offered a rich source of information not only on the voluntary reading habits of these pupils but also their many other after school activities, which suggested that an in depth analysis would be of value. The original intention of this project was therefore to analyse the diaries in depth and then make comparisons between pupils' reading habits and after school activities in 1984 and 1985. However, it soon became obvious that this would not be possible for three reasons:

1. The diary returns for 1985 were considerably lower than those for 1984 which reduced the number of diaries that could be paired.

2. Had the project analysed only those diaries that could be paired, an element of bias would have been introduced into the results.

3. 537 diaries were too many to be analysed in depth in the time available.

It was therefore decided that only 1984 diaries from three of the four primary schools would be analysed in depth – a total of 190 diaries in all. Using these diaries this project therefore set out to investigate

a) the after school activities of these 9-11 year olds and assess to what extent they influenced reading;

b) to discover as much as possible about the reading habits of these pupils.

The value of these diaries lay in the fact that they were only structured in so far as each day was divided into four time periods:

i) the time between getting home from school and before a meal;

ii) the time after a meal but before getting ready for bed;

118

iii)   the time between getting ready for bed and actually getting into bed;

iv)   and time in bed before going to sleep.

Within these time divisions the pupil could offer any information they liked. No questions were asked – the pupils were merely guided into making statements, for example:

This is the time I had my meal. . . .

These are some things I did after that.

     1. . . .

     2. . . .

     3. . . .

Much information was therefore obtained that might otherwise have been missed by a questionnaire. However such informal methods of gathering data can present problems when trying to convert what is essentially qualitative data into a quantitative form, since the pupil may have omitted to mention the very thing that the researcher is looking for. The findings of this research should therefore be treated with a certain amount of caution.

The analysis of these diaries was carried out with no knowledge of the area concerned. Although initially it was the author's intention to visit the Fleetville area this was eventually decided against for two reasons:

1.   Analysis of the diaries would be carried out with no pre-conceived ideas of what the findings might reveal. This would reduce the possibility of any bias creeping in.

2.   It would only have been possible to get to know the area and the schools as they were in 1987-88 and not as they were in 1984, when the diaries were completed.

The author has therefore relied entirely on the information given in Dina Thorpe's thesis.

The methodology used in this project will be outlined in E2. E3 will discuss the after school activities mentioned in the diaries and make comparisons between the schools. In E4 an assessment of the influence of various after school activities on reading will be made. E5 will analyse the data obtained from the diaries to see what can be learned about the reading habits of these pupils. Finally, the conclusions of this piece of research will be presented in E6.

E.2 Methodology

As the diaries were not very easy to handle the information contained in each of them was transferred to a data sheet a copy of which is included in Appendix 4. These were designed in such a way that for each pupil easy comparison of after school activities was possible, not only between the days of the week, but also between both the weeks that the diary was completed. On the reverse side of the data sheet separate lists were made of all the reading material mentioned, the television programmes watched, organisations attended and games played. A note was also made of the number of children in the family.

In order to estimate the amount of time spent on each activity analogue clocks had been included in the diaries for the pupils to fill in. However this proved difficult for many, and some did not attempt to do this at all. The information was therefore structured on the data sheets, and then subsequently into tables, in the same time divisions that were present in the diaries:

a) on getting home from school but before having a meal;

b) after having a meal but before getting ready for bed;

c) after getting ready for bed;

d) in bed.

Arranging the data in this way would facilitate the collection of numerical data such as:

i) How many book titles did each pupil list?

ii) How often did each pupil list reading as an after school activity?

iii) During what part of the evening were the pupils most likely to read?

iv) How many organised activities did each pupil attend?

It would also indicate if the emphasis on certain activities changed as the evening progressed.

Table E2.1   To show the number of diaries completed

	School 1	School 2	School 3	Total
Fully completed diaries	33	80	58	171
Incomplete diaries	5	6	8	19
TOTAL	**38**	**86**	**66**	**190**

Although some of the diaries were incomplete (see Table E2.1) they still contained much useful information. All of the diaries were therefore used for information concerning after school activities, organisations attended, weekend activities, type of reading material and titles of books and comics read. However only fully completed diaries were used when making comparisons between the number of times reading was mentioned as an activity, and other after school activities. Many of the pupils had not completed entries for the final Friday. It was therefore decided to ignore the final Friday in all diaries. In the discussion that follows therefore, the term 'fully completed diary' will refer to those diaries which have full entries for nine school days.

Several problems were encountered:

1. The pupils were only provided with space to mention three activities in each time division. Some activities may therefore have been omitted. The assumption made is that the activities mentioned are those that the pupil felt to be the most important, or which were the most memorable where the diary was filled in at school the next day.

2. For quite a few of the pupils the diaries lost their novelty value after the first few days. In some of the diaries this was obvious from the deteriorating quality of the handwriting and the amount of information offered. Other pupils continued to make full entries but expressed their irritation verbally — 'filled in this stupid thing' — and one girl showed her relief at finishing the diary by adding a large 'THE END' on the back cover. In many of the diaries therefore the first week was the most informative and possibly the most accurate.

E.3 After School Activities

Some pupils were highly motivated and filled their evenings with so much activity that even reading their diaries left one exhausted! Guy's diary is such an example.

DIARY NUMBER 1

Guy: who seemed to fill every minute with activity.
Brothers/sisters: one sister.
Likes best: making *Action Force* bases in the tree.
Membership of organisations: none.
Music lessons: violin and piano.
Sport: nothing mentioned.

Guy arrived home from school at approximately 4pm each day, switched on the television and watched *Batfink* (ITV 4.15pm). Apart from this no other television programmes were mentioned except for *Heman and the Masters of the Universe* on a Monday (ITV 4.20pm). The time between watching *Batfink* and having a meal (usually eaten between 5pm-5.30pm) was filled with either violin practice, piano practice, or both, drawing and/or playing with his *Action Force* or *Action Man.* He even mentioned train spotting on one occasion. Half an hour was usually spent on practising each musical instrument, and he had a violin lesson on a Monday and piano lesson on a Thursday.

After a meal more time was spent playing with *Action Force,* practising the piano if this had not been done earlier, and feeding, cleaning and playing with his gerbils. He then tidied away and got ready for bed somewhere between 7.30pm-8.30pm depending on whether or not there was a television programme he particularly wanted to watch – *Blue Thunder* (Mon. BBC1, 7.20pm), *Dr Who* (Wed. BBC1, 6.50pm) and *The A-Team* (Fri. ITV, 7.30pm) were mentioned.

Once ready for bed he spent between 15-30 minutes reading every night but one. The books he chose reflected his interest in action, and two were adult titles. The time he went to bed varied but was no later than 9pm. In bed he mentioned reading once and playing with *Star Wars* figures once. At the weekend he made a model helicopter, repaired his bike and had a friend round for lunch.

Reading: *Iceberg* (Clive Cussler)
　　　　Raise the Titanic (Clive Cussler)
　　　　The Machine-Gunners (Robert Westall)

However, there were others, like Louise, who were far less motivated.

DIARY NUMBER 2

Louise: whose main after school activity seemed to be watching television.
Brothers/sisters: two sisters.
Likes best: I like cooking, swimming and dancing.
Membership of organisations: none.
Music lessons: none.
Sport: none.

Louise arrived home from school at 3.55pm, changed and settled down to watch telvision. This was the only activity mentioned before the evening meal apart from one day when she said she did some painting, and another when she mentioned colouring the pictures in the After School Diary. The evening meal was eaten at 6.15pm after which Louise helped to clear away. She then watched more television, often returning to the television set after getting ready for bed, usually at about 8pm. On one occasion she mentioned playing Snakes and Ladders and Chess after the evening meal, and on another she went to the Junior School's Valentine's Day Disco. Bedtime was usually at 8.30pm. She never mentioned reading in the diary but in the section headed 'This is what I read today' indicated two book titles on the first Monday – *Lucy* (Joan Tate) and *Stig of the Dump* (Clive King), and one book title *Super Gran* (Forrest Wilson) on the final Friday. There is however no way of knowing whether these were read at home or at school.

In between these two extremes pupils showed considerable variation both in their motivation to take part in after school activities other than watching television, and in the type of activities in which they were engaged. The range of activities was so interesting that a full list of all those mentioned in the 190 diaries has been included in Appendix 5. In order to show how the choice of activities varied throughout the evening, these have been listed separately for each of the four time divisions described in chapter E1, and have been placed into priority order according to the number of pupils mentioning them on one or more occasions over the period of nine school days under analysis. In all time divisions except the last (in bed), watching television was as perhaps expected, the activity mentioned by more pupils than any other. Reading was however quite highly placed on each list although far fewer pupils mentioned it than mentioned watching television. Except after a meal, when more pupils indicated that they had attended a meeting of an organisation, reading appeared in second place on each list. It was however the most popular activity in bed.

In order to investigate the extent to which the after school activities chosen by the pupils varied between the different areas of Fleetville, and thus between the schools attended, a number of the more popular activities were selected and a comparison made between the schools. As different sized samples were being compared the number of pupils who mentioned each activity has been converted to a percentage. A breakdown of these selected activities is given in Table E3.1 for the period of time between arriving home from school and having the main meal of the evening. This shows that pupils at School 1 were less likley to practise a musical instrument, take part in any sporting activities, or do any kind of art or craft work, than pupils at either of the other two schools. They were however more likely to read.

Table E3.1   After School Activities Mentioned in the Diaries Breakdown of selected activities by school.
I. On getting home from school but before having a meal.

Activity	Percentage of Pupils Mentioning Activity		
	School 1	School 2	School 3
Watched television	100	96.5	92.4
Played with friend(s)	39.5	40.7	51.5
Read	52.6	45.4	37.9
Homework	10.5	11.6	48.5
Computer/electronic/video games	23.7	22.1	25.8
Colouring/painting/drawing/craft	7.9	23.3	25.8
Practised musical instrument(s)	7.9	25.6	21.2
Games (board/card/puzzles etc.)	18.4	17.4	19.7
Sporting activities	10.5	18.6	21.2
Tapes/tape recording/records	13.2	11.6	15.2
Imaginative role play games	7.9	7.0	9.1
Darts/snooker/table tennis	5.3	10.5	4.6
Lego/Meccano	5.3	8.1	6.1
A-Team/He-man etc. figures	5.3	5.8	6.1
Dolls/dolls house	5.3	4.7	6.1
Visited the library	0.0	7.0	4.6
Knitting/sewing etc.	0.0	7.0	3.0

Table E3.2   After School Activities Mentioned in the Diaries Breakdown of selected activities by school.
II. After having a meal but before getting ready for bed.

Activity	Percentage of Pupils Mentioning Activity		
	School 1	School 2	School 3
Watched television	92.1	94.2	92.4
Meeting of organisation	23.7	64.0	39.4
Read	50.0	48.8	33.3
Games (board, card/puzzles etc.)	15.8	37.2	30.3
Colouring/painting/drawing/craft	18.4	31.4	22.7
Homework	0.0	19.8	47.0
Computer/electronic/video games	26.3	24.4	21.2
Practised musical instrument(s)	7.9	24.2	25.8
Played with friend(s)	23.7	20.9	18.2
Sporting activities	7.9	14.0	18.2
Tapes/tape recording/records	13.2	15.1	12.1
Dart/snooker/table tennis	10.5	12.8	7.6
Lego/Meccano	7.9	10.5	7.6
A-Team/He-man etc. figures	5.3	8.1	3.0
Imaginative role play	10.5	2.3	4.6
Knitting/sewing etc.	2.6	8.1	4.6
Dolls/dolls house	0.0	8.1	4.6

More pupils at School 2 practised a musical instrument, while at School 3 playing with friends and doing homework seemed to be the most important activities listed after watching television. Similar differences can be seen in Table E3.2 in which activities are compared for the period of time between having the evening meal and getting ready for bed, the most obvious being that more pupils from School 2 mentioned attending meetings of organisations. When all the activities in this table are compared it is the pupils at School 2 who appear to have the most active lifestyles, and yet 48% of them mentioned reading at this point in the evening at least once during the period of time that the diaries were completed. This was considerably more than School 3 and nearly as many as School 1.

Although the diaries were mainly concerned with gathering information about after school activities, space was included for pupils to offer information about the weekend in the section headed 'These are some special things I did at the weekend'. In addition they were invited to give details of books read and television programmes watched. Some pupils wrote no more than a sentence or two, a few wrote what virtually amounted to an essay, others ignored this section altogether. Although many of the activities are similar to those mentioned after school, others such as fishing, gardening, horse riding and bird watching had not previously been listed. For interest therefore lists of weekend activities have been included in Appendix 6, again by school, so that comparisons can be made. Once again reading assumed a position of importance and was the most mentioned activity after television. The percentage of pupils at each of the schools who mentioned reading at the weekend was:

School 1   48%
School 2   70%
School 3   55%

Yet another opportunity for assessing how reading rated as an after school activity came from the first page of the diary where the pupil had been invited to complete the rhyme:

Down the garden, over the wall
This is what I like best of all.

....

The response to this produced a very wide range of 'likes' and favourite activities, with anything from 'cheese on toast' to 'skateboarding' being listed. Several of the pupils mentioned collecting things, such as coins, stamps and keyrings. Quite a few sports were listed, and many seemed to enjoy either listening to music or playing a musical instrument. There were some surprises too – 'drawing road maps and weather charts', 'designing fashion pictures', and even 'learning my tables'! Top favourites at each of the schools were swimming and reading, with watching television down to third or fourth place. Some pupils even specified the type of reading they liked best – 'reading fantasy books', 'reading C.S. Lewis books', 'Bengali books', and 'poetry'. Since they make such fascinating reading, lists of what the pupils at each of the schools said that they liked 'best of all' are included in Appendix 7.

E.4   After School Activities and Reading

Using evidence from the diaries this chapter will examine the influence that after school activities have on reading. This may be a positive one stimulating the pupil to read, or a negative one which either reduces the time that can be spent reading, or perhaps even decreases the motivation to read. Television has often been implicated in the latter. Alternatively reading may itself stimulate other after school activities.

Throughout the discussion that follows it should be remembered that the diaries were completed during the month of February. The emphasis on certain activities might be expected to change in the Summer months.

Table E 4.1 **The Frequency with which Pupils Listed Television Viewing as an Activity.** (Fully completed diaries only).

Number of pupils who watched television	Frequency in Days									
	0	1	2	3	4	5	6	7	8	9
Before the evening meal	5	0	8	6	15	16	24	25	42	30
After the evening meal	9	3	14	14	19	27	23	26	24	12

4.1 Television

The frequency with which the pupils listed television viewing as an activity is shown in Table E4.1.

From this it would appear that many pupils watched television regularly. However it was seldom the only activity listed in these two time divisions, and quite a few pupils watched much less frequently, preferring other activities such as playing with friends, music practice, games etc.

The usual pattern was for a pupil to return home from school, perhaps change, get a snack and switch on the television set. However many watched for only a short period of time before going off to do something else, returning later to watch favourite programmes. Evidence for this selectivity is shown in Table E4.2 where an indication is given of the number of pupils who mentioned watching each of the children's television programmes. It can be seen that some programmes were very much more popular than others, for example *Grange Hill, Blue Peter* and *Chocky*. Those pupils who watched for longer periods of time often combined this activity with another such as colouring, weaving, playing with dolls, and even doing homework and reading!

After the meal the television programmes watched were most probably dictated by adult members of the family and did not always interest the pupils. There were comments such as 'I saw a bit of *Dallas*', and 'I watched the end of *Coronation Street*', although it was clear that some pupils has sat right through the programmes they had mentioned. There were however some programmes screened in the early evening that many pupils made a point of watching, such as *Tucker's Luck, Dr Who, The A-Team* and *Knight Rider*. Other programmes mentioned by quite a few of the pupils were *Top of the Pops, The Living Planet, Treasure Hunt, In Loving Memory* and *Auf Wiedersehen Pet*. Several of the boys also mentioned watching sports programmes, and there seemed to be quite an interest in the Winter Olympics which were taking place at that time.

Television may have reduced the amount of time that some pupils spent reading, while a few who watched a considerable amount of television never mentioned reading at all. There was however some evidence to suggest that television had actually stimulated some pupils to read. Four annuals were mentioned — *Knight Rider, The A-Team, Jim'll Fix It* and *Match of the Day*, all of which related to television programmes. *Look-In: the Junior T.V. Times* was also being read by a few of the pupils. Several book titles mentioned in the diaries had previously been serialised on television, for example *Carrie's War* (Nina Bawden) and *The Secret Garden* (Frances Hodgson Burnett), and others related to television series, such as *Grange Hill rules — OK?, Super Gran* (Forrest Wilson) and *Anyone can draw* (Tony Hart). Other examples can be found in the full list of book titles mentioned in the diaries which is included as Appendix 8.

Five of the pupils did not have a television set. However there was no evidence to suggest that they read any more than those pupils who did. Bridget and Caroline were both members of large families, each having a total of five brothers and sisters, Bridget's reading was about average for the total sample, but Caroline only mentioned reading on two occasions. Timothy read a little of the same book every day, but always 'out loud to mummy'. However, in addition to their own book reading both Deborah and Miles had books read to them by their parents. This suggests that the absence of a television provides more time and opportunities for parents to encourage and promote the pleasures of book reading.

4.2 Games and Toys

Quite a few of the pupils mentioned playing board games and card games. These were played with members of the family, friends or even alone. The most popular board games were Chess, *Scrabble* and *Monopoly*, and one pupil mentioned reading a book on 'how to play better chess' (title not given). Other games mentioned were hand held electronic games, video games, darts, table tennis and snooker.

Toys favoured by the boys included Lego, Meccano and cars, while 21 girls mentioned playing with dolls or a doll's house. Interestingly though, almost as many boys (17) were playing with dolls in the form of *Action Force, A-Team, Star Wars* and *He-man and the Masters of the Universe* figures, and generally they spent much longer periods of time in this activity than the girls, often accompanied by one or two friends. As many of these pupils also played with Lego and cars, evenings were filled with imaginative play between favourite television programmes, with very little time left free for reading.

Quite a variety of imaginative role play games were mentioned — 'schools', 'houses', 'spaceships', 'police', 'army', 'cowboys and indians', 'smugglers', 'ghosts', 'offices' and even 'libraries'. Nicholas made a camp at the end of his garden and played there with his friends on several evenings after school. He was reading *Five on a Hike Together* (Enid Blyton) that week. Jonathan helped to make a camp in a friend's bedroom, while Sam and his friend Richard 'played rock climbing' on Sam's bed. Deborah played 'schools' on several occasions. During this time she was reading *First Term at Malory Towers, Second Form at Malory Towers* and *Third Term at Malory Towers,* all by Enid Blyton. Although much of the role play reflected real life situations, films or programmes watched on television, it would seem equally likely that book reading also influenced this activity.

Table E 4.2   Children's Television — The Programmes Mentioned in the Diaries.

BBC1 Programme		Number of Pupils			
		School 1	School 2	School 3	Total
4.20 *Tin Tin*	(each day)	13	28	7	48
4.25 *Tottie*	(each day)	3	24	9	36
4.40 *Finders Keepers*	(Mon.)	0	14	7	21
Jigsaw	(Tues.)	2	12	13	27
Rentaghost	(Wed.)	5	15	23	43
Fonz and the Happy Days Gang	(Thurs.)	7	16	20	43
Wildtrack	(Fri.)	0	4	11	15
5.05 *John Craven's Newsround*		0	20	12	32
5.10 *Blue Peter*	(Mon. & Thur.)	13	40	40	93
Grange Hill	(Tues. & Fr.)	17	68	43	128
Think of a Number	(Wed.)	3	8	18	29

ITV Programme		Number of Pupils			
		School 1	School 2	School 3	Total
4.15 *Batfink*	(each day)	19	47	21	87
4.20 *He-Man*	(Mon.)	21	41	14	76
On Safari	(Tues.)	8	19	14	41
Luna	(Wed.)	7	17	10	41
Do It	(Thurs.)	4	9	2	15
Sooty	(Fri.)	4	4	8	16
4.45 *Chocky*	(Mon.)	21	43	32	96
CBTV	(Tues.)	4	5	8	17
Razzamatazz	(Wed.)	3	5	1	9
This is Me	(Thurs.)	0	1	2	3
Freetime	(Fri.)	0	3	5	8

4.3 Computers

Not all of the pupils who mentioned playing computer games had their own computer, but had access to those belonging to friends. Two pupils acquired a computer of their own during the period that the diaries were completed. Some pupils spent a lot of time playing with their computers, others used them much less frequently. Most of the pupils would watch their favourite television programmes before starting a computer game. However, there were others, like Stephen, who would prefer to use the computer rather than watch television, usually commencing a game immediately on arrival home from school. Unfortunately his sister did sometimes wish to watch a particular programme! On Thursday his diary entry reads:

4.00pm I played Jetpac.

4.30pm Played *Hobbit*.

5.00pm Watched TV (because I had to).

The Hobbit seemed to be his favourite computer game and was often mentioned. It also stimulated his interest in the book. He indicates reading *The Hobbit* (J.R.R. Tolkien) in bed every night during the second week of the diary.

4.4 Pets

39 pupils mentioned having pets, several having more than one. These included dogs and puppies, cats and kittens, goldfish, hamsters, gerbils, guinea pigs, rabbits and even stick insects. Most took pet care very seriously — feeding them, cleaning them out, training them, walking them, grooming them, and of course cuddling and playing with those that could be cuddled and played with.

Interest in pets — particularly dogs, did promote reading. For example Katherine's list of books included the titles *Just a dog* (Helen Griffiths), and the Ladybird books *Learnabout dogs* and *Training your dog*.

4.5 Art and Craft

A variety of arts and crafts was mentioned in the diaries — painting, drawing, colouring, stencilling, badge making, model aeroplanes, pom-poms, necklaces, ear-rings, sequin pictures, puppets, bookmarks, sewing, knitting, tapestry, weaving etc. These activities often accompanied television viewing. There were only two books mentioned that related to these activities — *Anyone can draw* (Tony Hart), and 'a book on how to knit' (author and title not given). However there was evidence in Peter's diary that reading could influence what a pupil drew or painted.

DIARY NUMBER 3

Peter:- who preferred reading to watching television.

Brothers/Sisters:- one brother.

Likes best:- I enjoy reading, roll [sic] playing games and my scalextric.

Membership of organisations:- none.

Music lessons:- none.

Sporting activities:- none mentioned.

. . . . .

On arrival home from school Peter changed, had a snack and settled down to read, often reading for an hour. After this, and before the main meal eaten between 6.00pm and 6.30pm, he would play Chess or Othello with himself, draw, or play with an electronic game or his *Scalextric* set. On the first Monday he mentions visiting the library. His diary reads:

4.30pm Went to the library and got 5 *Dr Who* books and a book about the future.

After the main meal he usually returned to a book, again often reading for quite long periods and stopping only to draw or play an electronic game. His reading seemed to influence what he drew. For example:

Mon. 7.15pm I read my book
7.55pm Did a drawing of a monster
8.15pm Cut out my monster and put it with the other one.
Tues. 6.55pm Drew a monster called Kobold.

Both days he was reading *Dr Who and the Planet of the Spiders* (Terrance Dicks).

The only television programmes that Peter mentioned were *Batfink* and *The Discovery of Animal Behaviour* on the first Tuesday, *Dr Who* on a Friday, and *Saturday Superstore* at the weekend.

He continued with his reading after getting ready for bed every day, but never mentioned reading in Bed.

Reading:- *Explorer Encyclopaedia* (ed. Bill Bruce)
Dr Who and the Planet of the Spiders (Terrance Dicks)
Citadel of Chaos (Steve Jackson)
Forest of Doom (Ian Livingstone)
Dungeons and Dragons Basic Rule Book
Star Wars/Return of the Jedi Weekly (Comic)
The Empire Strikes Back (Comic)

4.6 Homework

The majority of pupils who listed homework as an activity were learning their spellings/dictation or tables. However a few pupils from School 3 indicated that they had done some English, and during the second week several pupils from School 2 mentioned *Griffiths* maths homework. The type of homework most likely to promote reading was that described by the pupils as 'topic homework'. For example, Roger mentioned working on a dinosaur topic, while Bridget and Margaret were busy researching for a topic on 'sugar'.

4.7 Organised Activities

The percentage of pupils at each school who regularly attended one or more organised activities each week such as music lessons, sports training sessions, or meetings of an organisation such as Cubs, Brownies, Youth Club, Red Cross etc., were:

School 1   37%

School 2   79%

School 3   64%

Table E 4.3   Organised Activities Mentioned in the Diaries.

Activity	Number of Pupils
Youth Club	31
Cubs	34
Scouts	9
Brownies	24
Guides	11
St. Johns Ambulance Brigade	7
Red Cross	1
Royal Society for the Protection of Birds	1
Woodcraft	1
Dog Training	1
Badminton Club	1
Dancing Lessons	7
Diving Club	1
Football practice/match	9
Gym Club	9
Judo	3
Karate	1
Netball	3
Swimming Club	17
Tennis coaching	3
Weight Training	1
Band Practice	5
Choir (Church)	1
Clarinet lesson	1
Drumming lesson	1
Flute lesson	2
Guitar lesson	2
Organ lesson	1
Percussion lesson	1
Piano lesson	14
Recorder lesson	1
Trumpet lesson	2
Viola lesson	1
Violin lesson	1
Church/Religious Meeting	2
Islamic Centre	1
Mosque	4

A full list of all the organised activities mentioned in the diaries is shown in Table E4.3. Of the 31 pupils who mentioned that they attended a Youth Club, 29 were pupils at School 2, which may account for the high percentage shown for this school. The low percentage of pupils at School 1 who left home in the evening to attend some form of organised activity, could be due to the fact that their numbers included a substantial proportion of children from ethnic minority groups, particularly Asian and Italian.

Many pupils listed more than one organised activity during each week, and several attended more than one on the same evening. For example Geoffrey went to a swimming club on a Monday, a piano lesson and Youth Club on a Tuesday, and a judo club on a Friday.

Since time spent at a meeting, music lesson or training session would obviously reduce the amount of time that could be spent reading, it was decided to use the diaries to investigate whether pupils who attended a large number of organised activities, read less than pupils who attended few or none. This was approached by comparing the number of times that reading was listed as an activity against the number of organised activities attended, and the results are presented in Table E4.4.

Table E 4.4   A Comparison of the Number of Times Reading was Listed as an Activity with the Number of Organised Activities Attended. (Fully completed diaries only).

Number of organised activities attended	Number of Times Reading Listed as an Activity					
	0	1-4	5-8	9-12	more than 12	Total
0	2	13	10	14	6	45
1	–	9	12	1	–	22
2	–	11	13	11	4	39
3	2	4	7	4	25	
4	–	6	6	8	1	21
5	1	3	4	1	1	10
6	–	1	1	–	–	2
7	–	2	2	1	–	5
8	–	–	1	–	–	1
9	–	–	1	–	–	1

No obvious correlation can be seen between the number of activities attended and the amount of reading undertaken — one pupil who attended five organised activities never mentioned reading, while another attending the same number of activities mentioned reading on twelve separate occasions. The conclusion reached is that if a pupil is motivated to read, they will find the time do so no matter how many organised activities they attend. Those who attended several organised activities seemed to be highly motivated at home too, and spent their free time playing Chess and other board games, tape recording, or playing with friends etc., rather than watching a lot of television.

There was some evidence to suggest that a few of these activities did promote reading. Suzie, a member of the St. John's Ambulance Brigade listed *Essentials of First Aid* (a book produced by that organisation) amongst her reading. She was also a Brownie and on more than one occasion mentioned reading *Brownies: their Book* (Palmer Cox), and a book on 'how to knit' — perhaps for a Brownies badge test? Quite a few of the pupils mentioned working for Cub, Brownie and Guide badge tests. There was no evidence to suggest that musical activities stimulated reading, but interest in sport certainly did, with the *Guinness Book of Soccer Facts and Feats* (Jack Rollin), *Football Quiz 1981-82* (Gordon Jeffery), *Learnabout Football* (John Baker) and 'a netball book' (author and title not given), all being mentioned.

DIARY NUMBER 4

Louise:- who led a very active life but still found time to read every day.

Brothers/sisters:- two sisters.

Likes best:- Playing with my rabbits and feeding my cat.

Membership of organisations:- Youth Club, St. John's Ambulance Brigade, and Brownies.

Music:- clarinet lesson.

Sporting activities:- Gym club.

. . . . .

Except for Friday when she stayed for Gym Club, Louise arrived home at 4.00pm and switched on the television set. The programmes she mentioned watching were *Tin Tin, Tottie: the Story of a Dolls House, Chocky, Blue Peter, On Safari* and *Grange Hill*. Other activities before the main meal included clarinet practice and playing computer games. After the meal, usually eaten between 5.00pm and 6.00pm. Louise went to Youth Club on a Monday, a clarinet lesson and Brownies on a Tuesday, and St. John's Ambulance Brigade on a Wednesday. She usually got ready for bed between 8.00pm and 9.00pm depending on what time these activities finished. She read every day but one, either after getting ready for bed, or in bed, completing one book before starting another.

Reading:- *Charlie and the Chocolate Factory* (Roald Dahl)
The Fiend next Door (Sheila Lavelle)
Happy Endings: Stories Old and New (Wendy Craig)

E.5 Reading

From the reading material mentioned in the diaries it was obvious that within this sample of 190 pupils existed not only a wide range of reading abilities, but also considerable diversity both in subject interest and in the type of material chosen. The book titles mentioned ranged from those belonging to reading schemes such as Sheila McCullagh's *1,2,3 and Away* right through to adult literature, and included titles in the Bengali language. Comics, annuals, magazines and newspapers were also read. The various types of reading mentioned by the pupils will be considered separately in the sections that follow.

5.1 Books

There has over the past 40 years or so been a growing interest in children's voluntary reading. One of the most important pieces of research into this, and one that has stimulated others to carry out research in this field, was the Schools Council research project under the directorship of Frank Whitehead. The results of this project were published under the title *Children and their Books* (1977). This project surveyed a randomly selected group of 7,800 children aged 10, 12 and 14 years at 197 primary schools and 201 secondary schools in England and Wales. Information was collected from the pupils by means of a questionnaire, with questionnaires also being sent to the schools concerned. Although the data for this project was collected in a completely different way, and the sample size was considerably smaller and concentrated in one area, it was nevertheless thought to be of interest to compare the information on pupils' book reading habits gathered from the diaries with the findings of Whitehead's report, and this will be done where appropriate in the discussion that follows.

In all 404 book titles were mentioned by the total sample of 190 pupils during the two weeks that the diaries were completed. Of these 88% were fiction and only 12% non-fiction. This proportion of narrative to non-narrative shows similarity to that indicated by the Schools Council project where non-narrative was found to account for 14.4% of the whole at 10+.

One of the factors that the Whitehead project found to be strongly linked with the amount of book reading was sex:

> At all ages girls read more books than boys, and at the same time there are fewer non-book readers among the girls than among the boys.

It was decided therefore to use the information in the diaries to test this observation and this was done in two ways. First all the book titles mentioned by each pupil were counted, and the results listed separately for girls and boys. These are given in Table E5.1 and suggest that if one uses the measure of the number of book titles mentioned, the girls did read more than the boys since the percentage of girls who mentioned three or more book titles was 15% greater than the boys. However these figures merely indicated the number of books that were in the possession of each pupil. There is no way of knowing how much of the books were read during the period that the diaries were completed. In addition they hide the fact that several pupils who only mentioned one title, were reading that title consistently every evening after school, and at the weekend too. This particularly applied to some of the boys. It was therefore decided to look at the number of days book titles were listed as having been read and then compare the differences between the sexes. These results appear in Table E5.2. The figures still indicate that the girls read more than

Table E 5.1 **To Indicate the Amount of Voluntary Book Reading Undertaken by Each of the Sexes as Evident from the Number of Titles Listed over the Two Weeks that the Diaries were Completed** (includes titles mentioned at the weekend)

Number of Book Titles Listed	Boys	% of Boys	Girls	% of Girls	Total	% of Total Sample
1	19	21	15	19	34	19.88
2	16	18	18	22	34	19.88
3	14	16	15	19	29	16.96
4	14	16	13	16	27	15.79
5	4	4	4	5	8	4.68
6	1	1	5	6	6	3.51
7	2	2	4	5	6	3.51
8	–	–	1	1	1	0.58
9	1	1	–	–	1	0.58
10	–	–	2	2	2	1.17
15	1	1	–	–	1	0.58
17	–	–	1	1	1	0.58
NONE	18	20	3	4	21	12.3
TOTAL	90	100	81	100	171	100

Table E 5.2 **To Indicate the Amount of Voluntary Book Reading Undertaken by Each of the Sexes as Evident from the Number of Days that Book Titles were Listed During the Two Weeks that the Diaries were Completed.**

Number of Days that book titles were Listed	Boys	% of Boys	Girls	% of Girls	Total	% of Total Sample
1	12	13	6	7	18	11
2	6	7	6	7	12	7
3	7	8	7	9	14	8
4	6	7	10	12	16	9
5	4	4	10	12	14	8
6	8	9	5	6	13	8
7	6	7	8	10	14	8
8	4	4	11	14	15	9
9	19	21	15	19	34	20
NONE	18	20	3	4	21	12
TOTAL	90	100	81	100	171	100
WEEKEND	37	41	45	56	82	48

the boys with 61% of the girls mentioning reading on five or more days out of the nine, but only 45% of the boys. It is however, interesting to note that out of the total sample of 171 pupils (fully completed diaries only), 20% read at some point in the evening on all nine days under analysis, and roughly the same percentage of boys as of girls. There appeared to be a considerable drop in the number of pupils reading at the weekend — 48% mentioning this as an activity, and of these slightly more girls than boys. Of those who did not mention reading books 18 were boys but only three were girls. However of these only four boys and one girl mentioned no reading material at all. The rest read comics and/or annuals, some quite extensively.

Yet another finding of the Whitehead project was that the amount of book reading was positively associated with smallness of family size. Since the pupils had been asked in the diaries to give the names of their brothers and sisters, it was also possible to test this observation. This was done by comparing the number of brothers and/or sisters a pupil had with the number of days that they had listed book titles as having been read. The results are presented in Table E5.3 and indicate that although there were more non-book readers during this period among the pupils with two or more brothers and/or sisters, there was very little difference between the number who read after school on six or more days over the nine day period, when compared with the pupils who had only one brother or sister.

Table E 5.3   Size of Family X Number of Days Book Titles were Listed

Number of brothers and/or sisters	Number of Days Book Titles were Listed							
	0	*1*	*2*	*3*	*4*	*5*	*6 or more*	*Total*
0	–	2	–	–	–	–	3	5
1	8	8	5	6	9	9	39	84
2 or more	13	8	7	8	7	5	34	82
								171

The Whitehead project also indicated social class and ability and attainment at school as being other factors which influenced children's book reading habits. These were however impossible to explore using the information in the diaries.

The majority of book titles mentioned in the diaries were for fiction, and a full list of those mentioned is included as Appendix 8. The taste in books was fairly typical for this age group — a mixture of humour, fantasy, adventure and mystery, short stories, animal stories, fairy tales and cartoon characters, with humour and fantasy predominating. Also included were a number of 'old favourites' such as *Black Beauty* (Anna Sewell), *The Railway Children* (E. Nesbit), and *The Secret Garden* (Frances Hodgson Burnett). Some pupils were however selecting at a lower reading level, while others chose titles intended for teenagers such as *The Fortunate Few* (Tim Kennamore), *Taran Wanderer* (Lloyd Alexander) and *Summer Dreams* (Barbara Conklin). Several pupils mentioned reading adult literature. In each case the title was referred to on several occasions which suggests that these books were actually being read. Proof of this came from Marion's diary. She was reading a novel by Barbara Cartland. On Thursday, after getting ready for bed, she wrote:-

I read a chapter of *The Golden Gondola.*

She then made an identical entry for Friday. But at the weekend after describing the dancing lessons she attended she put:-

After the dance I came home and I read some more of *The Golden Gondola*, it is about an important man who travels he went on a sailing boat and the ship is wreked and he manages to save a girl. The girl has no relations and she is poor and they try to get her a rich husband. [sic].

On Monday she arrived home from school at 4pm and continued reading this book for half an hour before watching the television.

Some authors were particularly popular with these pupils — Beverly Cleary, Alan Coren, Roald Dahl, Brian Earnshaw, E.W. Hildick, C.S. Lewis and Forrest Wilson to name a few. The most popular author was however Enid Blyton with no less than 46 of her titles being mentioned in the diaries — 37 of these being read by pupils at School 2; nine by pupils at School 3; and eight by pupils at School 1.

Some pupils mentioned several titles by the same author either 'dipping' into one and then another, or finishing one title before starting the next. Was it safer perhaps to stick with an author known and liked? Philip for example mentioned *Whale Adventure* (Willard Price) on Monday; was reading *Gorilla Adventure* (Willard Price) on Thursday and Friday; and then began *Volcano Adventure* (Willard Price) at the weekend, and he continued reading this title right through to the end of the second week.

Only 39 non-fiction titles were mentioned in the diaries (see Appendix 6b) although a further eight were indicated by subject, the author and title having been omitted by the pupil, e.g. 'a book on sugar', 'a computer book', 'a nature book' etc. The most popular non-fiction books were poetry books and books of jokes, for example *Silly Verse for Kids* (Spike Milligan), and *Up with School!* (Christopher Wright). Other titles could be related to either leisure interests or topics done at school and these have already been discussed. The distribution of the non-fiction titles between the sexes is given in Table E5.4.

One of the conclusions reached by Whitehead's project was that boys read much more non-narrative than girls. The above table is consistent with this finding with almost twice as many boys as girls reading non-fiction titles. There were only two boys and one girl whose reading consisted solely of non-fiction titles.

Table E 5.4 Number of Non-Fiction Titles Mentioned x Sex

Number of Non –Fiction Titles Mentioned		Boys	Girls
1		16	8
2		3	2
3		2	1
4		–	–
5		1	1
TOTAL	**22**	**12**	

Table E 5.5   Comics — Number of Titles Mentioned

Number of Titles mentioned	Boys	Girls	Total
1	27	6	33
2	7	10	17
3	5	1	6
4	–	1	1
5	–	–	–
6	–	–	–
7	1	–	1

5.2   Comics, Annuals and Magazines

A total of 57 pupils — 30% of the sample, mentioned reading one or more comic titles over the two weeks that the diaries were completed. Of these 57, 40 were boys and 17 were girls. Quite a few of the boys — 67.5%, had only mentioned reading one title. The girls however, though fewer in number, were much more likely to be reading two or more titles. A breakdown of the number of titles mentioned by each of the sexes is given in Table E5.5.

The comics being read could be grouped both according to the intended age range and by the content. Two girls mentioned reading *Twinkle*. This was however the only example of a comic for the four to seven age group. The comics aimed at the middle age range were very popular, although mainly with the boys. These included *Beano, Dandy, Beezer, Buster* and *Whizzer and Chips*, all full of strip cartoons with the emphasis on fun and humour. Of these *Beano* was by far the most popular.

The comics for older children could be separated according to the sex of the intended reader. Those for boys included *Eagle, 2000AD* and *Star Wars / Return of the Jedi*, all with the emphasis on action, fantasy and the supernatural; and *Roy of the Rovers* devoted exclusively to football. Those specifically for girls could be recognised as such by their titles, and contained far more realistic stories than the comics for the boys. These included *Girl, Judy, Mandy* and *Tammy*. Although one girl was reading *Star Wars / Return of the Jedi* and another girl *Spiderman,* none of the boys were reading comics intended for girls. The only examples of girls' teenage comics being read were *Blue Jeans, My Guy* and *Jackie*.

Also popular and with wide appeal both in age range and content was *Look-In: The Junior TV Times.* This contains a mixture of comic strips of favourite television characters, news and views about programmes, items on popular music, sport etc., and quizzes and puzzle pages. This was read by both sexes, but tended to be favoured more by the girls than the boys. All the comics mentioned in the diaries are listed in Table E5.6.

Those pupils who took more than one comic tended to take others in the same grouping. They were seldom mixed. For example Steven who read *Beano,* was also reading *Dandy* and *Whizzer and Chips*; James read *Eagle* and *Star Wars / Return of the Jedi.* Elizabeth reading *Tammy* also mentioned *Bunty* and *Mandy*; similarly *My Guy, Blue Jeans* and *Jackie* were all being read by Joanne.

Table E 5.6   Comics Titles Mentioned in the Diaries

Title	Number of Pupils Reading Each Title		
	Boys	Girls	Total
Beano	16	4	20
Beezer	1	–	1
Blue Jeans	–	1	1
Bunty	–	1	1
Buster	1	–	1
Dandy	8	1	9
Eagle	4	–	4
Empire Strikes Back	1	1	2
Girl	–	4	4
Jackie	–	3	3
Judy	–	1	1
Look-In	3	6	9
Mandy	–	1	1
My Guy	–	1	1
Roy of The Rovers	1	–	1
Spiderman	–	1	1
Star Wars/Return of The Jedi Weekly	10	1	11
Suzy	–	1	1
Tammy	–	2	2
Twinkle	–	2	2
2000AD	1	–	1
Whizzer and Chips	7	1	8
Wow	1	–	1
Title not specified	6	–	6

Comics could be, and were, read at any time, and often filled odd moments between other activities such as the short break that occurred after the children's television programmes had ended, but before the main meal was served. Some pupils read comics immediately on arrival home from school while others preferred to read them after getting ready for bed. The favourite place to read them was however in bed. It was not possible to estimate the length of time the pupils spent reading the comics in bed, however it is possible to suggest from the evidence in the diaries that at other times the pupils spent between five minutes and 15 minutes in this activity, and certainly no longer than half an hour. Only a few pupils mentioned reading comics at the weekend.

With only nine exceptions the pupils who read comics also mentioned reading books, most mentioning more than one title. The combination of book reading and comic reading showed considerable variation from the pupil who mentioned seven comic titles and read comics every day but no books, to the pupil who read books every day listing ten book titles, and who also mentioned reading two comic titles but on one day only. A total of 31 pupils did however mention reading books on more days than they mentioned reading comics, although generally the amount of book reading decreased as the number of comics read increased.

Of considerable interest was how the pupils' taste in comics compared with their taste in books. Pupils who preferred the humorous comics such as *Dandy* and *Beano*, also tended to look for humour in the books that they read. Included in the books they mentioned reading were titles such as *William Again* by Richmal Crompton, *Charlie and the Chocolate Factory* and other titles by Roald Dahl, *The Secret Diary of Adrian Mole* by Sue Townsend, and Forrest Wilson's *Super Gran*. Books by Enid Blyton were also popular with these pupils.

Boys who read comics such as *Eagle* and *Star Wars / Return of the Jedi* also sought for action, fantasy and the supernatural in the books that had been selected. Amongst the titles that they mentioned were *Haunted Houses* by Aidan Chambers, *Dr Who and the Planet of the Spiders* by Terrance Dicks, the *Dragonfall 5* books by Brian Earnshaw, Nicholas Fisk's books *Flamers* and *Trillions*, *A Wizard of Earthsea* by Ursula Le Guin, *The Edge of the World* by John Gordon, and *Fighting Fantasy Adventure Gamebooks* by Ian Livingstone and Steve Jackson, in which the reader as hero or heroine can choose the course of their own adventure.

The book titles selected by the girls who read comics such as *Girl, Tammy* and *Mandy* showed a similar emphasis on relationships, with school stories and books with horse riding, ballet, boy-friends etc, as the most popular subjects. Titles mentioned by these pupils included the *Witch's Daughter* by Nina Bawden, *Tiger Eyes* by Judy Blume, *The House on the Cliffs* by Ruth Dallas, *Samantha on Stage* by Susan Clement Farrar, *Saturday Went Wrong* by Tim Goodwin and Lois Lowry's *Find a Stranger, Say Goodbye*. There was no obvious correlation between taste in books and comics for the girls who were reading the teenage magazines such as *Blue Jeans*. However there were only three pupils reading comics from this group.

Only two pupils reading comics appears to have a poor command of the English language — the first a girl who in addition to *Beano* listed only titles from a reading scheme, and the second a boy who read *Whizzer and Chips* as well as a number of books in the Bengali language.

In addition to the comics many of the pupils were reading annuals, although some pupils mentioned reading annuals but no comics. These were either associated with a comic such as *Beano, Beezer, Blue Jeans, Jinty,* etc., or related to a television programme such as *Jim'll Fix It, Knight Rider, Match of the Day* and *Tom and Jerry*. The annuals that were being read are listed in table E5.7, and once again the popularity of the *Beano* is clearly illustrated. Like the comics annuals were more popular with the boys.

Only four adult magazines were mentioned in the diaries. (These were *Friend* (a Quaker magazine), *Good Housekeeping, The Micro User,* and *Reader's Digest*.

Table E 5.7 Annuals Mentioned in the Diaries.

Title	Boys	Girls	Total
A-Team	1	–	1
Beano Book	8	2	10
Beezer Book	3	–	3
Bimbo Book	1	–	1
Blue Jeans	–	1	1
Dandy Book	1	–	1
Krazy	1	–	1
Flash Gordon	1	–	1
Jim'll Fix It	1	–	1
Jinty	–	1	1
Judy Book	–	1	1
Knight Rider	2	–	2
Look-In Television Annual	–	1	1
Match of the Day	1	–	1
Superman	1	–	1
Tammy	–	1	1
Tom and Jerry	–	1	1

DIARY NUMBER 5

Robert:- an avid reader of comics.

Brothers/sisters:- one sister.

Likes best:- watching television and riding my BMX and playing with my *Star Wars* Figures.

Membership of organisation(s):- none.

Music lessons/practice:- nothing mentioned.

Sporting activities:- plays football with friends.

Pets:- cat and rabbit.

Games mentioned:- cards, darts, *Lego, Yahtzee, Pac-man, Atari.*

. . . . .

Usually watched *Tin Tin* (BBC 1, 4.20pm every day) on arriving home from school, but then often went out on his BMX bike, played with his friends (six mentioned) or his sister, fed the pets etc., before returning to watch favourite television programmes such as *Grange Hill, Blue Peter, Jigsaw* and *Chocky*. The evening meal was usually eaten at about 6.00 pm after which Robert sometimes helped with the washing up. The time between the evening meal and getting ready for bed was usually spent watching television, playing with *Star Wars* figures, or playing games with his sister. He got ready for bed at about 8.00 pm after which he read comics, played with the cat or his sister, or watched some more television. Bedtime was between 8.45pm and 9.30pm. Read comics and played with *Star Wars* figures (and the cat!) in bed.

Reading:- *Beano*
Dandy
Roy of the Rovers
Star Wars / Return of the Jedi Weekly
Whizzer and Chips
Wow
Nutty School Fun

5.3. Newspapers

24 of the pupils, nine girls and 15 boys, mentioned reading the newspaper in the section headed "This is what I read today". The titles mentioned were *The Daily Telegraph* (3), *The Sun* (2), The Guardian (1), *The Daily Mail* (2), *The Sunday Telegraph* (1), *The News of the World* (1), and *The Mid-Herts Citizen* (2). 15 pupils did not name the paper that they had "read".

Except for one girl who said that she had "read the T.V. bit in the newspaper", there were no clues as to what news items, articles, strip cartoons etc. interested the pupils. Nor was it possible to ascertain how long the pupils spent looking at the paper since only two of them had included a mention of this as an activity in the actual diary. Lucy's entry for Thursday read:

6.30pm   I read the paper.

6.35pm   I thought the paper was boring so I dropped it on the cat.

7.00pm   I read more of my book.

However Peter's reading material was mainly newspapers and magazines. His diary reads:

Week 1 Tuesday   6.45pm Read the newspaper
                         [*Daily Telegraph*]
         Wednesday 6.50pm Looked at some magazines and read the newspaper.
                         [*Mid-Herts Citizen, Good Housekeeping, Olympic Holiday Brochure*].
Week 2 Monday   7.30pm My mum went out to choir and I read the newspaper.
         Wednesday 7.00pm Look [sic] at the newspaper. [*Mid-Herts Citizen*]

He also mentioned that on several evenings he came downstairs to watch the *Nine o'Clock News* (BBC 1), after having got himself ready for bed, and *John Craven's Newsround* (screened each day at 5.05pm on BBC 1) was another programme that interested him.

Of the 24 pupils who mentioned "reading" a newspaper, eight also mentioned watching *John Craven's Newsround*, and 11 mentioned watching either the early evening news or the *Nine o'Clock News*. Only five of the pupils watched both. On the whole the impression gained from the diaries was that the news did not particularly interest children in this age group and there is evidence that several of the pupils who mentioned watching the early evening news on television, did so only because they happened to be present when adult members of the family were watching it — often during the evening meal.

Table E 5.8   To Show When and How Often the Pupils Read.

Number of pupils who mentioned needing	Frequency in days									Total	Total as % of total sample
	1	2	3	4	5	6	7	8	9		
a) on getting home from school but before having a meal	42	16	5	5	3	2	3	3	–	79	46
b) After a meal but before getting ready for bed	29	19	8	6	7	3	2	2	–	76	44
c) After getting ready for bed	27	25	16	7	4	5	4	1	–	89	52
d) In bed	26	25	18	9	5	4	8	2	6	103	60

5.4 When did the pupils read?

Although some pupils had failed to indicate when they had read the titles they had listed for each day, and so consequently the figures appearing in the tables that follow are likely to be an underestimate, an attempt was nevertheless made to assess from the diaries the frequency of reading within each of the time divisions over the nine school days under analysis. The results are presented in Table E5.8.

Out of a total sample size of 171 pupils (fully completed diaries only), 79 (46%) had mentioned reading after arriving home from school but before the main meal. However of these pupils, 58 (73%) had indicated reading on one or two days only — the majority only once. (Table E5.8a). Only three pupils fewer mentioned reading after a main meal but before getting ready for bed, however the number who read on more than one occasion showed a slight increase on the previous time divisions. (Table E5.8b). More than 50% of the total sample indicated reading after getting ready for bed with 42% of these pupils doing so on three or more occasions (Table E5.8c). The most popular time to read however was in bed with 60% of the total sample not only reading during this period but doing so much more frequently than in any of the previous time divisions. (Table E5.8d).

During the compilation of Table E5.8 it became obvious however that to treat the pupils as a total sample was to hide differences in the patterns of reading between pupils attending the three schools, each of which has an intake from a different part of the Fleetville area, and different attitudes within the school towards books and reading. So that a comparison could be made, the frequency with which the pupils mentioned reading in each of the four time divisions is listed separately for each school in Table E5.9.

Table E 5.9   To Show Variations in Patterns of Reading between the Three Schools (Fully completed diaries only).

% of pupils who mentioned reading	Frequency in Days									
	1	2	3	4	5	6	7	8	9	Total
(1) On getting home from school but before a meal										
School 1	18.2	18.2	6.1	6.1	6.1	3.0	–	–	–	57.7
School 2	23.8	7.5	3.8	2.5	3.1	–	3.8	3.8	–	46.5
School 3	29.8	6.9	–	1.7	–	1.7	–	–	–	39.6
(2) After a meal but before getting ready for bed										
School 1	21.2	6.1	9.1	3.0	6.1	3.0	3.0	3.0	–	54.5
School 2	17.5	15.0	2.5	5.0	3.8	2.5	1.3	1.3	–	48.9
School 3	13.8	8.6	5.2	1.7	3.5	–	–	–	–	32.8
(3) After getting ready for bed										
School 1	18.2	15.2	18.2	6.1	3.0	–	3.0	3.0	–	66.7
School 2	18.8	17.5	10.0	5.0	1.3	6.3	2.5	–	–	61.4
School 3	10.4	10.4	3.5	1.7	3.5	–	1.7	–	–	31.2
(4) In Bed										
School 1	15.2	15.2	6.1	–	3.0	3.0	–	–	–	42.5
School 2	20.0	17.5	10.0	3.8	2.5	2.5	5.0	2.5	2.5	66.3
School 3	8.6	10.4	13.8	10.4	3.5	1.7	6.9	–	6.9	62.2

The total percentage of pupils from School 2 who mentioned reading in each of these time divisions is similar or slightly higher than the average for the total sample of 171 pupils (see Table E5.8). However the averages shown for the frequency of reading a) on getting home from school; b) after having a meal; and c) after getting ready for bed, are for School 1 well above the averages for the total sample, while those for School 3 are considerably lower. Possible reasons for the observed differences will be considered as follows referring to the situation as it existed in February 1984 when the diaries were completed.

i)   *Availability of books — in school*

Although School 1 is furthest away from the Public Library the head teacher was 'highly committed to books and reading'. Here the library was centrally situated and the approach towards books and library use open and integral with the curriculum.

Although the intake at this school included 'a high percentage of children from multi-racial backgrounds, especially Asian and Italian' and therefore the reading of books

143

in the English language perhaps presented a problem to quite a few, the positive attitude of the school towards books was reflected in the amount of reading undertaken at home, with several of the pupils listing books from various reading schemes alongside other reading material. Encouragement may also have been forthcoming from parents anxious for their children to become fluent in speaking English. In School 3 the approach to library provision and use was entirely different. Here a Junior Non-fiction Library was situated in the small entrance hall to the school, while fiction stocks were held separately in each classroom. Access by the pupils to the total fiction stock of the school was therefore severely limited. The situation at School 2 fell somewhere between that at Schools 1 and 3, with fiction collections in classrooms, a rather 'antiquated' central library, and differing attitudes amongst the staff towards children's reading, the use of books and home loan, but with a newly appointed head teacher who saw one of his first priorities to be the creation of a new library within the school.

ii) Availability of books — the Public Library

School 2 is closest to the Public Library and more pupils from this school mentioned visiting the library in their diaries. Fleetville library was however only open 25 hours a week — Tuesdays, Thursdays, Fridays and Saturday mornings.

iii) After school activities

Fewer pupils at School 1 belonged to an organisation such as Cubs, Brownies etc., undertook sporting activities or played a musical instrument, than did the pupils at either of the other two schools. (See Tables E3.1 and E3.2). This suggests that these pupils read more often because they had more time to do so. However, although 64% of the pupils at School 3 took part in one or more organised activities each week, which might indicate a reason why they read less often, this was still fewer than the 79% of pupils at School 2 undertaking similar after school activities, and yet who still found time to read more often than the pupils at School 3. This suggests that for the pupils at School 3 lack of motivation may be a more important factor than lack of time.

iv) Peer group pressure

The popularity of certain authors for example Beverly Cleary, Alan Coren, Brian Earnshaw and C.S. Lewis, each of which was being read almost exclusively by the pupils of School 2, in addition to the majority of the Enid Blyton titles listed in Appendix 8a, suggests that the recommendations of friends are important here and may encourage reading. The pupils at School 3 spent a lot more of their time visiting, playing with and attending organised activities with friends than the pupils at either of the other two schools, and this may reduce the amount of time they have available in the early evening to spend in the activity of reading.

v) Parental influences on pupils' reading

The attitude of parents to books and reading is of considerable importance in influencing a child's motiviation to read. Some indication of the amount of parental involvement in their children's reading can be obtained from the attendance figures for the Fleetville Family Reading Group. It was the pupils from School 2, who along with their parents, were much more strongly represented than pupils and parents from either of the other two schools. The figures given by Dina Thorpe were as follows:-

School 1   4 pupils

School 2   30 pupils

School 3   15 pupils

5.5 How long did the pupils spend reading?

It was very difficult to estimate the length of time a pupil spent reading on any one occasion. Clocks were very often incorrectly filled in or not filled in at all, and there was no way of telling whether other activities filled the gap between reading being mentioned and the next activity indicated. Some pupils did however offer helpful comments on their reading. Lucy's diary for Thursday reads:

    4.00pm   I read two chapters of a book.
    4.20pm   I began to watch television.
and for Friday:
    6.20pm   Read a book.
    6.35pm   Stopped reading.

Then there was Zoe who went to bed at 8.30pm on the Monday and wrote:

    I read *Stig of the Dump* for atsackly [sic] half an hour an [sic] then went to sleep.

Rupa mention reading 'about three or four pages', but Roger's comment was much less helpful. He just put that he 'read for a little while'.

Using rough estimates of the length of time pupils at School 2 spent reading, other than in bed when specific evidence was not available, it can be suggested that few pupils spent more than half an hour in this activity, with many only reading for five minutes at a time. The average time spent seemed to be between ten and twenty minutes. One of the few exceptions to this generalisation was Michael, an avid reader, whose other after school activities seemed to take second place to reading.

DIARY NUMBER 6

Michael:- an avid reader of books.

Brothers/sisters:- one brother.

Likes best:- reading while drinking a very cool glass of un-fizzy lemonade.

Membership of organisations:- Youth Club.

Music lessons/practice:- nothing mentioned.

Sport:- nothing mentioned.

. . . . .

Michael arrived home from school somewhere between 4.10pm and 4.30pm. He watched some television selecting only those programmes he wanted to watch. He was critical too. On Monday he wrote:

4.35pm   Read a book. T.V. is boring on Monday.

The rest of his time was spent reading with occasional breaks to talk with his father, listen to the radio or a tape, and to go to Youth Club on a Monday. He even mentioned reading a book written by himself — *The spell book* by Michael — (my own origination)'! Michael's after school activities can best be illustrated by including some entries he made in his diary.

Wednesday   (arrived home from school at 4.10pm)
    4.25pm   Had juice and biscuits.
    4.40pm   Read some more of a book.
    6.40pm   Rushed down to watch *Dr Who — Resurrection of the Daleks.*
(Had a meal at 7.45 pm)
    8.15pm   Read even more of that book.
    8.30pm   Still reading book.
    9.10pm   Washed myself.
(Got ready for bed at 9.15pm)
    9.20pm   Listened to radio.
    9.30pm   Listened to part of a tape.
    9.40pm   Turned over tape.
(Went to bed at 9.45pm and went straight to sleep)

Friday   (arrived home from school at 4.30pm)
    4.40pm   Had juice and biscuits.
    4.50pm   Started watching T.V.
    5.30pm   Started reading a book.
(Had a meal at 7.20pm)
    8.05pm   Still reading.
    8.30pm   Still reading.
(Got ready for bed at 9.00pm)
    9.20pm   Picked up my book again.
    9.30pm   Told to get into bed.
    9.30pm   Sneaked a few more minutes.
(Went to bed at 9.40pm and went straight to sleep

Reading:- *The Cartoonist* (Betsy Byars)
    Arthur and the Bellybutton Diamond (Alan Coren)
    Arthur and the Great Detective (Alan Coren)
    Arthur v. the Rest (Alan Coren)
    Ordinary Jack (Helen Cresswell)
    Dragonfall 5 and the Haunted World (Brian Earnshaw)
    Jennifer, Hecate, Macbeth and me (Elaine L. Konigsburg)
    The Magic Grandfather (Jay Williams)
    Up With Skool! (Christopher Wright)
    Flash Gordon Annual 1981.
    The Micro User

E.6 Conclusion

The findings of this project can be summarized as follows:

1. In addition to watching television these 9 – 11 year olds engaged in a wide variety of after school activities both in, outside of and away from the home.

2. The choice of activities varied throughout the evening and between the different areas of Fleetville.

3. Reading was a popular activity both after school and at the weekend, and 32 pupils listed it amongst the things that they liked best.

4. There was some evidence to suggest that television viewing, board games, computers, art and craft, organised activities, pets and homework had stimulated reading. Reading in turn had probably given inspiration to drawing and imaginative role play games.

5. There was no evidence to suggest that a lot of time spent at organised activities reduced the amount of time spent reading. Motivation seemed to be of more importance here.

6. There was no evidence to suggest that the absence of a television at home increased the amount of reading undertaken by the pupils. There was however evidence to suggest that parents had more time or opportunity to encourage and promote the pleasures of reading.

7. The majority of book titles mentioned in the diaries were fiction, and the girls listed more book titles and read more often than the boys. However almost twice as many boys as girls mentioned non-fiction titles.

8. There was very little evidence in the diaries to suggest that the amount of book reading was positively associated with smallness of family size.

9. More than twice as many boys than girls were reading comics, and most of the pupils reading comics were also reading books.

10. Differing attitudes towards library provision in each of the three schools, the proximity of Fleetville library, after school activities, peer group pressure and parental influence may account for the observed differences in the patterns of voluntary reading between pupils attending each of the three schools.

11. It is estimated that the average length of time that a pupil spent reading on any one occasion was between 10 and 20 minutes. The most popular time and place to read was in bed at night.

Appendices

APPENDIX 1   Interview schedules

A   Basis of *Interview Schedule* for semi-structured interview of children who have attended the Family Reading Group to assess attitude to books and libraries.

PART I

1.   Had you ever been to Fleetville Library before you came to the Family Reading Group?

2.   IF YES, what kind of things did you go there for?
   prompt – books
            stories
            holiday activities
            class visit
            meet friends

3.   IF No – Can you remember the reason why you didn't go to the library?

4.   Do you borrow books from St Albans Central or any other libraries?

5.   What is the title of the book you are reading at the moment?

6.   Where did you get it from?
   prompt – library
            bought
            friend
            Family Reading Group

7.   Imagine someone has landed from another planet in your school playground and wants to know all about St Albans, and you have told them about all the different sorts of places in the town – what would you tell them about the library? And how would you describe librarians?
   What other sorts of things can you do in a library?
   What changes would you make to the library?
   What would you put in it?

PART II

1.   Who did you come to the Family Reading Group with?

2.   Whose idea was it to come to the meeting?

3.   Tell me about the part of the meeting which you enjoyed most of all.

4.   Did you bring any books home from the Family Reading Group for anyone else?

5.   What did your friends at school think of the Family Reading Group?

B   Basis of interview questionnaire for semi-structured interview of parents of children who have attended the Family Reading Group to assess attitude to books and libraries.

PART I

1.   Do you use the public library at all at the moment?
       YES – Fleetville
             St Albans Central
             Cunningham
             Marshalswick
             Trailer

       NO – Is there any special reason why you don't use the library?

2.   What kind of things do you find it useful for?
       prompt – records
             papers
             reference
             photocopying
             meeting friends
             societies
             storytimes

3.   Have you got a book on loan from the public library at the moment?

4.   Do you remember going to the library when you were young?
       prompt – where?
             who with?
             how often?

5.   Are there any books which you remember enjoying (or disliking) when you were young?

6.   Do you remember where they came from, or anything else about reading them?
       prompt – with family
             friends
             school
             ill
             holiday

7.   Can you tell me what you have been reading in the last week?
         prompt – books
                   papers
                   magazines

8.   What was the title of the last book you remember reading?

9.   Where did you get it from?
         prompt – library
                   bought
                   friend

10.   Do you ever give books to anyone else for presents?

PART II

1.   What made you come to the Family Reading Group?

2.   What did you think of the meeting?

3.   Which parts do you think the children enjoyed most?

4.   Which parts did you enjoy most?

5.   Do you think you will be coming to meetings in the future?

6.   Did you borrow any books from the Family Reading Group for
         yourself?
         other members of family?
         anyone else?

7.   Do you still read aloud to your children?

Final questionnaire for children who attended first Family Reading Group meeting.

1.   Have you any books on loan at the moment from the library?

2.   Have you joined a library since coming to the Family Reading Group?

3.   What is the title of the book you are reading at the moment?

4.   Where did you get it from?

5.   Who did you come to the last Family Reading Group meeting with?

6.   Did you bring any books home for anyone else in the family?

7. Why did you stop coming?

8. Have you or any of your friends started coming to the group because you recommended it to them?

9. Have you made any new friends at the meetings?

10. How would you describe the group to someone else?

11. Have you found anything out about libraries that you didn't know before?

12. Have you discovered any new kinds of books or authors?

13. On average you have read books a month from Family Reading Group. Is this more or less than usual?

Final questionnaire of parents who attended first Family Reading Group meeting.

1. Have you a book on loan from the public library at the moment?

2. Which was the last Family Reading Group meeting you came to?

3. Why did you stop coming?

4. Can you think of any way in which we could involve parents more? (or change meeting?)

5. Have any of your friends started coming to the group because you recommended it to them?

6. Have you joined a public library since coming to the meeting?

7. Did you borrow any books from the Family Reading Group for yourself – anyone else?

8. Have you looked at any of the children's books they have brought home – or read them with them?

9. Has your opinion on children's books altered at all since coming to Family Reading Group?

10 Have you noticed any difference in child's attitude to reading?

Basis of interview schedule for discussion at 'impact' interviews with children.

1. When you get home from the meeting what do you do with your books?

2. When did you start reading them?

3. When you chose these books which appeared to be the most interesting, next, etc.?

4. How did you feel when you were reading this book? (Happy, sad, puzzled, etc.?)

5. What do you think the author meant you to feel?

6. Did the book make you think about anything in particular? What?

7. Did it make you want to go off and do anything?

8. What was your favourite part of the book? Why?

9. Were there any parts of the book you skimmed over because they were boring?

10. Were there any parts of the book which you really didn't like? Why?

11. Have you read any other books which were like this one, by the same author?

12. Are there any books which you started reading but didn't finish?

13. Which bit were you up to when you stopped?

14. Why didn't you want to finish it?

15. Are there any books which you didn't read at all? Why?

16. Are there any books which you would like to read again? Which? Why?

17. Are there any books which you have read before?

18. Which of these books would you recommend to your friends?

19. Did anyone else in your family read any of the books?

20. Did you take any of the books to school?

21. Have you been reading anything else this week? Where did it come from?

Starting a Family Reading Group – Checklist

In your area, where would it be most appropriate to set up a Family Reading Group:
- in the library (open day or closed day)
- in the primary school
- in the secondary school
- somewhere else

What age group are you aiming to encourage (with parents)

Why this age (note previous links you may build on
or lost opportunities
or new developments
which make you feel that this group would be
    a) most responsive
    b) most in need of stimulus)

Would you intend to hold meetings
    – monthly (longterm)
    – weekly of fortnightly short term (i.e. during one school term)
    – other

What time of day for meetings (approx. length 1 hour + hour prep/clearing)
    – last hour of school day
    – immediately after school
    – evening

Which schools, book groups, youth groups etc. will you involve
    Bookstock – will you buy new stock – hardback/paperback
                  – will you use some of library or school's own stock
                  – will you need additional funding

Promotion – poster
            – leaflets
            – visit to nearby Heads
            – mention in school newsletter
            – class visit to nearby schools
            – mention at PTA talk or other

Who will you need to help at meetings
    – branch staff
    – SLS staff
    – parents

Where will you store books between meetings

Who will make coffee/orange

4 o'clock

5 o'clock

6 o'clock

My name is ....

My brothers and sisters are

called ....

....

Down the garden, over the wall

This is what I like best of all

....

....

....

7 o'clock

8 o'clock

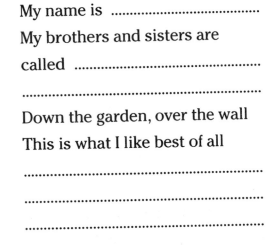

9 o'clock

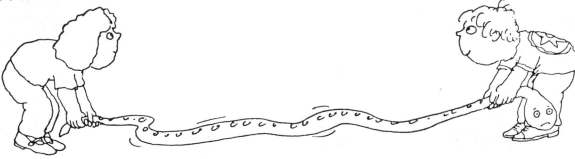

This is the time that I came home from school ......

These are some things that I did then

 1.

 2.

 3.

This is the time that I have my meal ....

These are some things that I did after that

1.

 2.

3.

157

This is the time I got ready for bed ....

These are some things that I did after that

 1.

 2.

 3.

This is the time I went to bed ....

This is what I did in bed

This is what I read today

This is what I watched on T.V. today

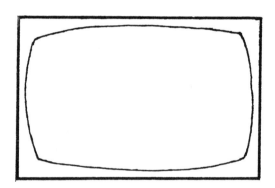
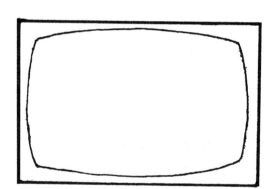

These are some games I played today

Notes on My After School Diary (given to Heads of Schools)

As prelude to a study of the part which reading plays in the leisure time activities of 9-11 year old children, the After School Diary aims to give a general survey of how they spend their time between arriving home from school and going to bed at night.

When the child is given the diary, please ask him to complete the first page, and explain that first thing each morning in school he can complete the diary for the night before. More eager children may like to keep notes in the evening of what they are doing ready to fill the diary in the next morning.

In the diary, children are asked to complete the approximate time they arrived home from school, ate their evening meal, got ready for bed and went to bed. There is space to enter three activities in each period of time – i.e. between mealtime and bedtime. This is to discourage a block entry of 'played games' or 'watched TV' for whole periods of time up to two or three hours, although, of course, there will be occasions when they will only be able to enter one activity. Full entries are to be encouraged, and there are spaces provided for children to list anything which they read each day – books, comics, newspapers, any TV programmes watched and games played – which could include 'football', 'snakes and ladders' and imaginative games.

The clock faces are provided so that we can gauge the percentage of time spent on each activity. It is appreciated that all children will not have enough consciousness of time, or telling the time, to fill in the clock face to show the time at which the activity took place. However, it would be most helpful if those children who can will fill in the clock faces with the time at which they started each activity (approximately!).

There is one sheet to be filled in with major events at the weekend, books read, TV programmes viewed and games played, but no timing is included here.

I would like to thank teachers and children for their cooperation. I hope that the children will enjoy filling in the diaries and colouring in the pictures. Please do not hesitate to contact me at work (West Herts Schools Library Service – Watford 27937) or at home – Hemel Hempstead 58722.

Dina Thorpe

Appendix 3

List of Family Reading Group Bookstock in order of Popularity

Pop Order	Title	Author	Publisher	Date of Pubn
21	Witch's Daughter	BAWDEN, Nina	Gollancz	1966
21	What Difference Does It Make Danny?	YOUNG, Helen	Armada Books	1983
21	Absolute Zero	CRESSWELL, Helen	Faber	1978
20	Marmalade Atkins in Space	DAVIES, Andrew	Thames-Methuen	1982
19	Bogwoppit	WILLIAMS, Ursula Moray	H. Hamilton	1978
19	The Cartoonist	BYARS, Betsy	Bodley Head	1978
19	Grinny	FISK, Nicholas	Heinemann	1973
19	Pinballs-1	BYARS, Betsy	Bodley Head	1977
19	The House that Sailed Away	HUTCHINS, Pat	Armada Books	1978
18	Animal Ghosts	(ed) DAVIS, Richard	Dragon Books	1982
18	Witches	DAHL, Roald	Cape	1983
18	Great Piratical Rumbistincation	MAHY, Margaret	Dent	1978
18	Dragons Live Forever	SWINDELLS, Robert	Hodder	1978
18	My Best Fiend	LAVELLE, Sheila	Armada Books	1980
18	TV Kid	BYARS, Betsy	Bodley Head	1976
17	Necklace of Raindrops	AIKEN, Joan	Cape	1968
16	School Trip	WILSON, Jacqueline	H. Hamilton	1984
16	Little Prince	SAINT-EXUPERY, Antoine de	Heinemann	1945
16	Pywacket and Son	WEIR, Rosemary	Abelard-Schuman	1980
16	Revolt at Ratcliffe's Rags	CROSS, Gillian	O.U.P.	1980
16	The Bongleweed	CRESSWELL, Helen	Faber	1973
16	Ogre Downstairs	WYNNE JONES, Diana	Macmillan	1974
15	Benjamin and Tulip	WELLS, Rosemary	Kestrel Books	1977
15	Clever Polly and the Stupid Wolf	STORR, Catherine	Faber	1979
15	The Turbulent Term of Tyke Tiler	KEMP, Gene	Faber	1977
14	Son of a Gun	AHLBERG, Allan and AHLBERG, Janet	Heinemann	1979
14	The great Smile Robbery	McGOUGH, Roger	Kestrel Books	1982
14	Supergran is Magic	WILSON, Forrest	Penguin	1983
14	Dog Days and Cat Naps	KEMP, Gene	Faber	1980
14	Sylvia Game	ALCOCK, Vivian	Armada Books	1984
13	The Multiplying Glass	PHILLIPS, Ann	O.U.P.	1981
13	Stig of the Dump	KING, Clive	Kestrel Books	1980
13	Mr Browser and the Comet Crisis	CURTIS, Philip	Andersen, P.	1981
13	Complete Father Christmas	BRIGGS, Raymond	H. Hamilton	1978
13	Ramona The Brave	CLEARY, Beverley	H. Hamilton	1975
13	Ghosts and Shadows	EDWARDS, Dorothy	Armada Books	1981
13	Just William	CROMPTON, Richmal	Macmillan	1983
13	King of the Copper Mountain	BIEGEL, Paul	Dent	1968
13	Spell Me a Witch	WILLARD, Barbara	H. Hamilton	1979
13	McBroom and the Great Race	FLEISCHMAN, Sid	Chatto	1981
13	Follow that Bus	HUTCHINS, Pat	Armada Books	1979
13	Dragon of Og	GODDEN, Rumer	Macmillan	1981
13	Flossie Teacake's Fur Coat	DAVIES, Hunter	Armada Books	1984
12	Bottersnikes and Gumbles	WAKEFIELD, Sydney	Pan Books	1984
12	Rectory Mice	MACBETH, George	Hutchinson	1982
12	Magic Doll and Other Stories	(Ed) LEWIS, Naomi	Magnet Books	1983
12	It's Too Frightening for Me	HUGHES, Shirley	Penguin	1980
12	Tottie	GODDEN, Rumer	Penguin	1983
12	Arthur and the Belly-button Diamond	COREN, Alan	Penguin	1981

12	*Ghosts and Hauntings*	(Ed) CHAMBERS, Aidan	Kestrel Books	1980
12	*Adventures of the ABC Mob*	WILSON, Forrest	Pepper P.	1983
12	*Square Bear*	WILLSON, Robina Beckles	H. Hamilton	1983
12	*Marvello Simpson and the Lost Uncle*	SULLIVAN, Mary	Evans Bros.	1980
12	*Ballet Shoes*	STREATFIELD, Noel	Dent	1977
12	*The Remarkable Feat of King Caboodle*	RICE, Hugo	Black	1978
12	*Runaway*	CROSS, Gillian	Methuen Chi Books	1979
12	*Fungus the Bogeyman*	BRIGGS, Raymond	H. Hamilton	1977
12	*Little Vampire Moves In*	BODENBURG, Angela Sommer	Anderson, P.	1982
12	*Olga de Polga*	BOND, Michael	Longman	1975
11	*Encyclopaedia Brown*	SOBOL, Donald J.	Angus + R	1982
11	*Ghost and Bertie Boggin*	SEFTON, Catherine	Faber	1980
11	*Littlenose the Marksman*	EARNSHAW, Brian		
11	*Horse*	GARDAM, June	Julia Macrae Books	1982
11	*Mr Browser and the Brain Sharpeners*	CURTIS, Philip	Andersen, P.	1979
11	*Oggy at Home*	LAWRENCE, Anne	Pan	
11	*The Adventures of Blunter Button*	ARKLE, Phyllis	Hodder	1980
11	*Arabella's Raven*	AIKEN, John	Hodder	1983
11	*The Hen Who Wouldn't Give Up*	TOMLINSON, Jill	Magnet Books	1979
11	*Ice Warrior and Other Stories*	CHAMBERS, Robin	Penguin	1978
11	*Two Village Dinosaurs*	ARKLE, Phyllis	Penguin	1981
10	*Emil & the Detectives*	KASTNER, Erich	Cape	1959
10	*Devil's Story Book*	BABBITT, Natalie	Carousel Books	1981
10	*Homeward Bounders*	WYNNE JONES, Diana	Magnet Books	1984
10	*Strangers at Follyfoot*	DICKENS, Monica		
10	*Prince of the Godborn*	HARRIS, Geraldine	Allen & Unwin	1983
10	*Farthest Away Mountain*	BANKS, Lynne Reid	Abelard-Schuman	1976
10	*Mary Poppins in Cherry Tree Lane*	TRAVERS, Mary	Collins	1982
10	*No Way of Telling*	SMITH, Emma	Bodley Head	1972
10	*Speckled Panic*	TOWNSON, Hazel	Andersen, P.	1982
10	*The Day They Stole The F.A. Cup*	SMITH, Bryan	Blackie	1982
10	*Albeson and the Germans*	NEEDLE, Jan	Armada Books	1981
10	*The Terrible Kidnapping of Cyril Bonhamy*	GATHORNE-HARDY, Jonathon	Evans Bros	1978
10	*Agaton Sax and the Scotland Yard Mystery*	FRANZEN, Nils Olof	Deutsch	1969
10	*Dragonfall 5 and the Empty Planet*	EARNSHAW, Brian	Methuen Chi Books	1973
10	*Flames in the Forest*	BOND, Ruskin	Julia Macrae Books	1981
10	*Silver Chair*	LEWIS, C. S.	Armada Books	1981
10	*On the Run*	BAWDEN, Nina	Gollancz	1964
10	*The Machine Gunners*	WESTALL, Robert	Macmillan	1975
10	*Lost Merbaby*	BAKER, Margaret	Penguin	1980
10	*Grandma's Own Zoo*	ARKLE, Phyllis	Hodder	1979
10	*Crimson Oak*	ALMEDINGEN, E. M.	Methuen Chi Books	1981
10	*Thirteen Clocks*	THURBER, James	H. Hamilton	1966
10	*Mrs Frisby and the Rats of Nimh*	O'BRIEN, Robert	Gollancz	1972
10	*Ice Palace*	SWINDELLS, Robert	Armada	1980
10	*The Bee Rustlers*	NEEDLE, Jan	Magnet Books	1983
10	*The Red Balloon*	LAMORISSE, Albert	Allen & Unwin	1980
10	*Just So Stories*	KIPLING, Rudyard	Anchorage, P. U.S.	1976
10	*Deadline for Mchurk*	HILDICK, E. W.		
10	*Great Rabbit Robbery*	HILDICK, W. W.		
10	*Evil Eye*	FISK, Nicholas	Hodder	1982
10	*Catfang*	FISK, Nicholas	Hodder	1981
10	*Magic Finger*	DAHL, Roald	Allen & Unwin	1978
10	*Stories for Ten's & Over*	(Ed) CORRIN, Sarah & CORRIN, Steven	Faber	1976

10	Peppermint Pig	BAWDEN, Nina	Longman	1978
10	Village Dinosaur	ARKLE, Phyllis	Brockhampton	1968
9	Ghosts and Bogles	STARKEY, D.	Bodley Head	1972
9	Spooks and Spectres			
9	The Adventures of Johnny Briggs	EADINGTON, John	BBC	1979
9	Ramona and Her Mother	CLEARY. Beverley	H. Hamilton	1979
9	London Snow	THEROUX, Paul	H. Hamilton	1980
9	Willie the Squowze	ALLAN, Ted	Cape	1977
9	The Haunting of Cassie Palmer	ALCOCK, Vivian	Armada Books	1982
9	Magician's Nephew	LEWIS, C. S.	Armada Books	1980
9	Raging Robots & Unruly Uncles	MAHY, Margaret	Dent	1981
9	Fatty Puffs and Thinifers	MAUROIS, André	Penguin	1972
9	The Battle of Bubble & Squeak	PEARCE, Philippa	Penguin	1980
8	Stitch in Time	LIVELY, Penelope	Penguin	1986
8	World Eater	SWINDELLS, Robert	Hodder	1983
8	Cat and Mouse Story	ROSEN, Michael and RUSHTON, William	Deutsch	1982
8	The First Family on the Moon	WALTERS, Hugh	Abelard-Schuman	1979
8	Railway Computer	WILLS, Jean	H. Hamilton	1983
8	Johnny Goodlooks	TULLY, John	Methuen	1977
8	On Stage Please	TENNANT, Veronica	Warne	1979
8	War of the Wizards	STOREY, Margaret	Faber	1976
8	The Spy and the Diabolical Plot	SAYER, Philip Freeman	Evans	1979
8	Hurricane	SALKEY, Andrew	O.U.P.	1979
8	Earthquake	SALKEY, Andrew	O.U.P.	1980
8	Tales from Aesop		Julia Macrae Books	1981
8	Biddy's Talking Pineapple	HOLIDAY, Jane	Hodder	1980
8	Dragonfall 5 and the Haunted World	EARNSHAW, Brian	Methuen	1979
8	Starring Sally J. Friedman as Herself	BLUME, Judy	Pan	1984
8	The Robber Hopsika	PIEGEL, Paul	Dent	1978
8	Tales of Polly and the Hungry Wolf	STORR, Catherine	Faber	1980
8	To the Wild Sky	SOUTHALL, Ivan	Angus & Robertson	1967
8	Star Kaats and the Planet People	NORTON, Andre and MADLEY, Dorothy	Hodder	1981
8	Nurse Matilda	BRAND, Christiana	Hodder	1973
8	Mystery of the Maya	MONTGOMERY, R.A.	Bantam	1982
8	Short Voyage of the Albert Ross	MARK, Jan		
8	Dracula: Bedtime Story Book	AMBRUS, Victor	O.U.P.	1981
8	Blackbeard the Pirate	AMBRUS, Victor	O.U.P.	1982
8	The HOBBIT	TOLKEIN, J. R. R.	Allen & Unwin	1970
8	House of Danger	MONTGOMERY, R. A.	Bantam	1983
8	Please Mrs Butler	AHLBERG, Allan	Kestrel	1983
8	Carrie's War	BAWDEN, Nina	Gollancz	1973
8	Catseye	NORTON, Andre	Gollancz	1962
8	Frantic Phantom	HUNTER, Norman	Puffin	1976
8	Space Hostages	FISK, Nicholas	Kestrel	1984
8	The Robbers	BAWDEN, Nina	Gollancz	1979
8	Dragonfall 5 and the Space Cowboys	EARNSHAW, Brian	Methuen	1972
8	William IV	CROMPTON, Richmal	Macmillan	1983
8	William Again	CROMPTON, Richmal	Macmillan	1983
8	Dr Who and the Ice Warriors	HAYLES	Target	1976
8	Ordinary Jack	CRESSWELL, Helen	Faber	1977
8	Prince Caspian	LEWIS, C. S.	Collins	1974
7	Thunder and Lightenings	MARK, Jan	Kestrel	1976
7	Outside Over There	SENDAK, Maurice	Bodley Head	1981
7	Shane McKeller and the Treasure Hunt	BURCH, T. R.	Heinemann	1979

7	*The You-Two*	URE, Jean	Hutchinson	1984
7	*The Last Battle*	LEWIS, C. S.	Bodley Head	1956
7	*The Horse and His Boy*	LEWIS, C. S.	Collins	1974
7	*Charmed Life*	WYNNE JONES, Diana	Macmillan	1977
7	*Lassie Come Home*	KNIGHT, Eric	Penguin	1981
7	*Flamers*	FISK, Nicholas		
7	*My Favourite Animal Stories*	DURRELL, Gerald	Beaver Books	1976
7	*Otherwise Known as Sheila the Great*	BLUME, Judy	Bodley Head	1979
7	*Goodnight Mr Tom*	MALURIAN, Michelle	Kestrel	1981
7	*Arthur and the Great Detective*	COREN, Alan	Puffin	1981
7	*The Grey Dancer*	FELL, Alison	Collins	1981
7	*Bagthorpe's Unlimited*	CRESSWELL, Helen	Faber	1978
6	*Conrad's War*	DAVIES, Andrew	Hippo	1980
6	*Supergran Rules OK*	WILSON, Forrest	Kestrel	1983
6	Fireweed	PATON WALSH, Jill	Penguin	1972
6	*Worzel Gummidge*	TODD, Barbara Euphraim	Penguin	1969
6	*Gemma*	STREATFIELD, Noel	Collins, Armada	1968
6	*Winnie the Pooh*	MILNE, A. A.	Methuen	1926
6	*The Silver Sword*	SERRAILIER, Ian	Cape	1956
6	*Minnow on the Say*	PEARCE, Philippa	O.U.P.	1974
6	*The Six Bullerby Children*	LINDGREN, Astrid	Magnet	1980
6	*The Voyage of the Dawn Treader*	LEWIS, C. S.	Collins	1974
6	*Dr Who – Time-Flight*	GRIMWADE, Leon	Target	1983
6	*Black Jack*	GARFIELD, Leon	Kestrel	1975
6	*Grimble*	FREUD, Clement	Penguin	1974
6	*Sunburst*	FISK, Nicholas	Hodder	1980
6	*Dragonfall 5 and the Hijackers*	EARNSHAW, Brian	Methuen	1975
6	*Stories for 9 year olds*	(Ed) CORRIN, Sara and Steven	Faber	1979
6	*Greyfriars Bobby*	ATKINSON, Eleanor	Penguin	1980
6	*Little Mookra*			
6	*Voyage into Danger*	JEFFRIES, Roderic	Hamlyn	1983
6	*Gowie Corby Plays Chicken*	KEMP, Gene	Faber	1979
6	*Day of the Starwind*	HILL, Douglas	Gollancz	1980
6	*The Abominable Snowman*	MONTGOMERY, R. A.	Bantam	1983
6	*The Indian in the Cupboard*	BANKS, Lynne Reid	Dent	1980
6	*Wizard of Boland*	B.B.	Kaye & Ward	1969
6	*Jennifer Hecate Macbeth and Me*	KONIGSBURG, E.		
5	*All My Men*	ASHLEY, Bernard	O.U.P.	1977
5	*Henry and Beezus*	CLEARY, Beverley	H. Hamilton	1980
5	*Shadow Guests*	AIKEN, Joan	Cape	1980
5	*The 9 Lives of Island Mackenzie*	WILLIAMS, Ursula Moray	Transworld	1980
5	*The Strange Affair of Adelaide Harris*	GARFIELD, Leon	Penguin	1974
5	*Charlie and the Great Glass Elevator*	DAHL, Roald	Allen & Unwin	1973
5	*The Wolves of Willoughby Chase*	AIKEN,Joan	Cape	1962
5	*Tommy Mac*	BARRY, Margaret Stuart	Kestrel	1977
5	*The Vanishment of Thomas Tull*	AHLBERG, Allan and AHLBERG, Janet	Black	1977
5	*Born Free*	ADAMSON, Joy	Chancellor P.	1986
5	*Astercote*	LIVELY, Penelope	Heinemann	1970
4	*Tales from the Panchantantra*	CLARK, L.		
4	*The Little Bookroom*	FARJEON, Eleanor	O.U.P.	1979
4	*Tigers Forever*	BOND, Ruskin	Julia Macrae Books	1983
4	*Stephen amd the Shaggy Dog*	BERESFORD, Elisabeth	Methuen	1976
4	*On the Banks of Plum Creek*	WILDER, Laura Ingalls	Penguin	1969
4	*The Little House on the Prairie*	WILDER, Laura Ingalls	Penguin	1969
4	*Danny Fox*	THOMSON, David	Penguin	1971
4	*The Voyage of the QV66*	LIVELY, Penelope	Heinemann	1978

4	*The Mouse and His Child*	HOBAN, Russell	Faber	1969
4	*The Ghost in the Water*	CHEETHAM, Edmund	Puffin	1982
4	*The Wizard of Earthsea*	LEGUIN, Ursula	Gollancz	1971
4	*Black Stallion*	FARLEY, William	Hodder	1975
4	*Break in the Sun*	ASHLEY, Bernard	O.U.P.	1980
4	*John Diamond*	GARFIELD, Leon	Puffin	1981
4	*Under the Autumn Garden*	MARK, Jan	Kestrel	1977
4	*Poachers Son*	ANDERSON, Rachel	O.U.P.	1982
4	*World Around the Corner*	GEE, Maurice	O.U.P.	1981
4	*Amazing Mr Blunden*	BARBER, Antonia	Penguin	1972
4	*Charlie and the Chocolate Factory*	DAHL, Roald	Allen & Unwin	1967
4	*Freaky Friday*	RODGERS, Mary	Puffin	1976
4	*Hi There Supermouse*	URE, Jean	Hutchinson	1983
4	*The Bugbear*	STORR, Catherine	Hamlyn	1981
4	*The Fiend Next Door*	LAVELLE, Sheila	H. Hamilton	1982
4	*The Borrowers*	NORTON, Mary	Dent	1975
4	*The Demon Headmaster*	CROSS, Gillian	O.U.P.	1982
4	*The White Mountain*	CHRISTOPHER, John	Puffin	1984
3	*The Witch of Candlewick*	ELLIOTT, Margaret		
3	*More William*	CROMPTON, Richmal	Macmillan	1983
3	*The Eyes of the Amaryllis*	BABBITT, Natalie		
2	*Song of Pentecost*	CORBETT, William	Methuen	1982
2	*Vandal*	SCHLEE, Ann	Magnet	1983
2	*Tod's Owl*	POTTS, Richard	Hodder	1982
2	*City of Gold and Lead*	CHRISTOPHER, John	Puffin	1984
2	*Treehorn's Treasure*	HEIDE, Florence Parry	Kestrel	1983
2	*Traveller in Time*	UTTLEY, Alison	Faber	1939
2	*Ask Oliver*	DICKS, T. R.	Picadilly Press	1984
2	*Sea Green Magic*	HOBAN, Russell		
2	*Time of the Ghost*	WYNNE JONES, Diana	Macmillan	1981
2	*Pool of Fire*	CHRISTOPHER, John	Puffin	1984
2	*Hollow Land*	GARDAM, Jane	Julia Macrae Books	1981
2	*The Mercury Cup*	BURCH, T. R.	Granada	1983
2	*Handles*	MARK, Jan	Kestrel	1983
2	*Julie of the Wolves*	GEORGE, Jean	Penguin	1976
2	*Hot Dog and other poems*	WRIGHT, Kit	Penguin	1982
2	*Tom Fobbles Day*	GARNER, Alan	Collins	1977
2	*Conrad*	NOSTLINGER, Christine	Andersen, P.	1976
2	*Boris the Tomato*			
2	*Genie on the Loose*	LEESON, Robert	H. Hamilton	1984
2	*Box of Delights*	MASEFIELD, John	Heinemann	1935
2	*Devil's Storybook*	BABBIT, Natalie	Transworld	1981

Bibliographic details are incomplete for some entries as stock is now dispersed, however this is a list of the basic stock titles.

APPENDIX 4   Example of data sheet

	HOME		MEAL		READY FOR BED		BED	
MON								
TUES								
WED								
THURS								
FRI								

WEEKEND

	HOME		MEAL		READY FOR BED		BED	
MON								
TUES								
WED								
THURS								
FRI								

166

	READING	T.V.	ORGANISATIONS	GAMES
MON				
TUES				
WED				
THURS				
FRI				
WEEKEND				

	READING	T.V.	ORGANISATIONS	GAMES
MON				
TUES				
WED				
THURS				
FRI				

BROTHERS/SISTERS:-   LIKES BEST:-

APPENDIX 5   After school activities mentioned in Diaries

1. On getting home from school but before having a meal.

Activity	Number of Pupils
Watched television	182
Played with friend(s)	84
Read	84
Went to the shop(s)	51
Homework	46
Computer/electronic/video games	45
Helped mother	41
Colouring/painting/drawing/craft	40
Practised musical instrument(s)/band practice	39
Games (board, card, puzzles)	35
Sporting activities	34
Pets (cleaning, feeding, walking, etc).	29
Played with brother/sister	27
Listened to tapes/tape recorded/played records	25
Played outside/ball/hopscotch/swings/roller skating	22
Imaginative role play games	15
Tidied bedroom	15
Darts/snooker/table tennis	14
Music lesson(s)	14
Lego/Meccano	13
Went on bike	11
A-Team/Action Force/He-man/Star Wars figures	11
Played with dolls/dolls house	10
Talked to mother/father	10
Visited the library	9
Knitting/sewing/tapestry/weaving	8
Played with cars/Scalextric	8
Listened to radio	7
Work for Cubs/Brownies/Guides	7
School/Tutor (e.g. Italian school, reading lessons etc.)	5
Visited Mosque/Islamic Centre	5
Dancing lessons	4
Hide and seek	3
Went to show/party	3
Looked after younger children	2
Looked at slides/took photographs	2
Wrote letter/phoned friend	2
Choir practice	1
Helped Dad	1
Train spotting	1

After School Activities Mentioned in the Diaries

2. After having a meal but before getting ready for bed.

Activity	Number of Pupils
Watched television	177
Attended meeting(s) of an organisation	90
Read	83
Helped mother/cooking	60
Games (board, card, puzzles, wordsearch, etc.)	58
Colouring/painting/drawing/craft	49
Homework	48
Computer/electronic/video games	45
Practised musical instrument(s)/band practice	41
Played with friend(s)	39
Disco at school (School 3 only)	34
Played with brother/sister	31
Sporting activities	27
Listened to tapes/tape recorded/played records	26
Darts/snooker/table tennis	23
Pets (cleaning, feeding, walking etc).	23
Tidied bedroom	18
Lego/Meccano	17
Music lesson(s)	12
A-Team/Action Force/He-man/Star Wars figures	11
Imaginative role play games	11
Knitting/sewing/tapestry/weaving	11
Played with cars/Scalextric	11
Went to shop(s)	11
Listened to radio	10
Played with dolls	10
Playing skipping/ball/hopscotch/marbles	9
Got brother/sister ready for bed	7
Helped father	6
Talked to mother/father	6
Went to see relative	6
Wrote letter/phoned friend	6
Hide and seek	5
Dancing lesson(s)	4
Work for Brownies/Cubs/Guides	4
Wrote limerick/poem/story	4
Hospital visiting	3
Went out on bike	3
Church/religious meeting	2
Choir practice	2
Dungeons and dragons	2
Talked to someone on C.B.	2
Domino rally with paperbacks	1
Made a light with battery, bulb and wires	1
Train spotting	1
Tutor class	1
Typing	1
Visited the library	1

After School Activities Mentioned in the Diaries

3. After getting ready for bed.

Activity	Number of Pupils
Watched television	122
Read	94
Computer/electronic games	27
Games (board, card, puzzles, wordsearch)	26
Homework	25
Colouring/drawing/craft	23
Filled in this/own diary	19
Played tapes/records	18
Pets (feeding, playing with)	16
Played with brother/sister	14
Practised musical instrument(s)	12
Snooker/darts	10
Talked to mother/father	10
Listened to radio	9
Lego	8
Dolls/dolls house	7
Tidied bedroom	6
Knitting/sewing	5
Played with cars/helicopter	5
A-Team/Action Force/He-man/Star Wars figures	4
Danced/did exercises/practised gym	4
Listened to a story	4
Put brother/sister to bed	4
Helped mother	3
Imaginative role play games	3
Looked at night sky through telescope/binoculars	3
Read to younger brother/sister	3
Wrote letter	3
Skipping/French skipping/marbles	3
Looked at stamp collection	2
Copied poem out of book	1
Learnt words for choir	1
Quiz with mother and father	1
Shorthand with babysitter	1
Talked French with mother	1

After School Activities Mentioned in the Diary

4. In bed.

Activity	Number of Pupils
Read	110
Filled in diary/journal (this one/own)	13
Watched television	10
Talked to brother/sister	9
Homework	8
Computer/Electronic games	7
Action Force/Star Wars figures	5
Listened to tapes/played records	5
Listened to radio	4
Played with cars	4
Pets (played with)	3
Colouring/drawing	3
Talked to friend	3
Talked to mother/father	3
Pillow fight	2
Puzzles	2
Crossword	1
Darts	1
Imaginative role play games	1
Looked through 3D viewer	1
Made my carpet	1
Made something for my doll	1
Played cards	1
Talked to teddy	1
Did a wordsearch	1

APPENDIX 6 Weekend activities mentioned in the Diaries

Weekend Activities Mentioned in the Diaries – School 1.

Activity	Number of Pupils
Watched television	36
Read	17
Went to town/shopping	11
Played with friend(s)	5
Swimming	5
Football/Cub football/match	4
Went to visit relative	4
Sunday School	3
Helped at home	2
Played with brother/sister	2
Took dog for a walk	2
Watched a video	2
Went for a walk	2
Went out on bike	2
Went to the club	2
Bengali school	1
Birthday party	1
Cooking	1
Dancing	1
Did an experiment	1
Dolls	1
Drawing	1
Friend stayed	1
Flew a kite	1
Helped in shop	1
Horse riding	1
Mosque	1
Played games	1
Played Dungeons and Dragons	1
Played on swings	1
Roller skating	1
Tidied bedroom	1
Went to a Sunday market	1
Went to London	1
Went to play in the woods	1
Went to reading lessons	1
Went to the lake	1
Went to the park	1

Weekend Activities Mentioned in the Diaries – School 2.

Activity	Number of Pupils
Watched television	71
Read	60
Played with friend(s)	20
Visited relative/relative came	13
Ice skating (organised trip)	11
Out on bike	10
Shopping/went to town	8
Computer	7
Football/Cub football/match	7
Disco/party	6
Went to church	5
Dancing class(es)	4
Craft	3
Judo/judo grading	3
Jumble sale	3
Outing	3
Drawing/painting	2
Electronic games	2
Gardening	2
Hide and seek	2
Pets (playing with/walking etc)	2
Played tennis	2
Rugby	2
Went for a walk	2
Went to the library	2
American football	1
Badminton (for under 11's boys single champs)	1
Cars	1
Chess	1
Choir	1
Cinema	1
Cooking	1
Fishing	1
Gymnastics	1
Homework	1
Imaginative role play	1
Mosque	1
Roller skating	1
Wrote funny poems	1

Weekend Activities Mentioned in the Diaries – School 3.

Activity	Number of Pupils
Watched television	53
Read	36
Went to town/shopping	17
Visited relative/relative came	16
Played with/tea with friend(s)	12
Swimming	
Swimming gala	6
Swam in Herts. Championships	
Birthday outing/party	5
Roller skating	5
Cooking	4
Football/Cub football/match	4
Homework	4
Ballet	3
Computer games/programming	3
Out on bike	3
Went to Crufts	3
Bird watching	2
Electronic/video games	2
Pets (cleaning etc).	2
Played rugby/rugby match	2
Played musical instrument at meeting	2
Boat and submarine game	1
Bonfire in garden	1
Chess	1
Church	1
Cross country race	1
Darts	1
Dolls	1
Helped mother	1
Horse riding	1
Ice skating	1
Judo	1
Karting	1
Lego	1
Made a new friend	1
Made a Valentine's day card	1
Played A-team	1
Played pool	1
Played squash	1
Played schools	1
Played with toy hospital	1
Sewing	1
Sunday School	1
Watched a video	1
Went to extra lessons	1
Went for a walk	1
Went to the swings and slides	1
Worked out a robber's dance to music	1

APPENDIX 7   What the pupils said they liked best of all

What the Pupils Said They Liked Best of All.

School 1

Basketball	(1)
Bengali Books	(1)
Climbing trees	(1)
Collecting key rings	(2)
Collecting things	(2)
Colouring	(1)
Computer games	(2)
Cricket	(1)
Cubs	(2)
Dancing	(3)
Drawing	(1)
Eating	(1)
Football	(11)
Games	(1)
Going out	(1)
Golf	(2)
Helping Mum	(2)
Horseriding	(1)
Listening to the radio	(1)
Little flowers	(1)
Maths	(3)
Music	(2)
Netball	(8)
Playing	(5)
Playing board games	(2)
Playing 'donkeys'	(1)
Reading	(12)
Riding my bike	(3)
Rounders	(2)
Rugby	(3)
Running	(1)
Scouts	(2)
Skipping	(1)
Stamp collecting	(1)
Swimming	(12)
Tennis	(1)
Watching T.V.	(7)
Writing	(3)
Writing to friends	(1)

What the Pupils Said They Liked Best of All.

School 2

Animals	(3)	Making Action Force bases	(1)
Anything to do with fantasy	(1)	in the tree	
Army	(1)	Making models	(1)
Art	(1)	Making music	(1)
Badminton	(1)	Making things	(1)
Beefburgers and chips	(1)	Meccano	(1)
Being small	(1)	Motor bikes	(2)
Bird watching	(2)	Music	(1)
Brownies	(1)	My pets	(1)
Cars	(1)	New year's eve parties	(1)
Chess	(1)	Our neighbours	(3)
Climbing frames	(1)	Painting	(1)
Coin collecting	(1)	Planting flowers	(1)
Computer games	(2)	Playing	(2)
Cooking	(3)	Playing guitar	(1)
Cricket	(1)	Playing piano	(2)
Cubs	(2)	Playing recorder	(2)
Darts	(1)	Playing with my friend(s)	(4)
Discos	(1)	Playing with my nephews	(1)
Discuss	(1)	Playing with my sister	(1)
Drawing	(3)	Poetry	(2)
Drawing road maps and	(1)	Reading	(8)
weather charts		Reading fantasy books	(1)
Dungeons and dragons	(1)	Reading the book *The Victor*	(1)
Eating	(3)	Riding my bike	(9)
Electronic games	(1)	Rock climbing	(1)
Exercise	(1)	Roller skating	(1)
Fishing	(1)	Rugby	(1)
Football	(11)	Running	(2)
Games	(1)	Sewing	(1)
Gardening	(2)	Skateboarding	(1)
Girls Brigade	(1)	Skipping	(2)
Going out	(1)	Snooker	(1)
Going to the cinema	(1)	Stamp collecting	(1)
Going to town with friends	(1)	Star Wars figures	(2)
Gymnastics	(1)	Swimming	(12)
Hide and seek	(1)	Tennis	(1)
History	(2)	Watching T.V.	(8)
Horse riding	(1)	Wildlife	(1)
Ice skating	(2)	World War II	(1)
Judo	(1)	Youth club (because you can	(1)
Lego	(2)	meet your friends)	
Listening to the radio	(3)		
Listening to tapes	(1)		

What the Pupils Said They Liked Best of All.

School 3

A-Team	(2)	Playing guitar	(1)
Acting	(2)	Playing piano	(1)
Animals	(1)	Playing trumpet	(1)
Art	(2)	Reading	(9)
Ballet	(3)	Reading C.S. Lewis books	(1)
Billy Joel Music	(1)	Riding my bike	(4)
Cheese on toast	(1)	Role playing games	(1)
Chess	(4)	Roller skating	(2)
Chocky (on T.V.)	(1)	Rugby	(2)
Collecting dolls	(1)	Scalextric	(1)
Computer games	(4)	Singing	(2)
Cooking	(2)	Snooker	(1)
Cricket	(1)	Sports	(1)
Culture Club	(1)	Star Wars fighting	(1)
Dancing	(3)	Swimming	(11)
Designing fashion pictures	(1)	Tennis	(2)
Disco dancing	(1)	Toys	(1)
Drawing	(2)	Trees	(1)
Fights with the boys	(1)	Video games	(1)
Fishing	(1)	Watching television	(9)
Football	(5)		
Going to clubs	(1)		
Guides	(1)		
Gymnastics	(2)		
Handwork	(1)		
Home evenings	(1)		
Homework	(1)		
Horseriding	(2)		
Housework	(1)		
Jellybeans	(1)		
'Just behind the tree by the shed'	(1)		
Learning my tables	(1)		
Lego	(1)		
Listening to music	(2)		
Making things	(1)		
My best friend	(1)		
My den	(1)		
My pets	(3)		
Playing	(3)		

APPENDIX 8   The book titles mentioned in the Diaries

Book Titles Mentioned in the Diaries — a number in parentheses denotes the number of pupils reading that title where this is more than one.

(a)   Fiction

Author	Title
ADAMS, Piers	*It's magic*
AIKEN, Joan	*Midnight is a place* *A necklace of raindrops* (2)
AINSWORTH, Ruth	*Lucky dip* *Rufty Tufty runs away*
ALCOCK, Vivien	*The stonewalkers*
ALEXANDER, Lloyd	*Taran wanderer*
ALLAN, Mabel Ester	*The Wood Street helpers*
ALLEN, Eric	*The latchkey children*
ALLEN, Judy	*The spring on the mountain*
ALVERSON, Charles	*Time bandits*
ANDERSEN, Hans Christian	*Fairy tales* (4)
ANDREW, Prudence	*Una and Grubstreet*
"BB"	*Little grey men*
BANKS, Lynne Reid	*The farthest away mountain*
BARRIE, J.M.	*Peter Pan*
BATEMAN, Robert	*Race against the U-boats*
BAUM, L. Frank	*Wizard of Oz* (2)
BAWDEN, Nina	*Carrie's war* *Rebel on a rock* *The robbers* *The witch's daughter*
BERESFORD, Elizabeth	*The wandering Wombles*
BLACKMORE, R.D.	*Lorna Doone* (2)
BLUME, Judy	*Tiger eyes*
BLYTON, Enid	*The adventures of the wishing chair* (2) *Brer Rabbit book* *Brer Rabbit's a rascal* *The children of Cherry Tree Farm* *The children of Willow Farm* *Claudine at St. Clare's* *The dog with the long tail and other stories* *Eight o'clock tales* *The enchanted wood* (2) *Famous Five* — title not specified (6) *First term at Malory Towers* (2) *Five are together again* *Five get into a fix* *Five get into trouble* *Five go off in a caravan* *Five go off to camp* *Five go to Billycock Hill* (2)

178

BLYTON, Enid/contd..	*Five go to Mystery Moor*
	Five have a wonderful time
	Five on a hike together (2)
	Five on a secret trail
	Five on a treasure island (3)
	Four cousins
	In the fifth at Malory Towers
	Island of adventure (2)
	Last term at Malory Towers
	Look out secret seven
	The magic faraway tree
	Mountain of adventure (3)
	Mystery of Holly Lane
	Mystery of the burnt cottage
	Mystery of the disappearing cat (2)
	Mystery of the missing man
	Mystery of the strange bundle
	Mystery of the strange messages
	Naughtiest girl in the school (3)
	River of adventure
	Second form at Malory Towers
	Second form at St. Clare's
	Secret island
	Secret Seven adventures
	Secret Seven and the fireworks
	Ship of adventure
	Sleepyland tales
	Third year at Malory Towers (2)
	Valley of adventure
	Wishing chair again (2)
BOND, Ruskin	*Flames in the forest*
BOND, Michael	*Olga da Polga*
BOWLES, Steve	*The power of hoodoo*
BRADBURY, Ray	*The small assassin*
BRIGGS, Raymond	*Fungus the bogeyman*
BURNETT, Frances Hodgson	*The secret garden*
BURNFORD, Sheila	*The incredible journey*
BURTON, Hester	*Through the fire*
BUTTERWORTH, Ben and STOCKDALE, Bill	*Danger in the mountains*
BYARS, Betsy	*The cartoonist*
CAMERON, Ann	*The Julian stories*
CAMPBELL, Joanna	*Secret identity*
CANNING, Victor	*Flight of the grey goose*
CARPENTER, Richard	*Catweasle and the magic zodiac*
	The ghosts of Motley Hall
CARROLL, Lewis	*Alice in Wonderland*
CARTLAND, Barbara	*Golden gondola*
CASS, Joan	*The witch and the naughty princess*
CHAMBERS, Aidan (ed.)	*Ghost after ghost*
CHAMBERS, Nancy	*Wildcat Wendy and the peekaboo kid*
CLEARY, Beverly	*Beezus and Ramona*

	Henry and Ribsy
	Ramona the pest
CLEAVER, Vera and Bill	*Grover*
COLLODI, Carlo	*Pinocchio*
COLWELL, Eileen	*Tell me a story*
CONKLIN, Barbara	*Summer dreams*
COOLIDGE, Susan	*What Katy did* (4)
	What Katy did at school
	What Katy did next
	Dorrie and the hallowe'en plot
COOMBS, Patricia	*Dorrie and the weather-box*
COREN, Alan	*Arthur and the bellybutton diamond* (2)
	Arthur and the great detective (2)
	Arthur v. the rest
	Buffalo Arthur
	Klondike Arthur
	Lone Arthur
	Railroad Arthur
CORRIN, Sara & Steven (ed.)	*Stories for 10's and over*
CRAIG, Wendy	*Happy endings: stories old and new*
CRESSWELL, Helen	*Bagthorpes unlimited*
	Ordinary Jack
CROMPTON, Richmal	*Sweet William*
	William again
CROWTHER, Robert	*The most amazing hide and seek alphabet book*
CUSSLER, Clive	*Iceberg*
	Raise the Titanic
DAHL, Roald	*Charlie and the chocolate factory* (3)
	Charlie and the great glass elevator
	Danny the champion of the world (2)
	Fantastic Mr. Fox (2)
	George's marvellous medicine (2)
	James and the giant peach
	The twits (4)
	The witches
DALLAS, Ruth	*The house on the cliffs*
DANBY, Mary (ed.)	*Armada ghost book*
DANN, Colin	*Animals of Farthing Wood*
DAVIES, Andrew	*Marmalade Atkins in space*
DAVIS, Gerry	*Dr Who and the Cybermen*
DAVIS, Jim	*Garfield the great lover*
DICKENS, Charles	*Oliver Twist*
DICKINSON, Peter	*The gift*
DICKS, Terrance	*Dr Who and the planet of the spiders*
DIGBY, Anne	*A horse called September*
	Summer term at Trebizon
	Tennis term at Trebizon
DOYLE, Sir Arthur Conan	*The hound of the Baskervilles*
	The lost world
DRAKE, Joan	*Miss Hendy's house*

DUMAS, Alexandre	*The three musketeers*
EARNSHAW, Brian	*Dragonfall 5 and the empty planet* (2)
	Dragonfall 5 and the haunted world (3)
	Dragonfall 5 and the highjackers (3)
	Dragonfall 5 and the super horse (2)
EDWARDS, Dorothy	*My naughty little sister*
FARLEY, Walter	*Black stallion*
FARRAR, Susan Clement	*Samantha on stage*
FISK, Nicholas	*Flamers*
	Grinny
	Trillions (3)
FOLLETT, James	*The Tiptoe boys*
FRY, Rosalie Kingsmill	*Snowed up*
GARNETT, Eve	*The family from One End Street*
GATTI, William	*Caesar's ghost*
GAVIN, Jamila	*Double dare* (2)
	Kamla and Kate
GEE, Maurice	*The world around the corner*
GOODWIN, Tim	*Saturday went wrong*
GORDON, John	*The edge of the world*
GOSCINNY, Rene and SEMPE, J.J.	*Nickolas and the gang*
GOSCINNY, R. and UDERZO, M.	*Asterix* (titles not specified (2)
	Asterix in Britain
	Asterix in Spain
GRAHAME, Kenneth	*Wind in the willows* (3)
GRENDER, Iris	*Did I ever tell you . . . ?*
GRICE, Frederick	*The Black Hand Gang*
GRIFFITHS, Helen	*Just a dog*
GRIMM Brothers	*Grimm's fairy tales*
HALL, Willis	*The last vampire*
HARGREAVES, Roger	*Little Miss Late*
	Little Miss Naughty
	Mr. Nosey
HARVEY, Anne	*A present for Nellie*
HEIDE, Florence Parry	*The shrinking of Treehorn*
HENTOFF, Nat	*This school is driving me crazy*
HERBERT, James	*The fog*
	The rats
"HERGE"	*Tin Tin* (titles not specified) (2)
HILDICK, E.W.	*The case of the nervous newsboy*
	The great rabbit robbery
	The menaced midget
HILL, Douglas	*Have your own extra-terrestrial adventure*
	Planet of the Warlord
HINES, Barry	*Kes*
HOOKE, Nina Warner	*The snow kitten*
HOUGH, Charlotte	*The holiday story book*

181

HUGHES, Shirley	*It's too frightening for me!* *Charlie Moon books* (titles not specified)
HUGHES, Ted	*Iron man: a story in five nights* (2)
HUGILL, Beryl	*Bring on the clowns*
HUNTER, Norman	*The dribblesome teapots and other incredible stories* *The home-made dragon and other incredible stories* *The incredible adventures of professor Branestawm* (2)
HURD, Edith Thacher	*Last one home is a green pig*
HUTCHINS, Pat	*The best train set ever* (2)
IPCAR, Dahlov	*A dark horn blowing*
JACKSON, Steve	*Citadel of chaos* *Starship 'Traveller'*
JANSSON, Tove	*Finn Family Moomintroll*
JARRELL, Randall	*The gingerbread rabbit*
JEROME, Jerome K.	*Three men in a boat*
JOHNS, W.E.	*Biggles and the black mask*
JOY, Margaret	*Hairy and Slug* (2)
KEMP, Gene	*The turbulent term of Tyke Tiler*
KENNEMORE, Tim	*The fortunate few*
KING, Clive	*Stig of the dump* (2)
KINGSLEY, Charles	*The water babies*
KIPLING, Rudyard	*How the alphabet was made* *The jungle book* *Just so stories*
KONIGSBURG, Elaine L.	*Jennifer, Hecate, Macbeth and me*
LAGERLOF, Selino O.	*Wonderful adventures of Nils*
LAVELLE, Sheila	*The fiend next door* (2)
LEESON, Robert	*Grange Hill rules. O.K.?*
LE GUIN, Ursula K.	*The farthest shore* *The tombs of Atuan* *A wizard of Earthsea* (2)
LEWIS, C.S.	*The horse and his boy* *The last battle* *The lion, the witch and the wardrobe* (4) *The magician's nephew* (2) *Prince Caspian*
LINDGREN, Astrid	*Pippi Longstocking* *The six Bullerby children*
LINGARD, Joan	*Strangers in the house*
LIVELY, Penelope	*The ghost of Thomas Kempe* Going back
LIVINGSTONE, Ian	*City of thieves* (2) *Forest of doom*
LOBEL, Arnold	*Frog and toad all year* *Grasshopper on the road* *How the rooster saved the day* *Owl at home*
LORD, John Vernon	*The giant jam sandwich*

LOWRY, Lois	*Find a stranger, say goodbye*
LYDECKER, John	*Dr Who terminus*
McBRATNEY, Sam	*Mark time*
McGOUGH, Roger	*The great smile robbery*
MAKIN, Irene	*Ponies in the attic*
MARK, Jan	*Hairs in the palm of the hand*
MARKS, James Macdonald	*Hijacked*
MAYNE, William (ed.)	*A book of giants*
MILNE, A.A.	*Winnie the Pooh*
NAUGHTON, Bill	*The goalkeeper's revenge and other stories*
NEEDLE, Jan	*The size spies*
NESBIT, E.	*The railway children* (2)
	The story of the treasure seekers
NEWMAN, Nanette	*That dog!*
NICHOLS, Beverley	*The wickedest witch in the world*
NORTON, Mary	*The Borrowers*
	The Borrowers afield
O'BRIEN, Robert C.	*Mrs Frisby and the rats of NIMH* (2)
O'BRIEN, Edna	*The rescue*
OLDFIELD, Pamela	*Adventures of the Gumby Gang*
PARKER, Richard	*Paul and Etta*
PEARCE, Philippa	*The battle of Bubble and Squeak*
PIENKOWSKI, Jan	*Robot: pop up book*
POPE, Joyce	*Deadly creatures*
PRICE, Willard	*Diving adventure*
	Gorilla adventure
	Volcano adventure
	Whale adventure
PROYSEN, Alf	*Mrs Pepperpot again*
PUDNEY, John	*The Hartwarp bakehouse*
	The Hartwarp light railway
RANSOME, Arthur	*Peter Duck*
ROBINSON, Joan G.	*The summer surprise*
ROMANES, Alexa	*Save the horses!*
ROTSLER, William	*Grease 2*
SAWARD, Eric	*Dr Who and the visitation*
SCHULTZ, Charles Monroe	*Charlie Brown, Snoopy and me*
	Its raining on your parade
	Charlie Brown
	That's life, Snoopy
SEFTON, Catherine	*The ghost and Bertie Boggin*
SEWELL, Anna	*Black Beauty*
SHARMAT, Majorie Weinmann	*Getting something on Maggie Marmelstein*
SMITH, Dodie	*Midnight kittens*
SOUTHGATE, Vera	*The princess and the pea*
	Snow White and the seven dwarfs

SPIELBURG, Steven	*Close encounters of the third kind*
SPYRI, Johanna	*Heidi*
STEVENSON, Robert Louis	*Treasure Island*
STONE, Ann	*The balloon people*
STORR, Catherine	*Lucy*
STREATFIELD, Noel	*Ballet shoes* (2)
	Curtain up
	The painted garden
SUSSEX, Rayner	*The magic apple*
SYKES, Pamela	*Come back Lucy*
	Flying summer
TENISON, Marika Hanbury	*The princess and the unicorn*
THOMAS, Frances	*Secrets*
TOLKIEN, J.R.R.	*The Hobbit* (4)
TOMLINSON, Jill	*The gorilla who wanted to grow up*
	The owl who was afraid of the dark
TOWNSEND, Sue	*The secret diary of Adrian Mole aged 13¾* (3)
TRAVERS, P.L.	*Mary Poppins*
TREASE, Geoffrey	*Cue for treason*
TRITTEN, Charles	*Heidi's children*
TWAIN, Mark	*Tom Sawyer and Huckleberry Finn*
WESTALL, Robert	*The machine-gunners*
WHITE, E.B.	*Charlotte's web*
WILDER, Laura Ingalls	*By the shores of Silver Lake* (2)
	The long winter
WILLIAMS, Jay	*The magic grandfather*
WILLIAMS, Ursula Moray	*Bogwoppit*
WILSON, Forrest	*Super Gran* (7)
	Super Gran is magic (2)
	Super Gran rules OK!
WOLF, Chris L. and MAIKOWSKI, M.F.	*Fire in the sky*
WOODWARD Ian (ed.)	*Ballet stories*
WYSS, Johann David	*Swiss Family Robinson*
YORK, Carol Beech	*I will make you disappear*
ZOLOTOW, Charlotte	*Janey*

APPENDIX 8

Book Titles Mentioned in the Diaries

(b) Non fiction

Author	Title
AHLBERG, Janet and Allan	*The ha ha bonk book*
AMERY, Heather, and FOLLIOT, Katherine	*1st 1000 words in French*
ATTENBOROUGH, David	*Discovering life on earth*
BAKER, John P.	*Learnabout football*
BOSWELL, Hilda (ed.)	*Treasury of poetry*
BRANDRETH, Gyles (ed.)	*Big book of jokes*
	Knight book of tongue twisters
	1000 Secrets: the greatest book of spycraft ever known
	Play it alone!
BRUCE, Bill (ed.)	*Explorer encnclopaedia*
CHAMBERS, Aidan	*Haunted houses*
COLE, William	*Oh, what nonsense!*
COX, Palmer	*Brownies: their Book*
CURRY, Jennifer (ed.)	*The Beaver book of skool verse*
DALY, Audrey	*Royal wedding*
DANBY, Mary	*Armada book of fun*
	Even more awful joke book
GOULD, Gill	*Animals in danger: disappearing animals of Europe*
HART, Tony	*Anyone can draw*
JEFFREY, Gordon	*Football Quiz 1981-82*
JEFFRIES, David (ed.)	*Superbikes*
LEAR, Edward	*Nonsense Omnibus*
LORD, Derek (ed.)	*Boy's Handbook*
MAYLE, Peter	*Where did I come from?*
MILLIGAN, Spike	*A book of Milliganimals*
	Silly verse for kids
MORLEY, Robert (ed.)	*Robert Morley's book of bricks*
PERRINS, Leslie	*Showing your dog*
PILKINGTON, Roger	*The facts of life for children*
REES, Nigel (ed.)	*Eavesdropping* (2)
ROLLIN, Jack	*Guiness book of soccer facts and feats*
St. JOHN AMBULANCE ASSOCIATION & BRIGADE	*Esssentials of first Aid*
SCOTT, Nancy	*Ladybird book of dogs*
WEBB, Kaye (ed.)	*I like this poem*
WESTON, Wynter	*Training your dog*
WRIGHT, Christopher	*The crack-a-joke book* (2)
	Up with skool! (3)

APPENDIX 9   *Woman's Hour* interview with Dina Thorpe

Announcer   Well, now we are going to move into the Public Library. Now any successful method of persuading children that reading is enjoyable must be a good one. The idea of the Family Reading Group, as its name suggests is to involve the whole family in the business of choosing a good book and Jill Burridge dropped in on her local group.

Jill   And what did you read Nicola?

Nicola   *The Witch's Daughter*

Jill   And was that good?

Nicola   Well I didn't like all of it. I didn't read it all, but I didnt't like the first bit.

Jill   Oh, what didn't you like?

Nicola   Well, I think it was the writing, the way it was written.

Jill   Was there another in your pile that you really did like?

Nicola   I liked that one.

Jill   That's the *Bee Rustlers* by Jan Needler. What was good about it? Exciting?

Nicola   Yes, well I think it was the dialect sort of, as well.

Woman's Hour now talks to Dina

Presenter   Dina Thorpe is one of the librarians who has set up the newly formed St Albans branch of the Family Reading Group and there are others well established in Hertfordshire, as well as Bedfordshire and Yorkshire. The groups usually meet in schools or private homes, but the St Albans branch is the first to be sited in the local library, where parents and children can come along once a month to browse through a wide selection of children's literature and then choose as many books as they like to take home.

Dina   It is quite difficult, especially when children see reading as something which is only connected with school, because we want children to see reading as something that is fun, and unless their friends are reading as well, and the book that they have got by the bed is the book that their friend's going to want to pick up and read, reading becomes rather a second rate activity. So that I think parents

186

have a part to play here in showing that they consider that reading is important. That they read themselves. That they bring books home and read and leave them lying around the house. That they talk to their friends about books and talk to their children about books as well. So that the whole thing generates its own enthusiasm and becomes catching.

Presenter   Although children of any age can go along to the evening meeting, Rosemary Dudgeon, the Children's Librarian, is especially concerned to involve 9 to 11 year olds.

Rosemary   Once the children have actually learned to read there is a drop-off in interest, because once they have got the book they can go into the corner and read it and so they are alright. You don't have to worry about them. They are reading, but in fact a lot of them might need just an extra push in this age range.

Presenter   Parents opt out at that stage you think.

Rosemary   I think they feel perhaps that it's time to maybe leave them on their own and just get on with it, but I think they could help just as well by encouraging them at this stage too.

Presenter   And the Family Reading Group is designed to give this encouragement. There are no off-putting rows of books on shelves. About two hundred books are set out on tables around the room and the children can pick and choose, recommending their own favourites to their friends on the way. The librarians also recommend to the group a selection of stories which they particularly enjoyed. So now that television takes up so much of children's spare time, Rosemary Dugeon is well aware of the need to promote the art of reading.

Rosemary   With a book, you can look at it whenever you want to, but with the television programme you must sit down for thirty-five minutes and watch it, but you can read your book whenever you like, at your own speed, at your own pace.

Presenter   Obviously the enthusiastic readers will be right with you from the start, but you want to encourage children who have stopped reading books as a regular thing to do after school. How will you give them the enthusiasm?

Rosemary   We hope we will give them the enthusiasm by letting them see how enthusiastic we are and be able to give them suggestions of things to read, because maybe they lack enthusiasm because they just don't know what to read and when they hear other people recommending books they will be encouraged to try them for themselves.

Woman's Hour now records Dina in action at a Family Reading Group.

Dina I bet you don't enjoy reading stories about librarians do you? Well I do you see, because I am a librarian, so every time I see a book that is written about librarians I pick it up and I read it. Well, the book that I have brought along to tell you about is a book which is written by a librarian as well, so that is probably why it is about a librarian. It's about a librarian who is kidnapped. It says — "One day Serena Laburnum, the beautiful librarian (Dina: All librarians are beautiful) was carried off by wicked robbers. She had just gone for a walk in the woods at the edge of the town, when the robbers came charging at her and carried her off. Why are you kidnapping me? she asked coldly. I have no wealthy friends or relatives, indeed I am an orphan with no real home but the library. That's just it said the robber chief. The city Council will pay richly to have you restored. After all, everyone knows that the library doesn't work properly without you. This was especially true because Miss Laburnum had the library keys."

Presenter A tantalising snippet was enough to attract a good number eager to take the book home and the children also had a chance to pass on their best read of the month to the rest of the group. For Michael it was Andrew Salkey's? *Hurricane.*

Michael It is set in the West Indies and there is a hurricane warning and it is all about the preparations they make for it and what happens. It gives a very good description for it all really.

Dina Do you like books with lots of description in them?

Michael Yes.

Dina Which bits of description are the best?

Michael I think after the eye of the hurricane had passed.

Back to the Programme

Presenter Of course, librarians all over the country have organised different clubs for children to encourage them to read, but the success of these Family Reading Groups depends upon parents being involved. Cecilia Obrist formed one of the first groups back in the 1950's and is now instrumental in encouraging the scheme to expand through her work with the United Kingdom Reading Association. She believes that the benefits go well beyond the books that the parents and children read.

Cecilia They actually talk to each other much more when they have been reading the same book, and the children find their problems in books and talk to their parents about them. For instance, we have one family where a middle child had read a book where there was a middle child who had problems and said "That's just the sort of thing that happens to me". And the parents realised that they were doing certain things that only applied to middle children.

Presenter   But what most parents appreciate is a good selection of books readily available. Most of us would admit that with the number of new books being published it is almost impossible to keep up-to-date with children's literature. So we tend to look back to the old favourites that we enjoyed when we were young and some of these, Rosemary Dudgeon feels, are better forgotten.

Rosemary   I listen out in the library when people come in with children and very often you know you've got a ten year old boy and somebody is with him and says "Oh yes, have you got any Biggles books?" and unfortunately occasionally we have and I feel sorry in a way that the children do have this sort of book introduced to them, but often parents might want their children to read books that they think are very worthy, but the children might not always enjoy them, so we feel we would like to offer them a very wide range. Things that might be quite easy but they will still actually gain quite a lot from.

Back to the Family Reading Group

Child   I have chosen *Animals of Farthing Wood* by Colin Downe, *Book of Spooks* and *Spectres* by Ruth Manning Sanders. I have read most of Ruth Manning Sanders' books and this is about the only one I haven't read.

Presenter   Have they got a good selection of books here tonight?

Child   Yes, very good.

Presenter   And Richard, which do you think you will tackle first of those three?

Child   That one; *Educating Marmalade.*

Presenter   Why is that?

Child   I like starting off with fun, exciting books.

Presenter   By the end of the evening, some of the parents had also picked up a selection of books for themselves, but I wondered if they would really find time to read them during the month ahead.

Parent   Well, hopefully. I usually have a lot of books on the go. I was going to read Alan Garner first. I haven't read any of those, but Richard's read *Elidor.*

Another Parent	I think its super because you don't always have time. Richard uses the library a lot, but I mean, I don't always have time to come up with him, so I think a meeting like this, once every five weeks; yes I think it is very good.
Presenter	And that report was by Jill Burridge. You can get more information about family reading groups from your local library.

APPENDIX 10   A list of useful organisations and journals

Journals

BOOKS FOR KEEPS
School Bookshop Association Ltd
1 Effingham Road
Lee
LONDON SE12 8NZ

The magazine of the School Bookshop Association. Six issues per year. Aimed at teachers, librarians and parents. Contains articles and reports, an 'author-graph' feature and has good reviews divided into basic age bands.

BOOKS FOR YOUR CHILDREN
c/o Anne Wood Ed.,
PO Box 507
Harbourne
BIRMINGHAM B17 8PJ

Three issues per year. Aimed mainly at parent. A less formal magazine containing feature articles on authors etc. The reviews are categorised by age.

CHILD EDUCATION
Scholastic Publications Ltd
Marborough House
Holly Walk
Leamington Spa
Warks CV32 4LS

Monthly, with a bimonthly supplement Infant Projects. Aimed particularly at teachers. Contains articles on current topics, on school subjects and on the development of literacy skills. The reviews are aimed at teachers and therefore of less use to the public librarian.

CHILDREN'S BOOK BULLETIN
Children's Rights Workshop
4 Aldershot Terrace
LONDON W8

For news of progressive moves in children's literature.

DRAGON'S TEETH
National Committee on
Racism in Children's Books
7 Denbigh Road
LONDON W11 2SJ

Anti-racist children's books magazine. Four per year. Aimed at teachers particularly. Contains articles tackling racism, sexism, violence etc. in books across the whole educational field. The reviews are broadly divided into Primary and Higher Education and are thorough but a bit variable in quality.

CHILDREN'S BOOKS OF THE YEAR

Selected and annotated by Julia Eccleshare, London Book Trust (see list of Organisations)

THE GOOD BOOK GUIDE
Braithwaite & Taylor Ltd
91 Great Russell Street
LONDON WC1B 3PS

Annual. Aimed at parents. Contains an overview of the year's best 600 approx. books categorised into overlapping age groups sub-divided by type. There is a handy further reading section for adults.

GROWING POINT
c/o Margery Fisher Ed
Ashton Manor
Northampton NN7 2JL

Six per year. Aimed at the professional. Wholly reviews. These are concise and direct, grouped only loosely by age level. Many of the books examined are reviewed in thematically grouped mini-articles.

INTERNATIONAL REVIEW OF CHILDREN'S LIBRARIANSHIP Taylor Graham Publishing 500 Gresham House 150 Regent St LONDON W1R 5FA	Two per year. Aimed at librarians. Contains longer articles on children's librarianship internationally. The books examined are for professionals, reviewed by librarians, authors and other specialists.
JUMP! The Magazine for Children Two-Can Publishing Ltd 27 Cowper Street London EC2A 4AP	A magazine aimed at 3-8 year-olds. Contains news and reviews and is aimed at teachers and parents.
JUNIOR EDUCATION Scholastic Publications Ltd Marlborough House Holly Walk Leamington Spa Warks CV2 4LS	Monthly, with bimonthly supplement Junior Projects. Aimed at teachers. Same content as Child Education (above).
MATERIAL MATTERS Hertfordshire Library Service County Hall Hertford	Review journal
SCHOOL LIBRARIAN School Library Association Liden Library Barrington Close Swindon SN3 6HF	Four per year. Aimed at teachers and school librarians. Contains articles on literature and on teaching. The reviews are fairly long and divided into age groups. There is a regular select list of recent articles in periodicals covering children's books and reading.
SIGNAL Thimble Press Lockwood Station Road South Woodchester Nr Stroud Glos GL5 5EQ	Three per year. Aimed at librarians mainly. The articles are lengthy and very literary.
SIGNAL SELECTION OF CHILDREN'S BOOKS	Annual. Surveys new books for the year. The reviews are by teachers, librarians and other specialists.
TIMES EDUCATIONAL SUPPLEMENT Times Newspaper Ltd Priory House St John's Lane LONDON EC1M 4BX	Weekly. Aimed at teachers and those generally involved with education. There is a small section on children's books weekly and three times a year there is a large review section, Children's Book Extra. The quality and up-to-dateness varies, but there are some excellent articles and features.
TIMES LITERARY SUPPLEMENT Times Newspapers Ltd Priory House St John's Lane LONDON EC1M 4BX	Weekly, with a two-weekly book reviews column. Aimed at a general readership. Twice a year there is a Children's Books Supplement. The value is similar to the TES.
TRIED AND TESTED	Three per year. Produced by the Centre for Language in Primary Education. The reviews are detailed and are very usefully supplemented by photographic illustrations of the gooks reviewed, clearly showing their layout, illustrations and type

presentation. There is no grouping by age or otherwise of the reviews, but the age range of the material examined is limited to Primary, and clear indexing makes all the reviews accessible.

This information has primarily been supplied by the Youth Libraries Group of the Library Association, whose permission to reproduce is gratefully acknowledged.

Organisations

Children's Book Foundation
Book Trust
Book House
45 East Hill
LONDON SW18 2QZ

Federation of Children's Book Groups
13 Yewdale
196 Harborne Park Road
Harborne
Birmingham B17 0BP

National Library for the Handicapped Child
University of London Institute of Education
20 Bedford Way
LONDON WC1H 0AL

Youth Libraries Group of the Library Association
Central Children's Library
Chamberlain Square
Birmingham B3 3HQ

and don't forget your local library — for address and telephone number see your telephone directory.

Bibliography

BIBLIOGRAPHY

AIKEN, Joan   (1988)   *In and Out of Wonderland*, Times Educational Supplement 15.1.88.

AMIS, Kingley   (1985)   *That Uncertain Feeling,* Penguin

ASTBURY, E A   (1972)   *Family Reading Groups in the East Riding,* <u>Library Association Record</u> 72 (12), 231-232

BAGNALL, Peter   (1986)   *Narnia Revisited*: The Future of Children's Books and of the Book Trade, <u>Bookseller,</u> 10 May 1986, 1864-1870.

BIRD, Jean   (1982)   *Young Teenage Reading Habits,* (BNB Research Fund Report: 9) British Library

BRITTON, James   (1977)   *The Nature of the Reader's Satisfaction.* In: <u>The Cool Web</u>, edited by Meek, Margaret, Warlow, Aidan and Barton, Griselda.
London: Bodley Head, 106-111

BULLOCK report   (1975)   *Language for Life,* HMSO

BURGESS, Anthony   (1962)   *A Clockwork Orange,* Heinemann

BUSH, Avril   (1983)   *Can Pupil's Reading be Improved by Involving their Parents?*
<u>Remedial Education</u> 18(4), 167-170

BUNNEL, Stan   (1981)   *Family Reading Groups,* Times Educational Supplement 27.5.80

BUTLER, Dorothy   (1980)   *Babies Need Books,* Bodley Head.

CALVINO, Italo   (1981)   *If on a Winters Night a Traveller . . . London,* Secker and Warburg

CARTER, Carolyn, J.   (1986)   *Young People and Books:* a review of the Research into Young People's Reading Habits,
<u>Journal of Librarianship</u> 18(1), 1-23

CHAMBERS, A   (1983)   *Introducing Books to Children,* Heinemann

CLARK, Margaret M   (1976)   *Young Fluent Readers,* Heinemann

COLE, John, YOUNG, Carol S.   (1978)   *Reading in America* Survey, Library of Congress

CRONIN, Blaise and MARTIN, Irene   (1983)   *Social Skills Training in Librarianship,* <u>Journal of Librarianship</u> 15(2), 105-121

| DIXON, Bob | (1977) | *Catching them Young,* Pluto Press |

| EDUCATION, SCIENCE & ARTS COMMITTEE | (1986) | *Achievement in Primary Schools Vol 1,* HMSO xxv-xxvii |

| EGOFF, Sheila, STUBBS, G T and ASHLEY, L F | (1969) | *Only Connect,* Readings on Children's Literature. Oxford University Press |

| FADER, Daniel | (1969) | *Hooked on Books,* Pergamon Press |

| FATCHEN, Max | (1985) | *Wry Rhymes for Troublesome Times,* Penguin |

| FEARN, Margaret | (1982) | *Promotional Activities and Materials for Children in an Urban Branch Library.* (Claim Report No 15) (British Library Research and Development Department Report 5707) |

| FRY, Donald | (1985) | *Children Talk about Books: seeing themselves as Readers,* Open University Press. |

| GAULT, Michel | (1982) | *The Future of the Book* (Part 2 – The Changing Role of Reading) Studies on Books and Reading No 9. UNESCO |

| GOFF, Martyn | (1982) | *The Media are A-Messing,* Bookseller, 7 September 1982, 1255 |

| GOW, David | (1988) | *Reading Between the Battle Lines,* Guardian 2.2.88 |

| GREEN, J.A. | (1913) | *The Teaching of English II Literature* (What boys and girls read) Journal of Experimental Pedagogy II |

| GRIFFITHS, Alex and HAMILTON, Dorothy | (1984) | *Parent, Teacher, Child, Working Together in Children's Learning,* Methuen |

| GRUNDIN, Elizabeth Hunter and GRUNDIN, Hands U (eds) | (1978) | *Reading: Implementing the Bullock Report.* United Kingdom Reading Association, Ward Lock |

| HAJDU, Jan | (1978) | (Quoted in Reading in America Survey, by Cole, John and Young, Carol S. Library of Congress) |

| HATT, Frank | (1976) | *The Reading Process,* Clive Bingley |

| HEATHER, P | (1981) | *Young People's Reading,* British Library Research & Development Report 5650 |

| HEATON, Maggie and BROWN, Brian | (1985) | *TV Culture,* Times Educational Supplement 17.5.85 |

| HEEKS, Peggy | (1981) | *Choosing and Using Books in the First School,* Macmillan |

| HIMMELWEIT, H T, OPPENHEIM, A N and VINCE, P | (1961) | *Television and the Child,* Oxford University Press |

| HOLLINDALE, Peter | (1974) | *Choosing Books for Children,* Elek |

| HORDER, Mervyn | (1984) | *Across the Duckpond,* The Bookseller, June 30th, 1984; 2677 |

HOWARD, Philip   (1988)   *Oh my Bunter of Long Ago,* Times 19.2.88

INGHAM, Jennie   (1981)   *Books and Reading Development,* Heinemann

JAMES, Robert   (1983)   *Libraries in the Mind: how can we see users' perceptions of libraries?* Journal of Librarianship 15(1), 19-28

KARL, Jean   (1971)   *Building Interests and Selecting books for Children.* In: Parents and Reading. International Reading Association 37-42

KATZ, Elihu, BLUMLER, Jay and GUREVITCH, Michael   (1973)   *User and Gratifications Research,* Public Opinion Quarterly 37(4), 509-523

KENNERLEY, Peter (ed)   (1979)   *Teenage Reading,* Ward Lock

LEESON, Robert   (1985)   *Reading and Righting,* Collins

LONG, Barbara H and HENDERSON, Edmund H   (1973)   *Children's Use of Time: some personal and social correlates,* Elementary School Journal 75 (Jan 1973), 193-199

LUNZER, E and GARDNER, K   (1979)   *The Effective Use of Reading* (Schools Council Project), Heinemann

MACLEAN, Juliet   (1985)   *A Study of Voluntary Reading Across the Secondary Age Range and of the Role of Groups formed in two Secondary Schools to extend and support Pupils' Voluntary Reading* MA Dissertation. Institute of Education, London University

McCLEAR, Mickey   (1982)   *Children's Libraries: The Literary Place,* In Review: Canadian Books for Young People 16(1) February 1982, 5-10

MANN, Peter   (1971)   *Book Buyers and Borrowers,* Deutsch

MEEK, Margaret   (1982)   *Learning to Read,* Bodley Head

MEEK, Margaret WARLOW, Aidan and BARTON, Griselda   (1978)   *The Cool Web,* Bodley Head.

MELNIK, Amelia and MERRITT, John   (1972)   *Reading Today and Tomorrow,* University of London Press in association with Open University Press

MORTIMER, Penelope   (1969)   *Thoughts Concerning Children's Books,* In: Only Connect, reading on children's literature, ed by Egoff, Sheila, Stubbs, G T and Ashley, L F. Open University Press 97-102

MOYLE, Donald (ed)   (1975)   *Reading: What of the Future?* United Kingdom Reading Association Ward Lock

OBRIST, Cecilia   (1984)   *How to run Family Reading Groups,* United Kingdom Reading Association.

PORTERFIELD, O V and SCHLICHTING, Harry F   (1961)   *Peer Status and Reading Achievement,* Journal of Educational Research 54(8) 291-297

RANKIN, Marie	(1944)	*Children's Interests in Library Books of Fiction,* Teachers College Columbia University
RHYS, Jean	(1983)	In: *Difficult Women* by David Plante. Atheneum
ROBINSON, Helen and WEINTRAUB, Samuel	(1973)	*Research Related to Children's Interests and to Developmental Values of Reading,* Library Trends Vol 22 No 2, October 1973
ROBERTS, Muriel	(1982)	*Read to Them,* In Review. Canadian Books for Young People 16(1). February 1982, 16-18
SMITH, Carl	(1971)	*Parents and Reading,* Perspectives in Reading, No 14. International Reading Association
SOUTHGATE, Vera, ARNOLD, Helen and JOHNSON, Sandra	(1981)	*Extending Beginning Reading* (Schools Council Project), Heinemann
STORR, Anthony	(1969)	*The Child and the Book* In: *Only Connect,* readings on children's literature: ed by Egoff, Sheila, Stubbs, G T and Ashley, L F Oxford University Press, 91-97
THORPE, Dina	(1982)	*Family Reading Groups.* Reading 16(3) 143-152
THORPE, Dina	(1986)	*Family Reading Groups: a critical analysis of the part played by parents, public libraries and their peers in encouraging children aged 9-12 to read for enjoyment,* (MPhil Thesis), Cranfield Institute of Technology, 1985-6, 27
TOTTERDELL, Barry and BIRD, Jean	(1976)	*The Effective Library,* Library Association
TUCKER, Nicholas	(1981)	*The Child and the Book,* Cambridge University Press
VENESS, T	(1962)	*School Leavers,* Methuen
WARLOW, Aidan	(1977)	*Kinds of fiction: a hierarchy of veracity. In:* The Cool Web, edited by Meek, Margaret, Warlow, Aidan and Barton, Griselda. Bodley Head 97-102
WATERLAND, Liz	(1985)	*Read with me: An Apprenticeship approach to reading,* Thimble Press
WHITEHEAD, Frank et al	(1977)	*Children and Their Books,* Schools Council Research Studies Macmillan
WIGMORE, Hilary	(1988)	*The Captive Reader,* Cranfield Press
WRAGG, Marie	(1968)	*The Leisure Activities of Boys and Girls,* Educational Research 10, February 1968, 139-144

Index

action and characterisation 86-7, 89, 93, 97, 99
active children 18, 54
'activity', reading as an 29, 115, 131
adaptations of books on TV 69, 85-6
adult books read by children 121, 133, 135
adventure books 87, 135
after school activities 53, 106, 118-46, 168-71
Aiken, Joan 46, 102
Aldeson, Brian 42
Alexander, Lloyd 135
Alhberg, Allan 87
allusions 19, 87
Ambrus, Victor 77, 88, 102
Amis, Kingsley 45
Andrew 28, 46, 78
    comments by 40, 48, 75-6, 84, 95, 98, 100
animal stories 69, 135
animals *see* pets
annuals 126, 133, 135, 137-40, 145
appearance of library books 45, 65, 70-1, 74
apprenticeship in readership 41, 46, 70, 83, 85, 103
    see also development as readers
art activities 56, 121-5, 128, 129, 146
Ashley, Bernard 85
Astbury, Eve 13
Atkinson, Eleanor 73, 75
attendance at FRG meetings 22, 34-49
    childrens' 23, 27, 43, 44
    parents' 23, 27, 42-4, 104
    swings in 46, 48, 49, 58-60
Auden, W H 99
author familiarity 64-5, 70, 76, 103, 136
'avid' readers 18, 53, 59, 78, 86, 140

Bagnall, Peter 115
Baker, John 132
Banana books 113
Barber, Antonia 71
barriers to library use 15, 37, 40-1, 109
Bawden, Nina 68-9, 73-5, 126, 139, 184
bed, reading in 55, 61, 78, 122, 138, 142, 147
'beginner' readers 73-4, 77-8, 83, 85, 87-90, 92-5, 99
Beginning to Read series 85
Bengali language books 124, 133, 129
Beresford, Elisabeth 71, 88
Bird, Jean 1-9, 24, 37, 109
Blackbird series 74
Blake, Quentin 88

Blume, Judy 95, 103, 139
Blumer, J 19
Blyton, Enid 45, 72, 77, 94, 103, 136, 139, 144
    Famous Five books 84, 126
    Malory Towers books 126
board games 55, 60, 122, 147
    chess 121, 126, 128, 131
book supply 12, 14, 16, 19
book trade 12-13, 116
Book Trust 116
books mentioned in diaries 178-85
Books for Keeps 72, 90
Books for Your Children 72, 90
Bookseller, The 19, 64
Booksellers Association 12, 13, 115
bookstock 16, 22, 109, 112, 113, 115
    FRG 28, 68, 71-3, 107, 161-5
'boring' books 47, 83, 84, 86
borrowed books not read 23, 28, 68, 69
borrowing
    systems and records 18, 22-3, 27-8, 32, 38, 40, 53, 67-8, 78, 108
    unrestricted 14-15, 28, 73, 77, 103, 107-8, 112-14, 116
    number of books 28, 73-6, 114
branch libraries 14, 15, 25, 27, 106
breadth of reading 13, 15, 103, 112
Bridget 126, 129
Briggs, Raymond 77, 88
Britton, James 10, 103
Brown issue system 27, 40
Bruce, Bill 129
Bullock Report, The 12, 42
Bunnell, Stan 104
Burgess, Anthony 94
Burridge, Jill 184-8
Byars, Betsy 70, 98
    The Cartoonist 68, 75, 95, 96, 103, 146
    The TV Kid 43, 68, 89, 95-6

Calvino 64
card games 126, 140
Caroline 126
Carroll, Lewis 75
Carter, Carolyn J 116
Cartland, Barbara 135-6
cartoons 102, 135, 137
Cartwheel series 113

Ceri 28, 65, 69, 75-7, 96
  comments by 66, 70, 94-5
Chambers, Aiden 139
characterisation and action 87, 89, 93, 97, 99
Childrens Book Action Group 115
Childrens Book Foundation 116
Childrens Book Trust 116
Childrens Librarians 15, 25-6, 47, 108-9, 114
choice of books 63-79, 81-90, 115
  by adults 15, 64-6
  by children 17, 18, 32, 65, 67, 74
  from prior knowledge of book 64-5, 69-70, 70-1
Choose Your Own Adventure series 75, 84
Clare 76
  comments by 39, 83, 85, 103
Cleary, Beverly 136, 144
Clement Farrar, Susan 139
'clubbable' nature of children 58, 94, 115
Cole 12, 54
'complete' reader 93
Conklin, Barbara 135
Consumer Research Study on Reading and Book
  Purchasing 64
comics 126, 129, 133, 135, 137-41, 146
community libraries 15, 24, 39, 109, 113, 116
community spirit 14, 27, 48
computer games 55, 123, 127, 132, 140
computerised literature search 19
computers 56, 60, 127-8, 147
Coren, Alan 136, 144, 145
costs
  of bookstock 22, 28
  of FRG 107-110
cost effectiveness of FRG 107-10, 112
covers of books 45, 65, 70-1, 74
Cox, Brian 12
craft activities 56, 60, 122-3, 125, 128, 146
Craig, Wendy 132
Cresswell, Helen
  Absolute Zero 28, 68, 73, 85, 94, 96
  Bagthorpe Saga 65, 70, 73, 75-6, 88, 94
  Ordinary Jack 75, 146
Crompton, Richmal 103
  William books 65, 75-6, 78, 86, 97-8, 113, 139
Cronin, Blaise 24
Cunningham Library 27, 37, 38
Curtis, Philip 95
Cussler, Clive 121

Dahl, Roald 43, 68-9, 113, 132, 136, 139
Dallas, Ruth 139
Davies, Andrew 97, 113, 189
  Marmalade Atkins in Space 47, 67-8, 70, 73, 86-7
Davis, Richard 69, 75
Deborah 126
'decoding' of books 11, 16, 83, 85, 89-90, 98, 102
development as readers 12, 17, 19, 29, 31-2, 82-3,
  88, 92
  see also apprenticeship
dialogue in books 19, 85, 87-8

Diaries, After School 18, 22-3, 52-9, 62, 78, 83, 94
  activities mentioned in 146, 168-71
  comparison of 30, 60-1, 103
  data sheet 166-7
  format of 153-7
  problems with 29-30, 38, 52-3, 118, 120
  timings in 77, 118-120, 142-5, 168-71
Dicks, Terrance 129, 139
discussion of books 23, 65, 82, 86
Dixon, Bob 46, 95
'doers' and readers 54
dolls and figures 126
Downe, Colin 189
Dudgeon, Rosie 26, 34-7, 47-8, 109, 189-90

Earnshaw, Brian 74, 84, 136, 139, 146
Eghoff, Sheila 72
electronic games 55, 123, 126, 128-9
Elizabeth 137
enjoyment of books and reading 10-11, 16, 19, 23,
  31, 73, 86-7, 92
  see also gratification
ethnic minorities 34, 36, 131, 143
Evans, Alan 66
exercise, physical 57, 59, 60
expectations of books 47, 85
experienced readers 19, 84, 93, 97, 98

fairy stories 93, 135
family 13-14, 18, 44, 48, 55-6, 60
  playing with 57, 61, 141
  size of 135, 147
  stable 95
Family Reading Groups (FRG) 22-3, 34, 42-4, 47-9,
  61-2, 67, 83, 102, 104
  bookstock of 28, 68, 71-3, 107, 161-5
  effectiveness of 61-2, 107-10
  non members 30, 36, 53-4, 56-7, 59-60, 103, 118
  research on 9-19, 52-3
  setting up 16, 22, 24, 153-4
fantasy books 70, 75, 92, 95, 97, 99, 124, 135
  and reality 19, 102, 110
fantasy games 55, 62
Fatchen, Max 87
favourite activities 29, 62, 124, 175-7
Fearn, Margaret 34
Ferguson, Ruby 45
fiction 18-19, 148, 178-85
  books 13, 143
  reading 11, 13, 16, 75, 135
figures and dolls 123, 141
fines, library 40, 105-6, 109, 113
Fisk, Nicholas 139
Fleetville 27, 48, 54, 92-3, 95, 104, 146
  schools in 18, 29, 34
  see also School 1; School 2; School 3; School 4
Fleetville Library 1, 14, 18, 24, 28, 36, 105, 107-9, 114
  opening hours 26
  possible closure of 26-7, 31
  proximity of 37
  use of 22-3, 26-7, 37-8, 62

Fleetville Family Reading Group (FFRG) 1, 14, 18, 29, 34, 58, 72, 87, 144
    members of 30, 60, 118
    records of 22, 23, 27-8, 52
    study of 16-17, 22-4, 27, 42
    video of 27
formula books 84
Frances 66
friends 50, 56-7, 115
    playing with 61, 121, 123-5, 131
Friends of Fleetville Library 27, 109
frightening books 11, 22, 86, 88-9
Fry, Donald 18
funny books 32, 73, 75, 86-8, 95, 113, 135-6, 139

games 55-6, 60, 125-7, 140
    see also board; computer; electronic; fantasy; video games
Garfield, Leon 69, 75
Garner, Alan 187
Gault, Michel 12, 83, 85, 92
    The Future of the Book 10, 64, 82
    on literacy 10, 82
Geoffrey 131
Goff, Martin 12
Gold 12, 54
Goodwin, Tim 139
Gordon, John 139
government spending 12, 26
gratification from reading 10-11, 16-17, 19, 74, 78, 84, 87, 92, 97, 102
Green, J A 71
Griffiths, Alex 12, 19, 42
Griffiths, Helen 128
Guy 121

Hajdu, Jan 54
Hamilton, Dorothy 12, 19, 42
Hart, Tony 126, 128
Hatt, Frank 10, 11, 18-19
'heavy' readers 52, 54, 62
helping at home 52, 56, 57, 60
Henderson, Edmund H 52
Herts County Finance and Resources Committee 26
Hildick, E W 75-6, 84, 100, 103, 136
Himmelweit 52
historical books 45
Hoban, Russell 73
Hodgson Burnett, Frances 126, 135
home and family 14, 18, 48
    books in 13, 44
    helping at 52, 56, 57, 60
homework 52, 56, 60-1, 123-5, 129, 147
Horder, Mervyn 64
House of Commons report 42
Hunter-Grundin, Elizabeth 82
Hutchins, Pat 68, 85, 88, 89, 99, 102

identification with characters
    see relating to story

illiteracy 12, 92
illustrations 88
imaginative play 55, 123, 126, 147,
impact interviews 18, 22-3, 31-2, 65, 69-70, 77, 93, 152-3
indoor activities 59
informality of FRGs 14, 17, 27, 49, 102, 119
information from books 11, 39, 41
infrequent readers 53
Ingham, Jennie 19, 44, 52, 53, 59
    Bradford Book Flood 32, 42, 65, 72
Ingham/Clift Reading Record Form 32, 65
interviews 18, 23, 29, 31, 53, 82, 86, 149-50
    with children 18-19, 22-3, 30, 32, 53
    with FRG members 18-19, 28, 53
    with parents 18, 22-3, 30, 32, 53
    with Woman's Hour 37, 186-90
    see also impact interviews

Jackson, Steve 129
James 137
Jane 48, 76, 102
    comments 59, 77, 89, 95, 96
Jeffery, Gordon 132
Joanne 137
John 48-9, 76
Jonathan 126
journals 19

Karl, Jean 42
Katz, E 10, 19
Kemp, Gene 70
Kennamore, Tim 135
King, Clive 122, 145
knowledge, library as store of 41
Konigsburg, Elaine L 145

Ladybird books 128
Lavelle, Sheila 132
Leach, Mark 25
Leeson, Bob 13, 19, 71, 72-3, 82
Le Guin, Ursula 75, 90, 100, 139
Lewis, C S 62, 74, 85, 126, 136, 144
Librarians 12-13, 24, 27, 34, 41-2, 72, 112, 114-5
    childrens 15, 25, 26, 46, 47
    choice of books by 15, 64-5, 72
    and schools 14, 25, 46-7
    time of 22, 24-6, 107
libraries, public 14, 16, 24, 36, 45, 73, 105-10, 112, 143-4
    access to 113-4
    attitudes to 23, 30
    childrens perceptions of 41-2, 106
    links with schools 25, 46, 116, 146
    use of see use of libraries
library clubs 25
library policies 16, 107
library services 12, 14-16, 19, 44-5, 108, 112
Library of Congress Study 12, 29, 48, 64
'light' readers 52

Lisa 48
literacy 12, 52, 85, 98, 115, 143
    adult 41
    defined by Gault 10, 82
Lively, Penelope 71
Livingstone, Ian 129, 139
Long, Barbara 52
Louise 28, 74, 76, 77, 122, 132
    comments by 42, 58-9, 66, 71, 83, 89, 96, 98
Lowry, Lois 139
Lucy 28, 74, 76, 77, 88, 145
    comments by 87, 98-9, 105

McCullagh, Sheila 133
McGough, Roger 66, 73, 77, 87, 102
McLean, Juliet 14
magazines 133, 137-41, 145, 149
Mann, Peter 38, 92, 94
Manning Saunders, Ruth 181
Margaret 129
Marion 135
Mark, Jan 71, 89
Marshalswick Library 27, 37, 38, 62
Martin 46, 76, 77, 88, 105
    comments by 41, 84, 99, 100
Martin, Irene 24
Mary 28, 66
Meek, Margaret 10, 12, 19, 77, 92
methodology of study 17-18, 21-32, 119-120
Michael 76, 145-6
    comments by 40-1, 66, 71, 84, 88, 95, 97, 188
Miles 126
Milligan, Spike 136
Milne, A A 77, 78
moderate readers 52
Moray Williams, Ursula 68, 73
Mortimer, Penelope 72
music 29, 56, 60
    learning 54, 57-9, 121-2, 124-5, 129-32, 144
    listening to 55, 57, 59, 124
mystery stories 135

Nancy Drew stories 45, 84
National Book League 12
Needler, Jan 186
Nesbit, E 135
Ness, Evelina 93
Nicola 35, 69, 76, 88, 89-90
    comments by 48, 58, 77, 85, 98, 102, 186
Nicholas 126
newspapers 19, 26, 40, 113, 115, 133, 141, 149
non-fiction 11, 35-6, 75, 105, 136, 185

O'Brien, Robert 73
Obrist, Cecilia 13, 188
opening hours at library 26, 31, 40-1, 106, 108-9, 113
Oppenheim 52
organised activities 29, 39, 48, 52, 54-60, 94, 129-32,
    144-7

PACT 12, 13
Pain-Lewis, Helen 15
parents 25, 27, 40, 69, 76, 78, 102, 104-6, 108, 112
    choice of books by 15, 16
    and children 42-4, 46, 56
    and childrens reading 13, 16, 19, 72, 104, 143-4
    involvement of 12-13, 19, 23, 34, 36, 42, 48-9, 115,
    146
    reading of 30, 44, 46, 64
        in childhood 16, 30, 42, 46
        of childrens books 43, 104, 115
    use of libraries 23, 44, 105
        as children 30, 45-6, 113
Pearce, Philippa 102
peer group influences 17-18, 47-9, 58, 66, 74, 143, 146
Peter 66, 128-9, 141-2
pets 56, 60, 102, 121, 130, 132, 147
    cats 140-1
    dogs 57, 75, 128
Philip 136
photographic record of FRG meetings 17, 27
picture books 72, 74, 88
plot and subplot 88
Plowden Report, The 13
poetry 136
popularity of books 67-9, 87, 92, 99
    FRG bookstock 161-5
Porterfield 48
practiced readers 19, 73, 77, 90, 99
Price, Willard 72
primary world of belief 92, 99
promotion of
    books 13, 15, 19
    library services 34, 114-5
    reading 18, 25, 58
    FRGs 16, 24-6, 29, 34-7
proximity to library 34-6
    Fleetville 37, 146
publishers 12

questionnaires 32, 82, 119, 149-53
    problems with 17-18, 52
    Whitehead's 17, 18, 28, 32, 133
'quick reads'

racism 46
Rankin, Marie 71
Ransome, Arthur 42, 72
readability 92
readership 19, 102
    see also apprenticeship in
reading
    as leisure activity 10, 16, 29, 52-6, 118
    attitudes to 23
    definition of 10
reality in books 19, 91-100, 102
recommendation of books 15, 18, 64-5 66-9
    by adults 67-9, 73, 47
    by children 14-15, 28, 48, 58, 65, 67-8, 97, 102-3,
    115, 143

recommendations of study 112-16
rejection of titles 71
relating to story, children 10-11, 17, 19, 82, 86-7, 90, 92-3, 95, 96, 103
renewing books 40, 67
re-reading of books 18, 69, 70, 84
Rhys, Jean 93
Richard 39, 126, 189
Robert 140-1
Robinson, Helen 92
Roger 76, 77, 105, 129
    comments by 66, 96, 145
role playing games 55, 62, 123, 126, 146
Rollin, Jack 132
Rosen, Michael 87
Ross, Tony 88
Rupa 144

St Albans Central Library 26-7, 37-9, 44, 107, 109
St Albans Book Group 34
St Johns Ambulance Brigade 57, 131
Salkey, Andrew 188
Sam 48, 126
    comments by 39, 49, 70
satisfaction from reading 10-11, 84
    see also gratification
Schlee, Anne 78, 79, 89
Schlicting 48
School Librarian, The 72, 190
School 1 34, 36, 122-4, 127, 131, 143-5, 172, 175
    comparison with others 29-30, 109, 120, 129, 136
School 2 35-6, 48, 123-4, 127, 131, 143-5, 173, 176
    comparison with others 29-30, 109, 120, 129, 136
School 3 35-6, 124, 143-5, 174, 175
    comparison with others 29-30, 109, 120, 129, 136
School 4 29-30, 36
school libraries 14, 25, 34-6, 45, 112, 143, 136
Schools Council 19, 133
schools
    involvement and cooperation 14, 34, 52, 143-4
    reading at 53, 69, 78-9
    transfer between 27, 30, 53-4, 60-2, 75, 118
Schools Library Association 34
Schools Library Services 14, 36
science fiction books 46, 72, 74, 75, 100
secondary world of belief 92-4, 99
Sendak, Maurice 74, 89, 96
serialisation of books on TV 126
series books 65, 66, 84-5
Sewell, Anna 135
sex differences in reading 133-4, 136-7, 139, 147
sexism in books 46
Shirley, Felei L 93
short stories 135
slow reading 83
social background 14, 15, 52, 95, 135
    ethnic minorities 34, 36, 131, 143
Southgate, Vera 44, 52, 53, 72, 87
Spencer, Margaret 82, 84
sporting activities 52, 123, 125, 126, 130, 143

football 57, 58, 140
gymnastics 29, 57, 58, 132
swimming 29, 54-5, 57-8, 122, 124, 131
starting a FRG 16, 22, 24, 153-4
Stephen 76, 102, 127
    comments by 67, 85, 94
Stevenson, Robert L 46
Storr, Anthony 11
Stuart 76, 83
    comments by 96, 97, 98
Sunday Times, The 12, 41
survival reading 10, 82, 83, 92
Sutcliffe, Rosemary 45
Suzie 131-2
Swindell, Robert 68, 73, 75

Tate, Joan 122
teachers 25, 35, 72, 108
    and reading 10, 14, 15, 65, 69
television
    adaptations of books 69, 85-6
    programmes 54-5, 71, 121, 129, 132, 140, 146
        childrens 61, 78, 125, 127, 138
        news 141-2
        sport 125
    viewing 52, 54, 60, 65, 87, 121, 126-9, 132, 136, 140-1
        in bed 55, 61
        combined with other activity 55, 125, 128
        effect on reading 147
        selective 146
terminal reading 11, 18-19
Thorpe, Dina 34, 118, 186-90
time spent reading 52-3, 77, 78, 106-7, 141-5
Tolkien, J R R 75, 76, 128
Tom 28, 65, 76, 78, 88
    comments by 61, 66, 70, 86, 89, 97-9
Totterdell, Barry 19, 24, 37, 109
Townsend, Sue 139
Townson, Hazel 43
toys 121, 126-7, 129
Tuchman, Barbara 54
Tucker, Nicholas 19, 82

use of Fleetville library by FFRG members 22-3, 27, 37, 38, 62
use of public libraries 37, 38, 41, 62, 105-7
    barriers to 15, 37, 40-1 109
    by adults 19, 23, 25, 38, 44, 105
    by children 23, 37
UK Reading Association 13, 188

video games 123, 126
video tapes 55
    of FFRG 27
Vince 52

Warlow, Aidan 19, 92, 93
Waterland, Liz 13
weekend activities 172-4
Weintraub, Samuel 92

Westall, Robert 66, 75, 121
Wigmore, Hilary 82
Woman's Hour interview 37, 186-90
word play 73, 87
Willard, Barbara 100
Whitehead, Frank 52, 135, 136
   Children and their Books 17, 19, 72, 87, 133
   'heavy' reader category 62
   questionnaires 17, 18, 28, 32
Williams, Jay 146
Wilson, Forrest 75-6, 122, 126, 136, 139
Wragg, Marie 52
Wright, Christopher 136, 145
Wynne Jones, Diana 70

Young, Helen 104

Zimmer, John S 12, 29, 48, 64
Zoe 145